Advanced Accounting Theory and Practice

Edited By

Kabiru I. Dandago, PhD, ACA

Published by
Adonis & Abbey Publishers Ltd
P.O. Box 43418
London
SE11 4XZ

http://www.adonis-abbey.com
Email: editor@adonis-abbey.com

First Edition, January 2009

British Library Cataloguing-in-Publication Data

A catalogue record for this book is available from the British Library

ISBN: 9781906704223(HB)/9781906704230(PB)

Advanced Accounting Theory and Practice

Edited by

Kabiru Isa Dandago, PhD, ACA

Adonis & Abbey Publishers Ltd

FOREWORD

I am greatly honored to be requested to write the foreword for this valuable book titled *Advanced Accounting: Theory and Practice.* The book is made up of fifteen chapters and presents scholarly works in the areas of accounting theory and practice with special reference to the Nigerian situation.

Although a great deal of original work has taken place in the area of accounting theory and practice as a result of globalization and advancement in ICT, there is still evidence of paucity and dearth of locally produced accounting texts and reference materials in Nigeria. As such the publication of this book on accounting theory and practice with a flavor of global and local touch is timely and should therefore be commended. The book is a testimony of the efforts of our academic colleagues under the tutelage of Dr. Kabiru Isa Dandago, an Associate Professor and a highly respected Chartered Accountant. I have had the privilege of associating with him in a number of academic endeavors, so I am happy to see that he has brought his competence and experience to bear on the quality of this book.

On the whole, the authors have clearly succeeded in explaining a lot of complex accounting theories, thoughts, and principles in a lucid and readable manner. I believe that accounting professionals, researchers and students at the tertiary level of learning will find the book greatly useful.

Professor A.S. Mikailu
Usmanu Danfodiyo University,
Sokoto, Nigeria

ACKNOWLEDGEMENTS

On behalf of the contributors to this penetrating book, I would want to express our sincere gratitude to the Bayero University, Kano-Nigeria management for their ever continuous encouragement for the promotion of scholarship in the University. Specifically, I thank the Vice Chancellor, Prof. Attahiru M. Jega, OFR, for his sincere understanding and support on the need for this and similar book projects, by any group of scholars in the University, to come to fruitful.

We sincerely appreciate the understanding and support demonstrated by the Dean of our Faculty (Social and Management Sciences), Dr Saddiq Isa Radda and the Head of our Department (Accounting), Hajiya Dije Muhammad Suleiman. They have given all the required moral and financial supports for the successful execution of the book project.

It is our pleasure and privilege to have a very scholarly foreword to the book written by Professor Aminu Salihu Mikailu, a former Vice Chancellor of two universities (Usmanu Danfodiyo University, Sokoto and Kaduna State University, all in Nigeria). We are very grateful for the compliments expressed by the eminent scholar on the book and on our humble selves.

We thank our English editor, Associate Professor Mustapha Ahmad Isa, for his critical English editing and for providing other useful editorial comments. Our sincere thanks are extended to everyone who helped and encouraged us in the production of this book. We trust that they will all recognize the parts they have played for the successful publication of this book.

Associate Professor Kabiru Isa Dandago, PhD, ACA
Editor

Contents

Foreword iv

Acknowledgements..v

Chapter 1
General Introduction
Kabiru Isa Dandago 9

Chapter 2
Statements of Accounting Standards in Nigeria: The Marriage of Accounting Theory and Practice
Kabiru Isa Dandago 19

Chapter 3
International Harmonisation of Accounting Standards
Aliyu Sulaiman Kantudu 43

Chapter 4
Accounting as a Language of Business
Kabir Tahir Hamid 71

Chapter 5
An Examination of the Classification of Accounting Theory by Levels
Muhammad Aminu Isa 81

Chapter 6
History of Accounting Thought
Muhammad Liman Muhammad 93

Chapter 7
Ethical Thoughts in Accounting
Ibrahim Magaji Barde 109

Chapter 8
Ethical Considerations in Accounting
Ahmed Bawa Bello 125

Chapter 9
Approaches to Accounting Thoughts
Kabir Tahir Hamid 139

Chapter 10
An Alternative Approach to Accounting Theory
Y. M. Salaudeen 151

Chapter 11
Classification of Accounting Theory by Stance
Junaidu Muhammad Kurawa 169

Chapter 12
Accounting Theory by Reasoning
Ibrahim Magaji Barde 183

Chapter 13
Accounting and Social Change
Muhammad Liman Muhammad 203

Chapter 14
Issues in Behavioral Aspects of Accounting
Junaidu Muhammad Kurawa 221

Chapter 15
Equity Theories and Objectives of Financial Reporting
Aliyu Sulaiman Kantudu 235

Selected Bibliography 255

About the Contributors 279

Index 282

Chapter 1

General Introduction

Kabiru Isa Dandago

Accounting is a discipline whose characteristics have a very long historical background and its applications have a well developed theoretical framework. It is a discipline that could be said to be the first to be recognized by humanity (first with Adam and Eve made to account for what they did in the paradise) and the only discipline that is to be demonstrated in the Hereafter, where everybody would be raised up as an accountant- to account for all he/she did during his/her life time on earth! Accounting is a service-providing discipline, making available information (especially financial) for various decisions to be guided. Owners, creditors, managers, prospective investors, government and its agencies, employees and even the general public seek accounting information on entities/organizations for the purpose of taking various informed decisions. As a process, accounting is about identifying (through proper record keeping), measuring (through preparation of financial statements) and communicating economic information (through publication or making known the statements so prepared) to give room for informed judgments and decisions by the target users of the information.

Accounting, therefore, demands high degree of study for it to be well developed to play the role expected of it in molding the way of life of the whole humanity and in shaping the whole environment, through the influence it exercises over the decision of everybody in the global environment. One important area of accounting to be studied is its theoretical background in relation to its practices by practitioners, policy makers, managers of businesses and others that can not do without the information it provides. This book attempts to deeply study the various theories of accounting and the theorists, with a view to appreciating why practitioners in the field of Accountancy behave in a particular way in producing or utilizing accounting information. The book is an attempt at studying the theoretical underpinnings of accounting in relation to its practices. This first chapter entitled

General Introduction is an overview of all the other 14 chapters in the book, with a view to appreciating their objectives, methodology, discoveries/breakthrough and policy recommendations.

The second chapter entitled **Statements of Accounting Standards in Nigeria: the Marriage of Accounting Theory and Practice,** by Kabiru I. Dandago, reviews all the 26 SAS issued so far by the Nigerian Accounting Standards Board (NASB), with a view to showing how the standards ensure the marriage of the theory of accounting and its practice in Nigeria. It highlights the objectives, scope and major provisions of each of the 26 standards issued by the NASB, as at December 2007. The chapter shows accounting standards as the foundation for all the theories emanating in the accounting discipline as developed by scholars and practitioners in the field. Accounting students at all levels are expected to master those standards if they are to be sound in accounting, generally, and in financial accounting , specifically.

The third paper entitled **International Harmonization of Accounting Standards,** by Aliyu S. Kantudu, assesses the reasons for diversity in accounting policies and practices across the globe. The objectives of the paper are to ascertain the role of International Accounting Standards Board (IASB) and other actors in the harmonisation process and to review the implications of the convergence between the IASB and the US-GAAP on the developing nations. The methods used for data collection and analyses are documentation and the author's practical experiences in international accounting. Text books, journal articles and the internet provide materials for the study. The results show that a gap exists between countries in terms of cultural, educational, social, political and economic development and these give room for remarkable differences in accounting practices and policies.

The paper shows that IASB is really the catalyst and vanguard of the harmonisation of accounting practices and policies worldwide. It is also noted that despite its meaningful and far reaching policies, the International Accounting Standards(IAS) issued by the IASB have been heavily influenced by organizations such as the FASB, SEC, IOSCO, etc. which as a consequence has resulted in the relegation of developing countries to the background. The paper recommends that appropriate authorities such as the government, accountancy professional bodies and academics in the field of accounting, in the developing countries, should form pressure groups aimed at getting larger representation on the International Accounting Standard Board, so as to exercise greater influence in the process of setting IAS that would adequately capture the peculiarities of developing economies. The paper believes that greater participation in the process would not only allow the voices and interests of developing economies heard, but would also allow them to participate fully in the harmonisation and convergence processes.

An important purpose of accounting is to communicate relevant economic information to permit informed judgments and decisions by users of such information. The communication of accounting information is accomplished by the use of specific words and techniques that are very much characteristic of a specific language. This is why accounting is referred to as the language of business. The success of the messages conveyed by the accounting language rests on the level of readability of those messages and their correct perception by users. These are the issues addressed in the fourth paper.

The methodology used in the paper entitled **Accounting as a Language of Business,** by Kabir Tahir Hamid, includes a review of literature on the subject matter with a view to facilitating the understanding of the classification of accounting theory by level: pragmatic (the study of the effect of language), semantic (the study of meaning of language), and syntactic (the study of the logic or grammar of a language). The paper concludes that the classification of accounting theory by level is important because it helps to ascertain the effect, meaning and logical sense of accounting information to users of the information. The paper recommends that the presentation of financial statements by firms in Nigeria should be made as simple as possible so as to enhance easy understanding and correct perception by the users of the information.

The fifth paper entitled **An Examination of the Classification of Accounting Theory by Levels,** by Muhammad Aminu Isa, examines the classification of accounting theory by levels, with a view to making readers appreciate the relevance of the study of language in accounting theory. This classification involves the study of syntactic, semantics and pragmatics, the major components of language study. The study deployed content analysis for making inferences from texts. The paper concludes that the use of this classification of accounting theory is important in enhancing the grammatical structure of accounting reports. All the three aspects of the classification are found to be useful and relevant to accounting theory. It is, therefore, recommended that scholars should be encouraged to make sufficient contributions to this facet of accounting theory to enhance the understanding of the language structures upon which meanings are constructed from accounting events.

The sixth paper entitled **History of Accounting Thought**, by Muhammad Liman Muhammad, looks into the history of accounting thought. It traces the origin of accounting concepts and principles that have been in application over time. The study largely placed emphasis on the documentary source of data. Therefore, relevant materials including, but not limited to textbooks, journals and conference proceedings were used. It is found that though the terms, concepts, conventions and postulates are interchangeably used by different scholars, they, however, convey the same message. In addition, though accounting principles, concepts, conventions and standards reflect the systems of thought required for governing and regulating accounting practices, this appears not to be the case in practice as many enterprises do not comply with their provisions. It is, therefore, recommended that since accounting practice does not only lie on the skill and competence of an accountant but largely dependant on his/her ability and desire to observe integrity and objectivity, accountants, in whatever capacity they find themselves, should not allow such fundamental qualities to be compromised.

The rate at which ethics is becoming an issue of prominent importance among all categories of people has drawn the attention of many professionals including accountants, philosophers, religious leaders and other professional groups to the core issue of ethics. There have been varying degrees of effort aimed at studying the basic root of ethics with a view to providing meaningful and acceptable explanations on what ethics is and what possibly constitutes it. The seventh paper entitled **Ethical Thoughts in Accounting,** by Ibrahim Magaji Barde, studies the bedrock of ethical thinking as well as the constituents of ethics itself. The paper adopts the library research method and primarily reviews current literature in the field. The paper establishes that ethics sprouted from the principles of benefit maximization or just as a duty on an individual. It, therefore, concludes that values such as religious, societal, professional and personal principles seriously affect ethics and can, therefore, play a vital role in molding it. The paper, therefore, recommends that those with influence such as religious leaders and professional bodies have a role to play in encouraging and, where possible, enforcing ethics among their subjects. In addition, accountants in the academics and in practice need to be engaged in training and retraining programmes for them to improve their performance and competence.

The eighth paper entitled **Ethical Considerations in Accounting,** by Ahmed Bawa Bello, seeks to discuss ethical thought in Accounting with a view to identifying the major attributes required for ethical behavior, the consequences of unethical behavior and the challenges that affect ethical issues in accounting. Secondary data were used and they were collected through various sites of the internet. Textbooks, journals and conference proceedings were also consulted. There is, however, the dearth of materials on empirical studies on ethical matters. Literatures were reviewed; analyses were carried out on various topical issues on ethics and the nine major ethical attributes (independence, integrity, rationality, objectivity, competence, morality, honesty, confidentiality and time consciousness).

It was identified that unethical behavior will result to loss of public confidence, loss of profit and, in some instances, complete loss of capital that may lead to liquidation. Corruption, fear of loosing client, poor remuneration, inaction on auditors report and accountants' advice and proliferations of "accounting professional bodies" are identified as the major challenges faced by genuine accountants and genuine professional bodies. It is recommended that accountancy Professional bodies should have active disciplinary Committee that could act objectively and fast on any disciplinary matter involving accountants and that they should have monitoring committees to monitor the activities of accountants.

Judgments and discretions are required by accountants in order to resolve accounting problems on which no standards have been issued, or on the ways of complying with standards. Although some studies have revealed that some managers left their posts on their own and would come to resolutions that are perfectly satisfactory to all concerned, other studies have shown that managers may want to manipulate earnings to embellish their performance with a view to enhancing their rewards. This creates a problem because of the fear users of financial statements have that management may use its accounting discretion to distort reported profits. This clearly demonstrates that accounting theory is often a matter of professional judgments made by accountants faced with specific accounting issues. Paper nine addresses these issues.

The methodology used in the ninth paper entitled **Approaches to Accounting Thoughts,** by Kabir Tahir Hamid, involves review of various write-ups on the subject matter to understand the various approaches that are used in resolving problems in accounting, with a view to ascertaining their continued relevance, in theory and in practice. The paper concludes that the approaches are still very useful, because they enable solutions of accounting problems at various levels, on which no standards are issued. Finally, the paper recommends that accountants in all walks of life should acquaint themselves with the approaches in view of their continuous relevance in solving issues in accounting profession.

The tenth paper entitled **An Alternative Approach to Accounting Theory**, by Yinka M. Salaudeen, attempts to establish the approaches used in constructing the various accounting theories. Using contents analysis to interpret the mass of literature available in the field of accounting theory formulation, it was found that different authors use different appellation to describe the same type of approach, and that no single approach is capable of being used for formulating an accounting theory but a combination of approaches. The recommendation of the paper to stem the multiplicity of approaches is for efforts to be geared towards reaching a consensus amongst the accounting community on the underlying assumption to accounting theory and, therefore, the approach to theory formulation in accounting.

The eleventh paper entitled **Classification of Accounting Theory by Stance: Descriptive, Prescriptive and Positive,** by Junaidu Muhammad Kurawa, attempts to provide a framework under which Companies and Allied Matters Act (CAMA 1990) and the Nigerian Accounting Standards could be classified within the Descriptive, Prescriptive and the Positive accounting theories. The paper provides an overview of the concepts and meaning of accounting theory as a background to this classification. Using content analysis of documentary secondary data, the paper establishes that accounting theories have an important role to play in determining the content of financial statements. These accounting theories could either be descriptive, prescriptive or positive. The two major theories considered in our analysis have descriptive features due to their origin (Nigerian laws, customs, and business culture) intent (to regularize long standing practice) and content (descriptive provision devoid of dynamism). The paper also establishes that CAMA represents an adaptation of the UK Companies Act (1948).

According to the paper, CAMA has failed to reflect the changing needs of the Nigerian business environment and, as a guiding rule; it has not kept pace with the changing needs of accounting information by users of financial reports. The Act does not contain provisions on changes in equity position or provisions on detailed items of income statement and cash flow statement. The local accounting standards, on the other hand, have not covered about twenty topics actively covered by IASs. The paper opined that the contents of accounting standard are descriptive and their intent is to regularize existing practice. In addition, they are neither logical deductions nor products of empirical findings. They fail the test of time and must be reviewed from time to time to keep abreast with the changing needs of the accounting environment. The paper recommends that it is imperative to consider the changing needs of information by users from time to time in developing accounting standards and rules.

The 20th Century industrial revolution rendered the pre-revolution bookkeeping and accounting techniques inadequate. These techniques had to be improved upon to capture issues resulting from expansion in business as a result of the revolution. Consequently, it becomes necessary for accounting theorists to develop and occasionally improve on accounting principles to address issues like depreciation, income recognition and accounting measurement.

The twelfth paper entitled **Accounting Theory by Reasoning,** by Ibrahim Magaji Barde, studies deductive and inductive reasoning, with reference to the works of MacNeal (1939) and Ijiri (1975), respectively, in developing accounting theory. The paper establishes that both deductive and inductive theories of Accounting place varying degrees of importance on different issues. While deductive theories are usually reformist and revolutionary in nature, inductive theories maintain the status-quo and merely suggest improvement to current accounting practice. The paper concludes that both deductive and inductive theories have positively impacted on developing and shaping accounting theory and practice. It recommends that accounting theorists, regardless of the approaches they use, need to place emphasis on the issues of reliability and objectivity in developing accounting theories that would stand the test of time.

The thirteenth paper entitled **Accounting and Social Change**, by Muhammad Liman Muhammad, examines the relationship between accounting and social change. It seeks to find out whether or not accounting principles, practices or methods that have evolved over time emerged spontaneously or were occasioned by events in the environment in which accounting operates. In conducting the study, the documentary source of data was used. Relevant materials including textbooks and journals were used. It is found that though developments in accounting are inventions of man, they are largely necessitated and influenced by the dynamic socio-economic and political environment of accounting itself. Accounting evolution is thus largely a response to the social changes of the time. It is recommended that since accounting is not a natural science, and it is practiced under different and unstable socio-cultural and other environments, in developing or modifying accounting principles, practices or methods, the peculiarities of such environments should serve as very useful guides.

The Behavioral aspect of accounting is one of the few areas that receive considerable attention, in recent times, from management of organizations, policy makers in government, other users of accounting information, researchers and academics. Its eminence, however, is due to the fact that accounting profession is greatly influenced by the behavior of individuals and organizations which could also impact negatively on the accounting system and functions.

The fourteenth paper entitled **Issues in Behavioral Aspects of Accounting**, by Junaidu Muhammad Kurawa, examines the contributions of scholars in the most notable area of behavioral aspect of accounting, namely, financial reporting and management fraud. The aim is to provide an insight into the dimensions and relative importance of this issue and how accounting practice could be enhanced through a better understanding of the behavior of individuals and organizations. It is emphasized that falsification of financial statement has led to a high incidence of corporate failure, which is attributed to management fraud resulting from insider activities with the intent to deceive the users of financial information. The paper recommends that users of accounting information should strive to gain a thorough understanding of the fundamental issues in behavioral accounting in order to be able to use accounting information with high degree of caution and perusal to avoid being misled by the providers of such information.

The fifteenth paper entitled **Equity Theories and Objectives of Financial Reporting,** by Aliyu Sulaiman Kantudu, reviews the equity theories of accounting with a view to establishing whether or not the theories are relevant to today's business arrangements and, secondly, to find out whether or not accounting standards set by the accounting standards bodies have regards to these theories in formulating accounting policies, especially as they relate to the objectives of financial reporting. Documental analysis .was used as the method of data collection. Results show that accounting standard setting bodies, in most countries, seem to present definitions of the objectives of financial reporting which are very similar to one another, that is, providing information useful for making economic decisions.

The guidelines regarding financial reporting and users provided by the local accounting standard setting bodies as well as FASB and IASB seem to revolve on the issues of the objectives of financial reporting, user groups, and user needs. Some of the propositions presented seem to support the entity theory or perhaps the residual equity theory, while others support the enterprise theory or the proprietary theory. The paper found that equity theories were developed some decades back.

Although very relevant in today's business arrangements, the enterprise theory is found to be more relevant to the current information needs of users of financial reports of entities. It is thus, recommended that accounting standards setting bodies should pay more attention to the enterprise theory, which is broader in concept, when coming up with the objectives of financial reporting for business entities in the future. Secondly, accounting policy makers should pay more attention to the fund theory in case of governments and not-for-profit organizations accounting standards.

This book has addressed substantially what accounting theories are all about and how they are to be put to practice, especially in Nigeria. It is one of those attempts at addressing the advanced accounting issues both in theory and in practice. Students of advanced accounting theory and practice at all levels, in the Universities and polytechnics, have cause to jubilate with the arrival of this book.

Chapter 2

Statements of Accounting Standards in Nigeria: The Marriage of Accounting Theory and Practice

Kabiru Isa Dandago

Introduction

The Nigerian Accounting Standard Board (NASB) is the government agency shouldered with the responsibility of issuing Statements of Accounting Standards (SASs) on various accounting topics. The Board was established in September 1982, at the instance and sponsorship of the Institute of Chartered Accountants of Nigeria (ICAN), having realized the necessity of setting local accounting standards that would take into account the customs, laws, level of economic development and other peculiarities of the country. The first SAS issued by the Board was on Disclosure of Accounting Policies, in 1982. The Board was made a parastatal of government, under the supervision of the Federal Ministry of Commerce, in May 1993. It was made an autonomous body in 2003, with the enactment of Act No.22, the NASB Act 2003. The composition of the institutions/organizations represented on the Board was enlarged from eight in 1984 to fourteen in 2003 and from thirteen council members to nineteen council members.

With SASs in place, preparers of financial statements in Nigeria are to de-emphasize compliance with the provisions of a similar International Accounting Standards (IASs). In other words, if there is any conflict between the provisions of an SAS on an accounting topic and those of an IAS, the conflict is to be resolved in favor of the SAS. An IAS on an accounting topic is applicable in Nigeria only where an SAS is not issued on the topic.

The 2003 NASB Act carries provisions on the institutional members of the Board, its sources of revenue, its sources of expenditure, its powers in the areas of setting Accounting standards and ensuring compliance with the standards and many other issues. With that law, the provisions of all the SASs issued by the Board are now legally binding on preparers of financial statements in Nigeria; non-compliance, therefore, would attract legal actions. The SASs are no longer to be treated as Generally Accepted Accounting Principles (GAAPs); they are to be complied with as legal provisions!

This Chapter highlights the Statements of Accounting Standards issued so far by the Nigerian Accounting Standards Board, with a view to appreciating the efforts made in Nigeria, through the Board, to marry accounting theory with accounting practice in all the sectors of the Nigerian economy. Some of the Standards are specifically addressing the accounting practices expected in specified industries of the economy, while others are addressing matters that are of general applications.

Overviewing the Statements of Accounting Standards

Statement of Accounting Standard 1: SAS I

On Disclosure of Accounting Policies

This Standard was issued to address the following points:

- The end product of financial accounting process is the preparation and publication of financial statements. A Substantial number of alternative postulates, assumptions, principles and methods adopted by a reporting entity in the preparation of its financial statements can significantly affect its results of operations, financial position and changes thereof. It is, therefore, essential to the understanding, interpretation and use of financial statements that, whenever there are several acceptable accounting methods which may be followed; those who prepare them disclose the main assumptions on which they are based.
- The purpose of the relevant provisions of the Companies and Allied Matters Act(CAMA) 1990(as amended to date) and this Statement is to assist any reader in the understanding and the interpretation of financial statements and the information disclosed therein.
- This Statement does not seek to establish accounting standards for individual items as these were appropriately dealt with by separate Statements of Accounting Standards that were issued subsequently by the Board.
- This SAS, therefore, addresses all the policies, methods, techniques or assumptions that are to be employed in the preparation of financial statements by enterprises, emphasizing that any policy, method, etc

adopted must be disclosed for the user of the financial statements to appreciate the bases of the accounting information being used.

Statement of Accounting Standard 2: SAS 2

On Information to be disclosed in Financial Statements

This standard was issued to address the following points:

- Accounting information about a business entity or enterprise is required by a variety of users. This need dictates the fundamental objectives of accounting and the mode of reporting accounting information.
- Firms, organizations or enterprises carry on business activities in a given economic, social and political environment and there is public interest in their operations. For instance:
  - (i) Individuals, Financial institutions or group of Investors need accounting information to determine the liquidity, profitability and viability of the enterprise.
  - (ii) Managers in an enterprise need accounting information to measure performance, plan and control operations.
  - (iii) Employees and customers of an enterprise need accounting information in order to assess the ability of the enterprise to produce goods or to render services on a continuous basis.
  - (iv) Governments and regulatory bodies need accounting information in order to be able to impose and collect taxes, to regulate certain business activities and to plan, execute and evaluate government projects.
  - (v) Quasi-government establishments need accounting information in order to meet their statutory obligations.

Thus, the information expected to be provided in financial statements could be quantitative and qualitative in nature, to aid users in making informed economic decisions. Financial statements are, therefore, expected to be simple, clear and easy to understand by all users.

Financial statements are the means of communicating to interested parties information on the resources, obligations and performances of the reporting entity or enterprise.

This Standard emphasizes on the minimum amount of information to be disclosed by preparers of financial statements to assist users achieve their various objectives. Meaningful information can be gathered, collated and presented in different forms. The format recommended in this SAS is expected to be the best practice in Nigeria.

Statement of Accounting Standard 3: SAS 3

On Accounting for Property, Plant and Equipment

This standard was issued with a view to addressing the following issues:

- Property Plant and Equipment, generally referred to as fixed assets, are those tangible resources of an enterprise which are employed in its operations. In many enterprises these assets are grouped into various categories such as land and buildings, plant and machinery, equipment. furniture, fixtures and fittings, vehicles, etc
- This Statement deals with accounting for property, plant and equipment under the historical cost concept and the revaluation of specific items of property, plant and equipment. It does not deal with the effect of changing pieces in accounting for these assets.
- This Statement does not deal with accounting for expenditure on the following items: (a) Regenerative natural resources such as forests, standing timber, cattle, etc (b). Non-regenerative resources such as mineral deposits oil and gas deposits, etc(c) Real estate development by property companies.
- This Statement makes brief reference to the accounting treatment (under certain circumstances) of: (i) Leasehold property; (ii) depreciation and property, plant and equipment and (iii) Capitalization of borrowing cost.

Statement of Accounting Standard 4: SAS 4

On Accounting for Stocks

This standard was issued to address the following matters:

- Stocks (otherwise referred to as inventories) are items of value held for use or sale by an enterprise and usually comprise raw materials and supplies used in production, work in progress and finished goods.

- Depending on the nature of an enterprise, the value of stocks may be substantial, surpassing or only second to that of property, plant and equipment.
- Appropriate classification and accurate determination of the quantity and cost of stocks are necessary for proper determination of the result of the operations of an enterprise and for presentation of current assets in its Balance sheet.

The use of several methods for valuing and reporting stocks gives rise to wide differences in the results of the operations of enterprises in the same line of business. This Statement seeks to narrow such differences by setting a standard for the valuation and presentation of items of stock in the context of the historical cost concept.

This Statement deals with the valuation and presentation of items of stock including livestock and agricultural produce.

This Statement does not deal with:

(i) Valuation under the replacement cost accounting concept;

(ii) Valuation under the inflation accounting concept;

(iii) Valuation of work-in-progress under long-term contracts;

(iv) Valuation of by-products.

(v) Valuation of forest Products.

Statement of Accounting Standard 5: SAS 5

On Construction Contracts

This standard addresses the following matters:

- The main issues involved in accounting for Construction Contracts are the timing, measurement and recognition of revenue and the asset created during construction.
- Costs on a Construction Contract may start to accumulate even before the contract is won. It is, therefore, necessary to determine the accounting treatment that should be accorded to such costs as soon as there is a convincing evidence that the contract will be won.

- The treatment of these costs may have a significant effect on the reported result of an accounting period and on the assets and liabilities of the reporting enterprise. Unless a correct treatment of such costs is adopted, it may lead to a wrong appraisal of the profitability of the construction contract.
- The period for the execution of a Construction Contract depends on the nature, type and size of the contract. Some contracts run for only a short period of time, as a result of which it may be more prudent to recognize the profit on such a contract only on completion. Some other contracts, however, may extend over two or more accounting periods of the enterprises, in which case, a meaningful basis has to be adopted for the determination of the proportion of profit that has been earned as at each accounting date and the value that needs to be reported in the financial statement as work- in-progress in the books of the contractor. Most of the provisions of this Statement apply to the Contractor.

This Statement does not cover: (i) Contracts that deal with the research into and the development of new products; (ii) Service Contracts that fall under job order costing; (iii) Property development projects including those often referred to in Nigeria as Contractor Financed Projects; and (iv) The treatment of Construction Contracts in the books of the Employer (Contractee) because the value of any Construction Contract can be easily determined by the Employer through the analysis of cash outlays and the liabilities accrued to the contract.

Statements of Accounting Standard 6: SAS 6

On Extraordinary Items and Prior Year Adjustment

This standard addresses the following matters:

- Two opposing views that have considerable support for determination of operating income in the year: (i) the Current Operating Performance Concept and (ii) the All-inclusive Concept in the recent past. There has been considerable diversity of views as to what constitute extraordinary and unusual items, prior year adjustments and how they should be treated in the accounts reporting entities.

The Primary objectives of this Statement are:

- To examine the issue involved in the determination of operating income in any given accounting period, and
- To prescribe the accounting treatment of extraordinary and unusual items and prior year adjustments as well as their appropriate disclosure in financial statements.

Statement of Accounting Standard 7: SAS 7

On Foreign Currency Conversions and Translations

This standard addresses the following issues:

- Organizations or individuals in Nigeria often engage in business dealings with governments, enterprises or individuals in other countries. These dealings may involve the payment, receipt or transfer of foreign currency or the creation of foreign currency assets and liabilities.
- In each transaction with a foreign party, the invoice price is usually quoted in terms of foreign currency which is not necessarily the domestic currency of that party. For the transactions to be reflected in the accounts of the Nigerian enterprise, there must be conversion of the amount into Naira.
- Transactions between parties in different countries generally require one party to purchase some foreign currency in order to settle its obligations. Between the dates of the initial transaction and the final settlement, there may be fluctuations in the exchange rate and this may result in a gain or a loss.
- A Nigerian Company maintaining a branch office in a foreign country or holding an equity interest in a foreign company must translate the accounting data expressed in foreign currency into Naira before the financial statements can be consolidate or combined.

The primary objectives of this statement are to provide uniform accounting treatment for:

(i) Foreign exchange transactions and,

(ii) The transaction by a Nigerian enterprise of the financial statements of its foreign branches, subsidiaries, associates, or joint ventures based in a country other than Nigeria.

Statement of Accounting Standard 8: SAS 8

On Accounting for Employees' Retirement Benefits

This standard addresses the following important issues:

- Many charitable organizations, governments and business establishments provide retirement benefits for their employees. Retirement benefits can consist of monthly payments to former employees or a lump sum upon attainment of a specified retirement age and may include additional payments in case of death or disability. Depending on the terms of a retirement benefit plan, some employers bear the entire cost of a retirement plan whilst other employers contribute a proportion of the cost of the plan with the employee bearing the remaining fraction.
- Some retirement plans are evidenced by a well articulated document forming a part of the total employment contract of employees. Some plans are not so clear and can only be inferred from the employers' policies or practices. In some countries, laws prescribe the minimum benefits payable to a qualified employee to protect the employee, but this is not presently the case in Nigeria.
- The main issues involved in accounting for retirement benefits are the determination of the: (i) amount due to employees before or after the date of implementation of a plan; (ii) amount of funding required in order to meet employees' entitlements upon retirement; and(iii) amount of information to be disclosed in financial statements.

The primary objectives of this statement are to narrow the differences in the methods or manner used in: (a) measuring the amount of retirement obligations under retirement benefits plans, (b) allocating the cost of the plan and recognizing resulting gains or losses to the accounting periods, and (c) disclosing as accurately as possible, the plan and the effects of the plan implementation on the reporting enterprise.

Statement of Accounting Standard 9: SAS 9

On Accounting for Depreciation

This standard addresses the following important issues:

- Property, plant and equipment, generally referred to as fixed assets, are those tangible resources of an enterprise employed in its operations. Each item of fixed asset usually has a limited useful economic life during which it can be profitably used in the operations of the enterprise. Depreciation is the cost of these fixed assets to operations. When the use of such an item of fixed asset is no longer of economic benefit to the enterprise, the item is usually retired or disposed of.

- The Purpose of this Statement is to provide a guide for uniform and acceptable methods of determining and reporting depreciation on Items of property, plant and equipment whether such items are stated at their historical costs or revalued amounts.

Statements of Accounting Standard 10: SAS 10

On Accounting By Banks and Non – Bank Financial Institutions (part 1)

This standard addresses the following important issues:

- In recent times, national attention has focused on the banking industry and the accounting practices followed by banks due to the: (i) importance of the sector in the industrial and commercial development of the economy, (ii) inconsistent accounting policies and reporting practices which make comparison of performance difficult, (iii) allegedly overstated profits reported by banks, (iv) survival problems of "troubled" banks, (v) probable shake-out that may be ahead as a result of increased competition in the industry, and (vi) resulting need to sustain public confidence in the banking sector.
- This Statement seeks to provide a guide for accounting policies and accounting methods that should be followed by banks in the preparation of their financial statements. Improved accounting and reporting practices are important in ensuring reliable financial statements that are comparable across the banking industry.
- This Statement (Part 1) focuses on three main areas of concern relating to accounting practices followed by banks namely:

(i) Income recognition

(ii) Loss recognition and

(iii) Balance Sheet Classification

Statement of Accounting Standard 11: SAS 11

On Leases

This standard addresses the following important issues:

- Leasing has in recent times in Nigeria become an attractive means of financing the acquisition and use of fixed assets such land, buildings, plants, vehicles, machineries and equipment. The attraction of leasing is heightened by the very high cost of fixed assets, the scarcity of foreign exchange to pay for imports, and the relative ease of access to credit facilities for leasing.
- At the time of issuing this standard, financial statements published in Nigeria contained little or no information on lease transactions, some of which involved huge annual financial commitments. There was the need, therefore, to consider appropriate treatments and disclosure of lease transactions in the books of both the lessor and the leasee.
- This Statement does not cover: (a) lease agreements pertaining to exploration for, or exploitation of, natural resources such as oil, gas, minerals, and timber; (b) licensing agreements relating to intellectual properties such as motion pictures, video recordings, plays manuscripts, patents and copyrights; and (c)leases in favour of contractor financing the development of landed property.
- The primary objectives of this Statement are: (i) to ensure that published financial statements contain sufficient information about lease transactions to make it possible for users of such statements to determine the effects of lease commitments on the present and future operations of the reporting enterprises; and (ii) to ensure uniform disclosure of terms and classes of leases in financial statements.

Statement of Accounting Standard 12: SAS 12

On Accounting for Deferred Taxes

This standard addresses the following important issues:

- Profits and other gains of business organizations are sometimes recognized in one accounting period but brought into taxation in another period. In this situation, there is need to consider deferred taxes and how to account for them properly in financial statements of the related periods.
- The Statement deals with accounting for deferred taxes on income and other gains in the financial statements arising from differences in the timing of income recognition and assessment. It relates primarily to the deferred tax aspects of companies income lax, capital gains tax and petroleum profits tax in Nigeria.

Statement of Accounting Standard 13: SAS 13

On Accounting for Investments

This standard addresses the following important issues:

- Organizations, in the course of their business operations, apply all or some of their resources in acquiring assets to be held for capital appreciation, income generation, or other purposes such as securing trading advantages.
- Many financial statements published in Nigeria do not disclose adequate information about the investment held by the reporting enterprises. This statement therefore seeks to provide a guide for the accounting treatment of investment transactions and their disclosure in the financial statements. Such investments do not enable the investor to exercise significant influence or control over the financial and operating decisions of the investee companies.
- This statement does not cover: (i) stocks/inventory covered in SAS No. 4;(ii) property, plant and Equipment covered in SAS No.3; accounting for leases SAS No. 11;(iii) Investment in pension benefit plans and Life Insurance Enterprises;(iv) Investment in subsidiaries and associates;(v)Investment in Joint Ventures;(vi) Goodwill, patents, trademarks and similar assets;
- The statement focuses on three main forms of investments, namely; short-term investments (current investments); long-term investments, and investment properties.

Statement of Accounting Standard 14: SAS 14

Accounting in the petroleum Industry: Upstream Activities

This standard addresses the following important issues:

- The petroleum industry occupies a very strategic position in the Nigerian economy as the nation's major provider of foreign income. The industry plays a major role in facilitating the economic development of the nation.
- To date there is no authoritative pronouncement on accounting rules to be followed in the industry, in spite of existing legislation. Since the oil companies operating within the industry come from different countries of the world, the industry has developed a wide diversity of accounting practices. There is, therefore, a need to develop an accounting standard to be used by all the companies within the industry in order to ensure the comparability of financial statements.
- Activities of the industry can be divided into two broad categories: upstream and downstream. Upstream activities involve the acquisition of mineral interest in properties, exploration (including prospecting), development, and production of crude oil and gas. Downstream activities involve transporting, refining and marketing of oil, gas and derivatives. This statement deals with accounting and reporting for upstream activities.

Statement of Accounting Standards 15: SAS 15

On Accounting by Banks and Non – Bank Financial Institutions (Part II)

This standard addresses the following important issues:

- This Statement seeks to provide a guide for accounting policies and accounting methods that are to be followed by Non-Bank Financial institutions such as: (i) Finance Houses/Companies; (ii) Bureau De Change; (iii) Mortgage Institutions; (iv) Discount Houses; (v) Stock Brokerage Firms; and(vi) Other Capital Market Operators.
- This Statement focuses on three main areas, namely:
  - (i) Income recognition;
  - (ii) Loss recognition; and
  - (iii) Classification and disclosures in Financial Statements.

- It is noted that Non-Bank Financial Institutions are an emerging and dynamic sub-sector of the finance industry, with new types of business constantly evolving. This Statement is intended to establish minimum accounting and disclosure requirements for existing business activities in the sub-sector.

Statement of Accounting Standard 16: SAS 16

On Accounting for Insurance Business

This standard addresses the following important issues:

- The primary purpose of insurance is to provide economic protection from identifiable risks that may occur during a Specified period. Insurance business can be divided into two main categories-general (also called non-life) and life (also called long-term).
- Among the types of risks commonly insured are: property damage, fire, accident, burglary and theft under non-life insurance: disability, survival and death under life assurance.
- The business activities of the Insurance Industry are unique and at the time the standard was issued, there was a wide diversity of accounting practices. There was, therefore, the need to set out uniform accounting standards for the industry in order to streamline the areas of differences and variations in accounting treatments so as to enhance the comparability and usefulness of financial statements.
- This statement establishes financial accounting and reporting standards for the financial statements of non-life arid life assurance undertakings. This statement is intended to apply to the financial statements prepared in accordance with the requirements of the Companies and Allied Matters Decree, 1990 and the Insurance Decree, 1997 but not to the regulatory returns drawn up for submission to the National Insurance Commission.
- This statement does not-cover the activities of: friendly societies; pension or provident funds; loss adjusters; and insurance brokers/agents.

Statement of Accounting Standard 17: SAS 17

On Accounting in the Petroleum Industry: Downstream Activities

This standard addresses the following important issues:

- Statement of Accounting Standard (SAS) 14 was issued in 1993 as part of efforts to enhance the comparability of financial statements prepared by companies operating in the upstream sector of the petroleum industry. In order to complete the standardization process for the industry, there is a need to develop an accounting standard for the downstream sector.
- This Statement, therefore, provides a guide on accounting practices and reporting formats to be followed by companies operating in the downstream sector of the Nigerian petroleum industry. Such companies include those engaged in: (i) Refining and Petrochemicals; (ii) Marketing and Distribution; and (iii) Liquefied Natural Gas.

Statement of Accounting Standard 18: SAS 18

On Statement of Cash flows

This standard addresses the following important issues:

- A statement of cash flow provides information about cash receipts and cash payments of an enterprise over a given period; it indicates the pattern of cash generation and utilization. It reveals how cash is generated from operations or through new capital raised and how payments are made for taxes, dividends, new investments and debts. It is designed to shed light on an enterprise's financial strength.
- The information provided in a statement of cash flows, if used with related disclosure and other information in the financial statements, will over a period assist users to: (i) assess the impact of its current transactions - operating, investing and financing activities - on its performance and financial position;(ii) assess the ability of the enterprise to meet its debt obligations, pay dividends and meet other claims;(iii) assess the ability of the enterprise to finance ongoing operations and growth from internal sources and determine the amount of external financing required;(iv) reconcile profit/loss and cash flow; and (v) assess the ability of the enterprise to generate positive net future cash flows.
- A Statement of Source and Application of Funds is based on movements in working capital components. Working capital encompasses cash, cash equivalents and other assets which are convertible into cash within an accounting year, such as debtors and stocks. The main reason why the Statement of Cash Flows is now regarded as a preferred parameter for evaluating corporate liquidity is that the Statement of Source and Application of Funds based on

movements in working capital can obscure movements relevant to the viability and liquidity of an enterprise. For example, a potentially disastrous decrease in cash available can be masked by an increase in stock or debtors. Enterprises may, therefore, run out of cash while reporting increases in working capital.

Statement of Accounting Standard 19: SAS 19

On Accounting for Taxes

This standard addresses the following important issues:

- Recent developments internationally in accounting for taxation of income and profits have created the need for the revision of the Statement of Accounting Standard No. 12: Accounting for Deferred Taxes. It has also been considered necessary to expand the scope of the standard to include all forms of taxes payable by business entities. This Statement, therefore, replaces the Statement of Accounting Standard No. 12.
- This Statement covers taxes on business organizations. These include Companies Income Tax, Petroleum Profits Tax, Capital Gains Tax, Value Added Tax and Education Tax.

Statement of Accounting Standard 20: SAS 20

On Abridged Financial Statement

This standard addresses the following important issues:

- Annual Reports and Financial Statements are the means of communicating to shareholders and other interested parties information on the financial resources, obligations and performance of a reporting entity or enterprise. Such information usually assists shareholders and other interested parties in assessing the financial liquidity, profitability and viability of the enterprise. According to SAS 2, financial statements consist of Statement of Accounting Policies, Balance Sheet, Profit and Loss Account or Income Statement, Notes on the Accounts, Statement of Cash Flows, Value Added Statements and Five -Year Financial Summary.
- In recent years, there has been demand by some shareholders and companies in Nigeria to reduce the size of annual report and financial statements as well as curtail the high cost of printing and mailing glossy financial statements. Section 355 of the Companies and Allied

Matters Act, 1990, allows companies to publish Abridged Financial Statements. The Act however, does not specify any minimum disclosure requirements of such statements.

- A review of abridged financial statements published before the issuance of this Standard has shown that their information contents are not uniform; their formats are unsatisfactory and some lack acceptable technical quality and comparability. The primary objectives of this Statement are to:(i) specify the minimum contents of Abridged Financial Statements;(ii) standardize formats for presentation of Abridged Financial Statements; and(iii improve comparability and usefulness of Abridged Financial Statements.

Statement of Accounting Standard 21: SAS 21

On Earnings per Share

This standard addresses the following important issues:

- Earnings per Share (EPS) refer to earnings per ordinary share. Basically, earnings per share is calculated by dividing the operating profit after tax of a company for a financial year by the number of outstanding ordinary shares of the company during that financial year.
- Operating profit or loss after income tax is the profit or loss for the financial year before extraordinary items and after applicable income tax expense. It is an amount of profit or loss that includes exceptional items but excludes extraordinary items.
- EPS is a performance indicator that is primarily of interest to existing and potential shareholders, and their advisers. An appropriate method of calculating earnings per share plays a major role in arriving at earnings growth over time, and the price earning ratio. These are crucial indices to financial decisions. The objectives of this statement therefore are :(a) to prescribe the method of calculating basic earnings per share and diluted earnings per share; and (b) to require disclosure of basic earning per share, diluted earnings per share and other related information.

Statement of Accounting Standard 22: SAS 22

On Research and Development Costs

This standard addresses the following important issues:

- Research and Development are activities directly related to long-range planning. The effectiveness of research and development expenditure may be assessed only in relation to the attainment of goals specified in the long-range plan. The spending of millions of Naira on research and development which invariably leads to all kinds of new products and services is important for the survival of most businesses. The world's level of development is the product of research and development. Usually, there is a long lead time between costs incurred and benefits received.
- The importance of research and development to any business cannot be over emphasized as many industries' survival and growth depend to a great extent on it. The measurement and treatment of the associated costs also affect the entity significantly. Some entities treat all research and development costs as expense in the year incurred; other entities in the same business treat the cost as intangible assets to be amortized over future years. These divergent practices, no doubt, prevent the financial statements of different entities from being readily comparable.
- The entities that are adopting the practice of writing off the cost of research and development rely on the provisions of Section 8(2) of schedule 2 to the Companies and Allied Matters Act, 1990 which stipulates that research and development costs shall not be treated as assets in any entities' balance sheet. However, those opposed to this practice opine that research and development costs are so significant that writing them off in one accounting year will distort the information content of the financial statements of the entity. They further argue that it will be a disincentive to investors who are really interested in the development of the economy.
- A review of the financial statements of some entities reveals that only a few entities carry the cost of research and development activities as asset in their financial statements whilst others do not. This, no doubt, creates problems of uniformity and comparability in financial reporting. Therefore, this Statement is expected to provide an acceptable and uniform accounting practice for reporting research and development costs.

Statement of Accounting Standard 23: SAS 23

On Provisions, Contingent Liabilities and Contingent Assets

This standard addresses the following important issues:

- There are many financial transactions with significant impact on the result of an entity that may not be concluded with certainty at the end of a financial year. There is, therefore, the need for management to provide details of such contingencies in order to make the financial statements more meaningful. This might not have been previously done appropriately due to reluctance to disclose confidential and sensitive information. Thus, details of the amounts involved and the probability of the occurrence of the events are not always disclosed to enable the user assess the most likely financial effect on an entity.
- Provision is an amount set aside to meet a known liability whose amount and timing cannot be estimated with a significant level of certainty. In contrast, contingency applies to a condition which exists at the balance sheet date but whose outcome will be confirmed only on the occurrence or non-occurrence of one or more uncertain future events not wholly within the control of the entity. There are some contingencies where the possibility of the ultimate outcome having a material effect on the financial statements is so remote that its disclosure could be misleading.
- A contingent liability is one which arises from past events and cannot be recognized in the current financial statements because it is uncertain that an outflow of resources will be required to settle the obligation. On the other hand, a contingent asset arises if it is probable that such past events, relying on certain future events, will crystallize in an inflow of economic benefits to an entity.
- In order to ensure systematic and consistent basis of accounting for provisions, contingent liabilities and contingent assets, there is need to standardize their recognition, treatment and disclosure in financial statements.

Statement of Accounting Standard 24: SAS 24

On Segmental Reporting

This standard addresses the following important issues:

- Activities of many organizations cut across different classes of businesses and geographical boundaries. It is expected that their financial report should give reasonable information about the classes and geographical boundaries of their businesses, where such businesses are significantly affected by the different classes or geographical boundaries.
- Financial statements are a means of communicating information on the resources, obligations, and performance of a reporting entity. Therefore, the information contained therein should enable users to understand the risks and conditions which have affected or may affect the performance and financial position of the entity.
- The current basic format of reporting as stipulated by the Companies and Allied Matters Act, 1990, does not provide for adequate information for effective analysis and comparison of entities whose operations cut across different classes of business and geographical boundaries.
- The objective of this Standard is to establish principles for reporting financial information by segment-information about the different types of products and services an entity produces and the different geographical areas in which it operates—to help users of financial statements:(a) better understand the entity's past performance; (b) better assess the entity's risks and returns; and (c) make more informed judgments about the entity as a whole.
- This Statement establishes acceptable guide for :(i) classification by segments in terms of business and location;(ii) determining what constitutes material segments; and(iii) formats for the presentation of financial statements by segments.

Statement of Accounting Standard 25: SAS 25

On Interim Financial Reporting

This standard addresses the following important issues:

- Section 334 of the Companies and Allied Matters Act, 1990 stipulates that the directors shall, in respect of each year of the company, prepare financial statements for the year. This could explain why most organizations publish only annual financial statements. However, there is always the need to have up – to – date information about an organization to enable proper analysis and sound investment decisions to be taken by the users of accounting information.

- Interim financial reports are accounting information covering the operations of an organization for a period less than a full financial year, developed at various points during the year. Such reports usually cover a period of three, six or nine months.
- In the course of the financial year, the most recent annual financial statements may be unsuitable for investment and credit decisions due to events that might have taken place since the end of the financial year. Interim financial reports provide vital information on the current state of a business and, therefore, enable prospective investors or analysts to assess the effect of trends of activities of the organization. The interim reports will reveal the smoothening effects of most annual reports and help to disclose the seasonal nature of the activities of the business.
- The Primary objectives of this Statement are to:
  - (i) Specify the minimum content of interim financial reports;
  - (ii) Identify the accounting recognition and measurement principles that should be applied in an interim financial report; and
  - (iii) Standardize the formats for presentation of interim reports.

Statement of Accounting Standard 26: SAS 26

On Business Combination

This Standard addresses the following issues:

- A business combination is the bringing together of separate entities or businesses into one reporting entity. The result of nearly business contributions is that one entity, the acquirer, obtains control of one or more other businesses, the acquirers.
- This Standard includes the following salient features:
  - (i) It requires all business combinations within its scope to be accounted for by applying the acquisition method.

(ii) It requires an acquirer to be identified for every business combination within its scope. The acquirer is the combining entity that obtains control of the other combining entities or businesses.

(iii) It requires an acquirer to measure the cost of a business combination as the aggregate of: the values, at the date of exchange, of assets given, liabilities incurred or assumed, and equity instruments issued by the acquirer, in exchange for control of the acquire.

(iv) It requires an acquirer to recognize separately, at the acquisition date, the acquiree's identifiable asset, liabilities and contingent liabilities that satisfy the following recognition criteria at that date, regardless of whether they had been previously recognized in the acquiree's financial statements:

a. In the case of an asset other than an intangible asset, it is probable that any associated future economic benefits will flow to the acquirer, and its value can be measured reliably;

b. In the case of a liability other than a contingent liability, it is probable that an outflow of resources embodying economic benefits will be required to settle the obligation, and its value can be measured reliably; and

c. In the case of an intangible asset or a contingent liability, its value can be measured reliably.

(v) It requires the identifiable assets, liabilities and contingent liabilities that satisfy the above recognition criteria to be measured initially by the acquirer at their fair values at the acquisition date, irrespective of the extent of any non-controlling interest.

(vi) It requires goodwill acquired in a business combination to be recognized by the acquirer as an asset from the acquisition date, initially measured as the excess of the cost of the business combination over the acquirer's interest in the net value of the acquiree's identifiable asset, liabilities and contingent liabilities recognized in accordance with (d) above.

(vii) It requires disclosure of information that enables users of an entity's financial statements to evaluate the nature and financial effect of:

a. business combination that were effected during the period;

b. business combinations that were effected after the balance sheet date but before the financial statements are authorized for issue.

(viii) It requires disclosure of information that enables users of an entity's financial statements to evaluate changes in the carrying amount of goodwill during the period.

- This Standard includes specific requirements clarifying that the value of an intangible asset acquired in a business combination can normally be measured with sufficient reliability to qualify for recognition separately from goodwill. If an intangible asset acquired in a business combination has a finite useful life, there is a presumption that its value can be measures reliably.
- This Standard requires the acquiree's identifiable assets, liabilities and contingent liabilities recognized as part of allocating the cost of the combination to be measured initially by the acquirer at their fair values at the acquisition date. Therefore, any non-controlling interest in the acquiree is stated at the non-controlling proportion of the net fair values of those items.
- This Standard requires goodwill acquired in a business combination to be measured after initial recognition at cost less any accumulated impairment losses. Therefore, the goodwill is not amortized and instead must be tested for impairment annually or more frequently if events or changes in circumstances indicate that it might be impaired.
- This Standard requires the acquirer to reassess the identification and measurement of the acquiree's identifiable assets, liabilities and contingent liabilities and the measurement of the cost of the combination if, at the acquisition date, the acquirer's interest in the net value of those items exceeds the cost of the arise only rarely and the acquirer is usually required to fully justify that excess.

Conclusion

Accounting standards all over the world are set with a view to ensuring uniformity in the way businesses prepare and present their financial statements for the use of various interested parties. The unified financial statements would allow for comparative analysis on the performance of competing business organizations. The standardization, therefore, has the primary objective of ensuring objective comparison of the performance of enterprises before investment and other decisions are taken by users.

This chapter gives a highlight of the major issues contained in the 26 Statements of Accounting Standards (SAS) issued AS AT 31st December, 2007 by the Nigerian Accounting Standards Board (NASB), with a view to showing the efforts so far made, in Nigeria, to ensure good marriage between theory and practice in the field of Accounting. Each of the 26 SASs contains some background information on the theoretical or conceptual aspects of the Accounting topic addressed, including definitional issues, before outlining how the issues are to be practicalized by relevant enterprises in Nigeria and beyond to ensure standardization and uniformity in application.

While kudos should be extended to the NASB, there is the need for the Board to work harder and meet up with the challenge of catching up with the level of standardization attained at the international level by the IASC.

Chapter 3

International Harmonisation of Accounting Standards

Aliyu Sulaiman Kantudu

1. Introduction

Technological advancements and the transmission of information, people, goods and services have not only reduced the world into a global room but have also resulted in companies striving to raise capital in the global market place, which calls for worldwide comparable financial statements in order to facilitate the free flow of capital across national borders. As a consequence, global competition has led many firms to look out increasingly to new investors and markets to finance the expansion and modernization needed to keep pace and advance in world markets. Likewise, investors look out increasingly to other countries to broaden their investment opportunities and diversify risks. As a result, the need for internationally comparable financial statements and, therefore, internationally comparable accounting standards, has never been greater (FASB, 2002). Because of these developments companies, especially those that conduct businesses that cut across national boundaries and source capital to finance growth in world markets, have parties with differing and diverse information needs, spread across the globe, interested in what they are doing.

Thus, any communication from the companies to the stakeholders requires the use of a universal language which will effectively enhance the transmission of the result of operations to the ultimate users periodically, for the purpose of decision making. But due to the fact that both the companies and stakeholders have different nationalities, cultures, languages, norms and standards, etc, any attempt at communicating raises a number of issues. First, the user would not only be required to be multi- lingual and multi-cultural but must also be knowledgeable in all the standards, norms, laws, rules, regulations, etc applicable to financial reporting across the world or hire at exorbitant cost, the services of experts, to translate, contrast, etc before he invests in the shares of any company. This to a greater extent would not only constrain foreign investments but also allow a free flow of capital across the globe.

Secondly, viewing it from the stand point of companies, in the absence of global standards, they must not only contend with different accounting standards, laws, etc, but must bear the burden of translating their financial reports into different languages, currencies, etc in all the countries they have operations, which may rather be a hard if not an impossible task.

In other words, without global accounting standards, comparing financial statements of different companies in different countries may not be possible, even with an understanding of the standards of the countries' accounting procedures, data may not be available to make the information comparable. The result is that the values and measurements for the same economic event may be presented quite differently. This could have a large impact on many decisions a company or investor makes, for instance, the decision to acquire an overseas operation, an analyst's rating of creditworthiness of a company, global investment opportunities or use of overseas suppliers. With the move to a more global free market economy, however, one of the important elements is the comparability of financial statements. However, one of the continuing barriers to globalization is the difference in accounting standards across the world (Kantudu, 2006). These differences make it difficult to compare financial statements from companies operating in different countries or continents. With the increase in investments being made across national borders, there has been increasing attention not only to the financial comparability of companies, often in two or more different countries, but also globalization of accounting standards.

For the purpose of this paper the method of analysis adopted is descriptive analysis. The study, thus, relies heavily on the use of secondary data, whereby text books, journal articles, the internet, etc provide material for the study.

The major objectives of this paper are first, to assess the factors responsible for the diversity in accounting standards at global levels; second to explore the role played by IASB and others in the harmonisation process; third to identify the benefits of harmonisation of accounting standards; fourth to identify the weaknesses of IASB as a global standards – setting body; and lastly, to examine the implications of convergence on the developing countries. In order to achieve these objectives the paper has been divided into five sections. Section one is an introduction. Section two presents a conceptual framework and literature review. Section three focuses on methodology. Section four is a discussion of results, while section five contains the summary and conclusions drawn from the results.

2. Literature Review and Conceptual Framework

2.1 The Concept of International Accounting

The aim of international accounting is to achieve a complete standardisation of accounting principles internationally. Riahi-Belkaoui (2000) referred to it as world accounting and defines it as the broadest concept of international accounting which directs international accounting "to the formulation and study of a universally accepted set of accounting principles." Similarly, Iqbal, Trini and Elmallah (1996); and Wolk, Tearney and Dodd (2001) define it as accounting for international transactions, comparisons of accounting principles in different countries, harmonization of diverse accounting standard worldwide and accounting information for the management and control of global operations. This definition encompasses financial management, tax audit and other areas of accounting additionally; it takes into account broader conceptual issues involving contrasts among different accounting standards as well as harmonization of diverse accounting principles throughout the world.

Accounting standards according to the Webster's Dictionary of English Language means a model to be followed or imitated, established by customs and concept. In the same vein, Mueller; Gernon and Meek (1991) see accounting standards as the rules which govern the preparation of financial statements. They are the Generally Accepted Accounting Principles. Impliedly, this means that standards are relevant rules, principles and procedures that should guide the conduct of its members. In accounting for instance, there are standards like Statement of Accounting Standard (SAS), International Accounting Standard (IAS), Statement of Standard of Accounting Practice (SSAP), etc. Similarly, globalization has been defined by Friedman (2000) as the inexorable integration of markets, nation-states and technologies to a degree never witnessed before in a way that is enabling individuals, corporations and nation-states to reach around the world farther, faster, deeper and cheaper than ever before, and in a way that is enabling the world to reach into individuals, corporations and nation-states farther, faster, deeper and cheaper than ever before. The driving idea behind globalization is free-market capitalism. Thus, globalization has its own set of economic rules—rules that revolve around opening, deregulating and privatizing economies, in order to make them more competitive and attractive to foreign investment.

Consequently, convergence, according to Ruder (2001) is the effort of the IASB to examine the standards promulgated by the national standard – setter of the various countries, utilize the expertise of these national standards – setters of the various countries and promulgate the best standards. And harmonisation has been seen as the attempt, to bring together different systems, is seen as the process of increasing the comparability of accounting practices by setting limits on much they can vary (Choi, Frost and Gray, 2002). Also, Wolk, Tearney and Dodd (2001)defines accounting as the art of recording, classifying and summarizing in a significant manner and in terms of money transactions and which are in part at least of financial character and interpreting the result thereof. The purpose of financial accounting therefore, is to provide economic information useful for decision making not only for private use but for the benefit of all categories of users like shareholders, financial institutions, creditors, tax authorities potential investors etc. It should be noted however that this information must posses some qualities such as relevance, understandability, accuracy, timeliness, reliability, objectivity and completeness and such information is often communicated through a medium called financial statement.

2.2 Factors Influencing Accounting Standards

The environment in which a country operates shapes its accounting practices (Nobes, Mueller, Gernon and Meek; 1997 and Radebaugh and Gray, 1997). "Just as nations have different histories, values, and political systems, they also have different patterns of financial accounting development" (Nobes, Mueller, Gernon and Meek 1997) and as a consequence, there are not two countries, which have the same accounting practices (Roberts, Weetman and Gordon, 1998). The following subsections give an overview of the variables which can cause differences in accounting practices:

First, there is external financing which has three main sources for external capital as shareholders, banks and government (Hill, 1999; and Ali and Hwang, 2000). The importance of each source of capital varies from country to country. In some, investors are the major source, in others, the banks play a greater role and in some others, the major provider of funds is the government. For instance, in countries like Germany and Italy banks provide companies with capital. In countries like England and the United States shareholders provide companies with capital. The government is the provider of capital in countries like France and Sweden (Hill, 1999; and Gernon and Meek, 2001). This diversity of capital providers means that accounting practices differ in order to satisfy the needs of the capital providers. For instance, under the bank or credit oriented financial systems, countries have a few very large banks that supply most of the capital needs of businesses. The financial reporting is oriented towards creditor protection with limited information as much of the necessary information is communicated through personal contacts and direct visits. Even though financial reporting is more limited, it is still required by the government for public disclosure (Gernon and Meek, 2001).

Similarly, in the market-oriented countries, financial reporting is an important source of information on how well a company is doing. Because stockholders are the main source of capital, but lack the ability to communicate directly with management, the financial reports serve as a source of communication to the owners. Emphasis in the financial reports is on more disclosure, determining profitability and cash flow (Hill, 1999; Radebaugh and Gray, 1997; Gernon and Meek, 2001). The governmental influence on financial reporting is oriented toward decision making by government planners, as the national government plays a strong role in managing the country's resources. Businesses are expected to carry out the government's policies and macroeconomic plans and therefore the financial reports reflect how these government policies and plans are being accomplished (Gernon and Meek, 2001).

The Second variable is the Legal System obtained in a particular country. The legal system used by a country is another factor that influences its accounting system. Nobes, Mueller, Gernon and Meek (1997) observe that the accounting world can be divided into "those countries, which have a 'legalistic' orientation toward accounting and those with a 'non-legalistic' orientation." The non-legalistic approach is found in countries, which use common law, where accountants (professional organizations) arrange accounting rules. Hence, it is the private sector, which determines accounting and not the law. The task of the legal system in these countries is to give an answer to a specific case rather than to formulate general rules for the future (Choi, Frost and Gray 2002). The legalistic approach can be found in countries, which use the so called code (or codified) law. Contrary to the common law, the codified law system needs to develop rules in detail for the accounting and financial reporting (Nobes, 2000). This means that "Accounting rules are incorporated into national law and tend to be highly prescriptive and procedural" (Choi, Frost and Gray 2002). In these countries the role of law is to describe behaviour, which is considered acceptable in the society (Gornik-Tamaszewski and McCarthy, 2003).

It should be noted that the U.S., Canada or the U.K. belong to the common law countries and France or Germany for example to the codified countries. The laws of Scotland, Israel, South Africa, Nigeria, Quebec, Louisiana and the Philippines contain elements of both systems (Nobes and Parker, 2000).

Third among these variables is the nation's culture. Culture is another major factor which causes differences in accounting systems. Moran, Harris and Stripp (1993) and Zarzeski, (1996), note that "accounting systems are ethnocentric...based on cultural assumptions about human behaviour". Thus, it can be argued that a good knowledge of a country's accounting system is to be found in understanding its cultures and values. For example, in the United States the accounting system is based on the idea that people will strive for increased amounts of discretion and responsibility. In a highly paternalistic environment, such as the Middle East, competition is undesirable, and therefore, the accounting system is adjusted to reflect the difference. Other differences include difficulty of training in some countries, as well as language and currency translations (Moran, Harris and Stripp., 1993).

Hofstede (1991) compared cultural behaviour in an American company, which was represented in over 50 countries. His aim was to define characteristics of national culture with the help of four dimensions: (a) large versus small power distance (which measures the degree of inequality in society and to what extent members of a society accept that the power in an organization is distributed unequally); (b) strong versus weak uncertainty avoidance (which assumes that humans are unsure about their future and therefore tend to use rules, laws and rituals to a certain degree to reduce uncertainty, this dimension is therefore the level to which people are uncomfortable with ambiguity and an uncertain future); (c) individualism versus collectivism (which dimension describes whether members of a society have a very close relationship in the collective or if members of a society care for themselves and their family first, this dimension asks whether the I or we prevails); and (d) masculinity versus femininity (this dimension measures whether a society is more determined by masculine values as for example performance and achievement or by feminine values as relationships and caring). Hofstede finds that national culture influences the behaviour of accountants and therefore the nature of accounting practices.

In the same vein, Zaraeski (1996) conducted a study looking at cultural influence upon accounting and found that the secretive nature of a culture relates to the level of accounting disclosure practices across some countries. Similarly, Helgesson (1996); Roberts, Weetman and Gordon (1998); and Nobes and Parker, (2000) refer to the study of Hofstede in order to explain how national culture could influence accounting practices of countries. They found that in a country with high uncertainty avoidance, efforts are made to minimize uncertainty. This means in the area of accounting that rules and regulations tend to be rather explicit, detailed, prescriptive, all comprising and rigid. Individualism affects accounting in terms of disclosure practices and income measurement rules. It depends on the dimension of individualism, how willing people are to accept rules and controls from above.

Another influence on accounting practices can be called `factor of accident of history`. Accidents of history refer to rules of practices of accounting, which developed due to crisis or shocks of systems in general. To such kind of accidents of history belong for example, collapse of companies or financial crisis like in the beginning of the 1920`s when the German and US stock markets collapsed. In the United States this accident of history resulted in the creation of the Securities Exchange Commission and stricter accounting regulations in order to protect the shareholder, and in Germany the same accident leaded to Accounting regulations, which protect the creditor (Nobes and Parker, 2000). Other factors falling under this category include among others the following:

Fifth is the political and economic ties existing between countries. Political and economic ties with other countries play another important role in shaping accounting practices. Just as products and ideas are imported and exported, so are accounting systems. According to Riahi-Belkaoui (2002), "Since early history....accounting has been transmitted from one country to another ... generating specific national accounting system that has exhibited both similarities and differences". For example, the movement of accountants between United States and Great Britain led to many similarities between these two countries (Roberts, Weetman and Gordon 1998). Countries that have heavy trade between them tend to have similar accounting systems. For example Mexico's major trading partner is the United States. Therefore, the accounting systems in Mexico are very similar to those in the United States. Besides the United States, another significant force in worldwide accounting has been the United Kingdom. Almost all former colonies of Great Britain have an accounting system patterned after the UK. France and Germany have had similar influences although not to the extent of the UK (Gernon and Meek, 2001).

Sixth is the level of Inflation obtained in a country. A further complicating factor, that causes variation in the accounting system, is the level of inflation. Many countries use an historical cost perspective based on an assumption that currency is relatively stable. In countries with high economic growth and hyperinflation, as for example in South American countries, inflation has a big influence on accounting practices as well. For example, a practice of general price-level adjustments instead of traditional practices of historical cost measurements can be found there (Nobes and Parker, 2000). Countries in inflationary economies routinely have to write up their assets, rather than relying on historical cost measurement, which assumes that the currency does not loose value over time. Therefore it is a more useful Accounting Practice in countries with a stable currency (Gernon and Meek, 2001).

The Seventh area of difference is the size and complexity of business enterprises, sophistication of management and the financial community, as well as, the general levels of education. The more complex the business enterprises are the higher-level accounting skills are needed to understand and record business transactions. Hill (1999) points out that accounting in developed countries might be more complex and sophisticated than in less developed countries. This is because the developed nations tend to have large, highly educated and skilled workforce that can perform complex accounting functions and, complex organizations whose accounting problems are far more difficult than those of small firms found mostly in the developing countries. For the fact that the majority of multinational corporations are headquartered in the wealthy, industrialized nations, including Japan, Germany, Great Britain, and the United States, in emerging market economies, however, developing accounting expertise has a high priority (Radebough and Daniels, 2001; Hill, 1999; and Gernon & Meek, 2001).

Eighth is the system of taxation obtained in a country. The key question here is to ask, how much taxation regulations determine accounting measurements?(Achleitner, 2000). In countries like the U.S., U.K. and Netherlands there is no interplay between tax and accounting law. When Accounting Standards are developed, the only focus is how to conduce the information function. Questions about taxation are not considered in those countries (Achleitner, 2000). On the contrary, however, in nations such as France and Germany, tax and accounting Systems are ruled equal (Nobes and Parker, 2000). There is the principle of decisiveness in continental European 20 countries. This means that the profit of the balance sheet is at the same time the foundation to snap income taxes (Achleitner, 2000).

3. An Overview of Harmonization Efforts

Having viewed the factors causing diversity in accounting standards and policies across the globe, we turn our attention to identifying the vanguards responsible and the role they played in the process of harmonization. This is because in the international accounting literature, it was stated several times that the IASB plays an important role in the harmonization process (Choi, Frost and Gray, 2002; and Kleekämper, Kuhlewind and Alvarez 2002).

However it is worthy of note that the first move for harmonisation of accounting standards has been traced to Kraayenhop (the father of the movement) who in 1959, according to Samuels and Piper (1985) releases his article arguing for some degree of international uniformity on accounting principles as opposed to rigid uniformity (see table 1, in the appendix). But full movement started with the formation of the 'Group d' Etudes' in 1961 to support the European Union in accounting questions (Choi, Frost and Gray, 2002). It was this development that triggered the formation of 'Accountants' International Group' in 1966 in order to analyze and to vanquish differences in accounting between Canada, U.S. and U.K. (Kleekämper, Kuhlewind and Alvarez 2002).

4. The IASB and Harmonization of Accounting Standards

No study has captured the rapidity in the development of international accounting under the IASC (now IASB) more adequately than Stolowy (1997) when he states that "in twenty-five years, international accounting has outgrown its childhood and adolescence to become a young adult, and its growth is reflected in the large quantity of accounting literature in the sphere".

The IASC was formed in 1973 "to formulate and promote accounting standards for harmonization of accounting worldwide" (Sempier, Chandler and Dalessio, 1991). The formation IASC was the result of an agreement by accountancy bodies in Australia, Canada, France, Germany, Japan, Mexico, the Netherlands, The United Kingdom and Ireland, and the United States in 1973 (IASB, History, 2003). In order to accomplish this, the IASC compiled accounting standards that were common practices in many countries and labeled them International Accounting Standards, which according to SEC (2001) allowed for multiple alternative treatments for one transaction, limiting comparability of statements even if they were in compliance with IASs. By 1977, it had expanded to eleven countries, and the International Federation of Accountants (IFAC) was formed. While the IASC remained autonomous, it worked in conjunction with the IFAC. By 1981, the IASC and IFAC agreed that IASC would have full and complete autonomy in the setting of international accounting standards" (IASB, History, 2003).

Subsequently, the International Organization of Securities Commissions (IOSCO) joined the Consultative Group in 1987, by which time the IASC started the comparability project. This project as Beresford (1992); and Street and Gray (1999) note represented a new stage in the IASC's work, as it moved from 'consensus' standards to 'normative' standards". They further argue that even though, the project was released in 1993, it failed to receive the IOSCO's endorsement, this is because the IOSCO did only agree to the list of core standards and endorsed the Cash Flows Statement (IASB, History, 2003). As if not enough, the IASC continued to work on core standards in 1994; and by 1995 had a new agreement with IOSCO to complete the core standards by 1999, after which the IOSCO may consider endorsing IASs for cross-border offerings (IASB, History, 2003). By 1998 when the core standards were completed, countries (Belgium, France, Germany and Italy) allowed large companies to use IASs domestically. It was not until 2000, after an extensive review, that the IOSCO recommended that its members allow issuers to use the 30 IASC standards in their cross-border offerings and listings.

A study by Larson and Kenny (1999) which looked at 24 countries that were in both the 1991 and 1993 studies, showed that during these periods only three countries, Ireland, Spain and Brazil, adopted accounting standards that moved away for IAS. Six countries, Belgium, France, Australia, New Zealand, Singapore, and the United States, made national changes that did not move them either further from or closer to IASs. There were, however, eleven countries, Channel Islands, Denmark, Netherlands, Sweden, Switzerland, United Kingdom, Canada, Japan, Korea, Mexico, Nigeria and South Africa, that adopted new standards that brought them closer to IASs. Another four countries did not report making any changes in their accounting standards. Larson and Kenny (1999) concluded that IASs in 1993 were easier to comply with as the international standards allowed more alternatives. Even in 1995, the IASs were limiting alternatives and therefore compliance with IASs was easier to accomplish in the earlier years.

Consequently, in 1998, more countries such as France, Germany, Italy and Belgium developed legislation to allow both domestic and international companies to utilize IASs (Practer, 1998), and the Swiss were already allowing multinationals to use IAS for domestic reporting purposes. The Arab Society of Certified Accountants, made up of 22 Arab nations, signed a declaration supporting IAS as the national standards in 1997. Australia, Canada, and Malaysia planned on adopting harmonization approaches by 1998. A number of African and former Soviet Union countries were already using IASs directly as the basis for national standards. The World Trade Organization has also announced its support for use of IASC. Most major stock exchanges around the world, except the ones in the U.S., were accepting statements that were in compliance with IASs. Thus, the only few major holdouts, in 1998, included Japan, United Kingdom and the United States.

Although, the U.K. planned on retaining their own standards until the IASs had been tested in practice, the London Stock Exchange, however, allowed companies to list utilizing IAS without reconciliation with U.K. accounting standards. Finally, even the United States, while still holding to their own standards, had reduced the differences between U.S. GAAP and IASs as early as 1998 (Practer, 1998).It was not until 1999, in the course of developing its core standards, and after agitations from Financial Accounting Standards Board (FASB), the American Institute of Certified Public Accountants (AICPA) and the SEC that it (IASC) needed to be a truly independent standards setting body (Oliverio, 2000); that the IASC recognized deficiencies in its organizational structure. This is because as Bloom (2000) notes both the FASB and IASC envisioned high quality international standards that would make financial statements transparent and comparable, but the two bodies had different methods for achieving the standards. It was a result of pressure from FASB and others, in 1999, the IASC began restructuring to a 14-member board under independent trustees, of which 12 members would be full-time. The IOSCO endorsement gave the IASC an increased prominence in the setting of international accounting standards (Oliverio, 2000). The members of IASB (including the sub- division of the members into models) and those that sit on its board, trustees and advisory board are shown in the appendix, tables 2a to 2h and 3.

Furthermore, with the new restructuring, on April 1, 2001, the IASC changed to IASB and assumed the new responsibilities of setting accounting standards that are designated as International Financial Reporting Standards (IFRS). Also during 2001, the European Commission presented legislation to require the use of IASC Standards for all listed companies no later than 2005. (IASB, History, 2003).

4.1 The Role of the IASB in the Harmonisation Process

The IASB from the literature review has been seen to be the sole vanguard of Harmonisation. How it does this is a question whose answer is not far to find. This is because a glimpse at the works of Choi and Mueller *(1992)*; and Kleekämper, Kuhlewind and Alvarez (2002), and others, reveal the following as the work efforts and achievement of

IASB: (a) development of 33 Accounting Standards; (b) co-operation with national standard-setters; (c) IOSCO Endorsement; (d) EU regulation; and (f) co-operation of IASB and FASB. These points are briefly explained below:

Development of Accounting Standards: Although, the number of standards issued by IASB was 41, about eight were withdrawn, either because they have been overtaken by events or have merge d with another, in a bid to enhance the effectiveness and quality of the IAS. Similarly, IASB has also issued seven International Financial Reporting Standards (IFRS) (see the appendix A table 1). Kleekämper, Kuhlewind and Alvarez (2002) argue that the remaining so far 33 standards are used on a rather broad level. The IASB encourages countries without accounting standards to use IAS in order to eliminate differences to IAS. In appendix A Tables 1 and 2, one can see the standards and those countries, which already accept the IAS for preparing their financial statements

Co-operation with national standard-setters: The review of literature has also shown that the IASB uses several approaches to work close with national standard-setters. First, are the eight national standard-setters which are represented in the board of the IASC foundation. Here, they have the responsibility to take active part in the announcing and revising of International Standards. Second, there is the SAC, which invites organizations and interest groups, not represented in the Board, to take part in the process. Third, is the approach of the due-process which enables the participation of a variety of individuals and organizations as national standard-setters, financial analysts, stock exchanges and other users of the financial statements.

The IOSCO Endorsement: The recommendation of the IOSCO to its members to allow multi-national companies to use IAS for cross-border offerings was a rather important step for the world-wide acceptance of the IAS. It opened the door for IAS to be used by companies for listings on international capital markets. All member organizations (such as U.S.-SEC, Financial Services Authority of the U.K. or Australian Securities and Investments Commission) had to accept companies that prepared their financial statements in accordance with IAS. Since the IAS has only the character of recommendations, Ruder (2001) argues that the IASB needed the support of other organizations to make an acceptance of their standards possible and this was done by the IOSCO's endorsement in 2000.

Co-operation of IASB, FASB, EU and others: The announcement of IASB and FASB to work together in order to design a single set of global accounting rules in 2002 (IASB, 2002), is seen as another breakthrough for the acceptance of IAS. This is because the U.S. capital market is considered to be the most important in the world (Turner, 1999) and the U.S. standards are the best in the world (FASB, 2002). The efforts of the IASB in influencing the FASB to accepts its standards is commendable, for the fact that the FASB has been bent for years not accept any other standards of less quality, like IAS and insisted that a convergence would take place only on the basis of U.S.-GAAP (Investors Relations Business, 2002; IASB, 2002, SEC, 2002). The implication of an acceptance of IAS on that US market without reconciliation to US-GAAP would in our view motivate companies as well as regulators of other countries to further consider the use of IAS. Secondly, the declaration by EU that it will require from all listed European companies to prepare consolidated statements in accordance with IAS by 2005, is another commendable achievement of IASB towards harmonisation.

4.2 Weaknesses of the IASB and Harmonisation Efforts

Although, the IASB has been playing a very important role in the harmonisation processes, some limitations or weaknesses could be identified in its role as the vanguard of harmonisation; These are: (1) close relationship of IASB to philosophies of the Anglo-American Model; (2) convergence means only to harmonize IAS and U.S.-GAAP; and (3) developing countries are neglected (Muller, Gernon and Meek 1991; Roberts, Weetman and Gordon 1998; Muller, 1997; Epstein and Mirza, 2001; and Kleekämper, Kuhlewind and Alvarez 2002). These points are briefly explained below:

Close relationship of IASB to philosophies of the Anglo-American Model: It is often argued that the standards of the IASB belong to the Anglo-American Model which has been attested by the fact that the IASC was formed in 1973 out of initiatives from Canada, the United States and the United Kingdom in order to prevent the accounting philosophies of the continental- European model from gaining too much power (Muller, 1997). Thus, it seems not astonishing that the IASB is criticized for having a too close relationship with the United States and that the IASB spread in a hidden way, principles of the British-American model (Muller, Gernon and Meek 1991); as exemplifies by the IOSCO Endorsement (Kleekämper, Kuhlewind and Alvarez 2002). Another aspect, which supports the feeling that Americans and other countries of the Anglo- American model mainly influence the IASC foundation, can be seen, when the members of the Board and the Trustees are considered. For instance out of the 19 members of the trustees, US alone has five, EU, 6 while the rest of nations one member, except for Japan, which has two members. Similarly, a further look at the composition of the IASB's board members reveals that of the 14 members, the United States has 4 members, all other countries only represented with one member, except U.K., which is represented as well with four members. The implication of this is that countries of the Anglo-American Model represent 10 voices, whereas the others have 4. A further look at the members of the advisory council of the IASB, as shown in the appendix, table 3, is quite revealing, for it tells the same story. This vividly and clearly contradicts the rules relating to the appointment of members of the IASB, which said that the Trustees shall appoint Board members to ensure that it is not dominated by any constituency or regional interests.

Convergence means only eliminating the differences existing between IAS and U.S.-GAAP: A large body of existing literature (for example Ruder, 2001; Bloom, 2000; Zeff, 2002; Campbell, 2002; Industrial Relation Business, 2002; Zeff, 2002; Baker, 2003; and LaShaw, 2004) talks of a convergence of IAS/IFRS and U.S.- GAAP as the main activity of the IASB in the future. We see the risk of such development, that it would be against the aims of the IASB, to bring about the convergence of national Accounting Standards (Epstein and Mirza, 2001), for it would neglect standards of other nations and in our opinion such development would not auger well with the harmonisation and international acceptance of IAS. This is more so for the fact that U.S.-GAAP is not conforming to the directives of the EU (Kleekämper, Kuhlewind and Alvarez 2002). And consequently should IAS and U.S.-GAAP actually converge, there will be critics from the European side, because then the IAS will not be conforming to the EU directives. Such a development we note would conflict the area of harmonisation and we think that in order to achieve a harmonised global set of accounting standards all participants has to be given fair hearing and need accept changes to their old systems.

Developing countries have been neglected to the Background: The IASB has been criticized severally for the under representation of developing countries in the development of international standards and the apparent overrepresentation of the interests of developed nations on the board (Roberts, Weetman and Gordon 1998). For instance both the foundation members of the IASB as well as of the trustees are mainly from the western world such as Europe, the U.S., Canada and Australia. Therefore, the implication of harmonisation and convergence on the developing countries is that they will be reduced to the position of followers or dumping ground. Hence, one can even wonder whether their suggestions, initiatives and circumstances would be heard and considered.

5. The Role of other International Actors in the Harmonisation Battle

The role of the FASB should not be underestimated in the harmonisation process. FASB is the "principal body that writes the Generally Accepted Accounting Principles (GAAP) by which the financial statements of the U.S. companies must be prepared" (Nobes, Mueller, Gernon and Meek). These standards are officially recognized by the Securities and Exchange Commission and the Institute of Certified Public Accountants (FASB, 2002) in a comparison between the IAS and the U.S.-GAAP; this strengthens the importance of the U.S. -GAAP, because the SEC does not allow the IAS without reconciliation to U.S.-GAAP (Oliverio, 2000). However, it is the division and rivalry between the American-British model and the European-continental model, which prevents the U.S.-GAAP to take over the role as an international Accounting standard (Nobes, Mueller, Gernon and Meek). At least officially it is believe that U.S.-GAAP will not be the International Accounting Standard, however, attention has to be drawn on the argument, that the IAS is influenced from the standards of the FASB (Reiner, 2001).

Similarly, the UN and the OECD are both international public bodies which are interested in the financial statements of companies. Both have established working groups. Whereas the OECD includes only experts from industrial countries, the United Nation has as well experts from developing countries, and consequently, the United Nations is heavily represented by developing countries it has to protect their rights and ensure that they are provided with enough information (Wolk, Tearney and Dodd 2001). They further argue that the UN has as well released accounting standards. However, contrary, to the accounting standards of the IASB, the standards of the UN are rather unknown. The OECD had never the attention to write generally accepted Accounting principles. The role of the OECD is more the one of a catalyst (Nobes, Mueller, Gernon and Meek). That means that it is looking at the accounting practices of member countries in order to encourage greater harmonisation and comparability of financial statements (Nobes, Mueller, Gernon and Meek).

6. Benefits of Harmonisation of Accounting Standards

The world needs a single, uniform, globally applied and enforced set of standards of financial accounting and reporting. The benefits derivable from this, include as discerned from the works of Flower (1997); Barker, (2003); Sutton (1997); Street, Nicholas and Gray (2000); Schwartz (2001); Dzinkowski (2001); Wolk, Tearney and Dodd (2001); Campbell, Hermanson and McAllister (2002) Garrido, Leon and Zoio (2002); MaClenahen, (2002); FASB (2003); Gornik-Tamaszewski and McCarthy (2003), IASB, History 2003); and LaShaw (2004), among others, the following:

To Multinational Companies and International Investors:

(i) Ability to make a useful and meaningful comparison of investment portfolios in different countries.

(ii) Easy consolidation of financial statements. The need to present or publish financial statements in different countries' standard will be done away with. Hence, the confusions in the interpretation of accounting reports are also eliminated.

(iii) Better management control would be improved, because harmonization would aid internal communication of financial information.

(iv) Appraisal of foreign enterprises for take-over and mergers would be more straightforward.

(v) It would be easier to comply with the reporting requirements of overseas stock exchanges.

(vi) A reduction in audit costs might be achieved.

(vii) Transfer of accounting staff across national boarders would be easier.

(viii) Standardisation will improve the level of competition amongst capital markets around the world and consequently reduce the cost of capital as there will be no difficulties in financial analysis. This will go a long way in supporting and boosting cross-border financial transactions, securities trading and direct foreign investments etc.

To Governments and National Standard Setting Bodies

(i) Countries would save time and money as they can adopt International Accounting Standards in full. This is especially more so with developing countries. This is because the preparation of accounting standards involves considerable cost. It would therefore, not be economical for each country to have a separate process. What this means is that, in countries that do not have a national standards-setting board or the resources to undertake the full process of accounting standards, the IASB outputs will suffice.

(ii) Ability to counter transfers pricing by multi national companies as these companies could not 'hide' behind foreign accounting practice, which are difficult to understand.

(iii) Easy to calculate the tax liability of investors, including multinationals who receive income from overseas sources.

(iv) Ensures availability of high quality and well-researched standards to countries which otherwise could not have afforded to issue standards.

(v) Ensures accountability and transparency of operations of enterprises in different countries.

(vi) Assist governments in attracting international investors as adoption of IAS enables international investors easy monitoring of overseas investments.

To Regional Economic Groups

(i) Promotion of trade within the region through common accounting practices.

(ii) Ability to compile meaningful data on the performance of various enterprises within the region.

(iii) The aforementioned points would enhance the confidence on reports of businesses by individual investors, banks, government and other interested parties as there will be no cases of different profit figure in different countries for a given transaction.

Summary and Conclusion

In this paper, an attempt was made to re-iterate the significance of international accounting and harmonisation to managers of business entities, other users of the financial report and governments. The concept of harmonisation and international accounting, including, the role of IASB and other actors in the harmonisation process, its purposes and the weaknesses of IASB as a global standards setting body have been discussed. Factors affecting international accounting, harmonisation and its implications on the developing countries as well as the differences between IASs and US- were also analyzed.

From the analysis of related literature and interpretation of data, the researcher concludes that a gap exists between countries in terms of cultural, educational, social, political and economic, development, and by extension accounting practices and policies. Also IASB is really the catalyst and vanguard of the harmonisation of accounting practices and policies worldwide, which through its open door policies and cooperation with national standard setters, IOSCO, EU, FASB, SECs, accountants, etc., has issued 33 standards addressing different and diverse accounting issues. Similarly, the paper notes that IAS is not only beneficial to international firm but investors, regional economic groupings but also governments and national standards setters as well, this is because accounting standards are an important element in the expansion of global business and the ease of trading across borders. It is further noted that despite its meaningful and far reaching policies, the IAS has been heavily influence by organizations such as the FASB, SEC, IOSCO, etc., which as a consequence has resulted to utter neglect of developing countries to the background. It is obvious that accounting policies and practices are by product of culture, legal system, level of inflation, size and complexity of business enterprises, in deed foreign technology has proven difficult to transfer, if at all, at a very exorbitant costs and extra efforts in the form of training and infrastructural facilities, etc., thereby justifying the need to involve all and sundry in the crusade.

It is against this background that this paper finds it surprising that no serious efforts are made by government, academics and professional cycles especially, in the developing countries, regarding the implications of harmonisation process as well as consultations with the IASB and other bodies aimed at enhancing equal representations on the IASB's board and trustees of the less developed nations, so that their voice is heard. This, it is believed, would allow a fair treatment to member nations, such that no constituency or regional interests would dominate the IASB board. Lastly, the paper calls on the appropriate authorities such as the Government, professional bodies and academics in the developing countries to commission research and studies in an area which the researcher considers a neglected topic in the international harmonisation process is the participation of developing countries in the policy making of IASB.

References

Ali, A. and Hwang, L. S. (2000): Country-specific factors related to financial reporting and the value relevance of accounting data, *Journal of Accounting Research,* 38 (1), 1 – 21, Spring. June.

Achleitner, A. (2000): International-Accounting-Standards: In Campbell, J. E., Hermanson, H. M. and McAllister, J. P. (2002). The high road: Obstacles to international accounting standards convergence. *The CPA Journal,* May.

Barker, R. G. (2003): Global accounting is coming. *Harvard Business Review,* April 24 – 25.

Bloom, R. (2000): An analysis of: Two vision statements on international accounting standard setting. *The Ohio CPA Journal,* January – March 24-26.

Campbell, J. E., Hermanson, H. M. and McAllister, J. P. (2002): The high road: Obstacles to international accounting standards convergence. *The CPA Journal,* May 20 – 24.

Choi, F.; Frost C.; Gary, K. (2002): International Accounting, Prentice Hall, New Jersey, 4th edition.

Choi, F.; Mueller, G. (1992): International Accounting, Prentice Hall, New Jersey, 2nd edition.

Dzinkowski, R. (2001): Bridging the GAAP. *Financial Management,* March 28-29.

Epstein, B.; Mirza, A. (2001): IAS, Interpretation and Application, John Wiley & Sons, New York.

FASB (2003): *Convergence with the International Accounting Standards Board (IASB)*: http://www.fasb.org/intl/convergence_iasb.shtml

FASB (2002): *News Release,* http://www.fasb.org/news/nr102902.shtml

FASB(2002): *Memorandum of Understanding,* http://www.fasb.org/news /memorandum.pdf.

FASB (2002): http://www.fasb.org/news/nr102902.shtml.

Flower, J. (1997): The future shape of harmonization: the EU versus the IASC versus the SEC. *The European Accounting Review* (6)2, 281 – 303.

Garrido, P., Leon, A. and Zoio, A. (2002): Measurement of formal harmonization progress: The IASC experience. *The International Journal of Accounting,* Pp 37, 1 – 26.

Gebhardt (1999): The Evolution of Global Standards of Accounting CFS Working Paper No. 2000/05, December.

Gernon, H. and Meek G. K. (2001): *Accounting: An International Perspective (5th ed.).* New York: Irwin/McGraw-Hill.

Gornik-Tamaszewski, S. and McCarthy, I. (2003): Cooperation between FASB and IASB to achieve convergence of accounting standards. *Review of Business,* , Spring 52 –59.

Hill, C. (1999): *Competing in the Global Marketplace*; Irwin McGraw Hill, Boston, 3rd edition.

Hofstede, G. (1991): *Cultures and Organizations*: Software of the Mind, McGraw-Hill Book Company, New York.

Iqbal Z., M. Trini and Elmallah A. E. (1996): *International Accounting* - A Global Perspective. South-Western.

IASB(2003): *History* http://www.iasb.org.uk/cmt/0001.asp?s=9361665 &sc={9B72C21D-C641-4CA1-8F4E-CAEC8B3EF6C6}&n=90.

IASB(2003.)*RestructuringIASC(1997/1999:)*http://www.iasb.org.uk/cmt/0 001.asp?s=9361665&sc={9B72C21D-C641-4CA1-8F4E-CAEC8B3EF6C6}&n=91.

Investor Relations Business (2002): FASB, IASB to Converge Standards, *Investor Relations Business*, 2002, Pp11-18.

Kantudu, A.S. (2006): Application of Employee retirement Benefits by Quoted Firms in Nigeria, An Unpublished Ph.D. Theses submitted to Department of Accounting, Ahmadu Bello University, Zaria.

Kleekämper, H.; Kuhlewind, M.; Alvarez, M. (2002): In LaShaw, M. N. (2004), The Convergence of Generally Accepted Accounting Principles and International Financial Reporting Standards, Anderson University.

Larson, R. K. & Kenny, S. Y. (1999): The harmonization of international accounting standards: Progress in the 1990s? *Multinational Business Review*, Spring Pp1-12.

Larson, R. K. & Larson, L. L. (2001): Coming to terms with international accounting standards. *Internal Auditor*, February Pp 43 – 47.

LaShaw, M. N. (2004): *The Convergence of Generally Accepted Accounting Principles and International Financial Reporting Standards*, Anderson University.

MaClenahen, J. S. (2002): GAAP goodbye? PWC's CEO wants to scrap rules-based accounting for global guidelines. *Industry Week* http://www.findarticles.com

Moran, R. T., Harris, P. R., Stripp, W. G. (1993): *Developing the global organization,* Houston: Gulf Publishing.

Maier-Siegert; E.:(2001): http://www.legamedia.net/legamail/2001/01-06/0106_maier-siegert- erns_bvbctagung_01.php2002-12-16.

Mueller, G. (1997): Harmonization Efforts in the European Union, *In*: *International Accounting and Finance Handbook,* edited by Choi, F. (1997), Wiley and Sons, New York, 7th edition.

Mueller, G.; Gernon, H.; Meek, G. (1991): Accounting – an International Perspective; Richard D. Irwin, Inc; Homewood, 2nd edition.

Nobes, C.; Parker, R. (2000): Comparative International Accounting, *Financial Times-* Prentice Hall, Hartlow.

Nobes, C. (1999): Towards a General Model of the Reasons for International Differences in Financial Reporting, In: *International Accounting and Comparative Financial Reporting*, edited by Nobes, C. (1998), Edward Elgar Publishing Limited, Cheltenham.

Nobes, C; Mueller, G; Gernon, H; Meek, G. (1997): Accounting an International Perspective, Richard D. Irwin, Inc; Chicago, 4th edition.

Oliverio, M. E. (2000): The new structure of international accounting standards. *The CPA Journal*, May Pp20-26, 91.

Practer, P. (1998): International accounting standards. *The CPA Journal* 68(7), 14-20.

Reiner, E. L. (2001), Fusing together financial standards. *Treasury and Risk Management*, March, July, Pp53-54.

Radebaugh, L.; Daniels, J. (2001): *International Business, Environment and Operations*, Prentice Hall, London, 9th edition.

Radebaugh L.; Gray S. (1997): I*nternational Accounting and multinational enterprises*, John Wiley and Sons, New York, 4th edition.

Riahi-Belkaoui, A. (2002): *International Financial and Managerial Accounting*, Westport, CT: Quorum Books.

Riahi-Belkaoui, A. (2000): Accounting Theory, Thomson Learning – Business Press, Padstow, Cornwall, 4th edition.

Roberts, C.; Weetman, P.; Gordon P. (1998): International Financial Accounting – a comparative approach, *Financial Times* Pitman Publishing, London.

Ruder, D. (2001): Worldwide Convergence in Accounting, Auditing, and Independence Standards, S. 1-22,

Samuels, J.; Piper, A. (1985): *International Accounting: A survey*, Croom Helm, London.

Schultz, J.; Lopez, T. (2001): "The impact of national influence on accounting estimates: Implications for international Accounting Standard-setters", *The International Journal of Accounting*, 36, pp. 271-290.

Schwartz, D. (2001): What price global accounting standards? *The CPA Journal*, May, Pp 41- 48.

SEC (1997): *Report on promoting global preeminence of American securities markets*, October. http://www.sec.gov/news/studies/acctgsp.htm.

SEC, (2001):http://www.sec.gov/news/speech/spch511.htm)752002-12-12.

Sempier, R. N., Chandler, R. & Dalessio, A. (1991): "Harmonization of Auditing Standards". In F. D. S. Choi, *Handbook of International Accounting*, pp 14.1-14.24 New York: John Wiley & Sons, Inc.

Stanko, B. B. (2000): "The case for international accounting rules". *Business & Economic Review* July – September,. 21- 25.

Street, D. L. and Gray, S. J. (1999):"How wide is the gap between IASC and U.S. GAAP? Impact of the IASC comparability project and recent international developments". *Journal of International Accounting, Auditing & Taxation* 8(1), 133-1

Street, D. L., Nichols, N. B. and Gray, S. J. (2000): "Assessing the acceptability of international accounting standards in the U. S.: An empirical study of the materiality of U. S. GAAP reconciliations by non-U.S. companies complying with IASC standard". *The International Journal of Accounting* 35 (1), 27 – 63.

Stolowy, H. (1997): The definition of international accounting through textbook contents, a paper presented at the 8th world congress of the international association for accounting education and research (IAAER) Paris, France, October.

Sutton, M. H. (1997): "Financial reporting in U.S. capital markets: International dimensions". *Accounting Horizons* 11(2), 96-102.

Turner, L. (2001): Disclosure and Accounting in a Global Market: Looking to the Future, S.124, source: http://www.law.north western.edu/contexec/srgie/sections/Turner_Paper.pdf2003-01-11.

Wolk, H.; Tearney, M.; Dodd, J. (2001): *A Conceptual and intestinal Approach: Accounting Theory*, South-Western College Publishing, 5th edition.

Zeff, S. (2002): "Political Lobbying on Proposed Standards: A challenge on the IASB", *Accounting Horizons,* Vol. 16 Issue 1, March 2002, Pp 43& 9.

Zarzeski, M. T., (1996): "Spontaneous harmonization effects of culture and market forces on accounting disclosure practices". *Accounting Horizon vol. 10,* March, Pp 20

APPENDIX A

Table 1: Summary of International Accounting Standards

IAS	STANDARD	Date Issued/ Revised
IAS 1	Presentation of Financial Statements.	1975/97
IAS 2	Inventories.	1976/93
IAS 3*	Consolidated Financial Statement (Replaced by IAS 27 & 28 in 1998)	
IAS 4*	Depreciation Accounting (Withdrawn in 1999)	
IAS 5*	Information to be Disclosed in Financial Statements (Suspended by Revised IAS 1)	
IAS 6*	Accounting Responses to Changing Prices (Suspended by IAS 15)	
IAS 7	Cash flow Statements	1979/92
IAS 8	Net Profit for Loss for the Period, Fundamental Errors & Changes in accounting policies.	1979/93
IAS 9*	Research & Development Costs (Superseded by IAS 38, in 1998)	1993
IAS 10	Events after the Balance-sheet Date.	980/94
IAS 11	Construction Contracts	1980/93
IAS 12	income Taxes	1981/96
IAS 13 *	Presentation of Current Assets & Current Liabilities (suspended by Revised IAS 1}	
IAS 14	Segment Reporting	1983/97
IAS 15*	Information Reflecting the Effects of Changing Prices (Withdrawn in 2003)	
IAS 16	Property, Plant and Equipment	1983/93–98
IAS 17	Leases	1984/97
IAS 18	Revenue	1984/93
IAS 19	Employee Benefits	1985/95–98
IAS 20	Accounting For Governmental Grants & Disclosure of Government Assistance	1984/94
IAS 21	Effects of Changes in foreign exchange rates	1985/93
IAS 22*	Business Combinations (Suspended by IRS 3, in)	1985/95–98
IAS 23	Borrowing Costs	1986/93
IAS 24	Related Party Transactions	1986/94
IAS 25*	Accounting for Investments (Superseded by IAS 39 & 40)	
IAS 26	Accounting & Reporting by retirement benefit plans	1988/94
IAS 27	Consolidated Financial Statements & Accounting for Investments in Subsidiaries	1990/94
IAS 28	Accounting for Investments in associates.	1990/98
IAS 29	Financial Reporting in Hyper-inflationary economies	1990/94
IAS 30*	Disclosures in the Financial Statements of Banks & Similar Fin. Inst.(Superseded by IFRS 7)	1991/94

IAS 31	Financial Reporting of Interests in joint ventures.	1992/98
IAS 32	Financial Instruments Disclosure.	1996/98
IAS 33	Earnings Per Share	1997
IAS 34	Interim Financial Reporting	1998
IAS 35*	Discontinuing Operations (Superseded by IFRS 5)	1998
IAS 36	Impairment of Assets.	1998
IAS 37	Provisions, Contingent Liabilities & Contingent Assets	1998
IAS 38	Intangible Assets	1998
IAS 39	Financial Instruments: Recognition & Measurement	1999
IAS 40	Investment Property	2000
IAS 41	Agriculture	2001
IFRS 1	First-time Adoption of IFRSs.	
IFRS 2	Share-Based Payments.	
IFRS 3	Business Combinations	
IFRS 4	Insurance Contracts.	
IFRS 5	Non-Current Assets held for Sale & Discontinued Operations	
IFRS 6	Exploration for & Evaluation of Mineral Resources.	
IFRS 7	Financial Instruments: Disclosures.	

Source: Comparative International Accounting, Nobes, C. and Parker, R. Prentice Hall (2006); and Unshackling Accountants, Myddelton, D.R., The Institute of Economic Affairs 2 Lord North Street Westminster London sw1p 3lb (2004).

NB: Where two dates are given (e.g. 1986/94) this denotes date of first issue followed by date of revision. Where three dates are given (e.g. 1985/95–98) the third date relates to further revision. The IAS in asterisk are withdrawn, suspended or superseded by other standards.

Table 2: Members of IASB

Australia	Iceland	Paraguay
Austria	India	Peru
Bahamas	Indonesia	Philippines
Bahrain	Iraq	Poland
Bangladesh	Ireland	Portugal
Barbados	Israel	Saudi Arabia
Belgium	Italy	Singapore
Bolivia	Jamaica	South Africa
Botswana	Japan	Spain
Brazil	Jordan	Sri Lanka
Canada	Kenya	Sudan
Chile	Korea	Swaziland
Colombia	Kuwait	Sweden
Croatia	Lebanon	Switzerland
Cyprus	Lesotho	Syria
Czech Republic	Liberia	Taiwan
Denmark	Libya	Tanzania
Dominican Republic	Luxembourg	Thailand
Ecuador	Malawi	Trinidad and Tobago
Egypt	Malaysia	Tunisia
Fiji	Malta	Turkey
Finland	Mexico	United Kingdom
France	Netherlands	United States of America
Germany	New Zealand	Uruguay
Ghana	Nigeria	Zambia
Greece	Norway	Zimbabwe
Hong Kong	Pakistan	
Hungary	Panama	

Source: IASB, 2002

Chapter 4

Accounting as a Language of Business

Kabir Tahir Hamid

1. Introduction

Accounting has often been perceived as the language of business. Laurie (1990), as cited in Belkaoui (1995), refers to it as a process of bidirectional and interpersonal communication. As a result, when we study systematically the users of this language we need to ask what kinds of meaning are communicated to them, and what coordinated functions the use of this language permits. Language is not just talk, it is a way of seeing the real world.

This perception of accountings as a language is emphasized in most accounting textbooks. Horngren, as cited in Belkaoui (1995), observes that accounting is a language with a special vocabulary aimed at conveying the financial information of organizations. To understand both corporate and public financial reports therefore, a reader must learn the fundamentals of accounting language.

Similarly, Anthony and Reece (1975) are of the view that as in the case with every language, there are differences of opinion among accountants as to how a given event should be recorded just as there are differences of opinion among grammarians as to many matters of sentence structure, punctuation, and choice of words. It should be noted that, as against the flexible nature in which a language can be spoken from time to time, in accounting, the concept of consistency requires that once a method has been adopted, it should be used consistently, unless there are obvious reasons that make it necessary to go for a change. And where a method is changed, the accountant should report the reasons and effect of such change on the financial position of the business.

Classification of accounting theory by level relies on the notion that accounting is the language of business. It is used in the business world to describe the transactions entered into by all kinds of organizations. Hendriksen and Van Breda (2001) suggest that there are three questions that should be asked about the words and phrases that make up a language. These questions are: what effect will the words have on listeners? What meaning, if any, do the words have? And, finally, what logical sense do the words convey to the readers and listeners?

Answers to each of the above questions form part of the study of language. Pragmatics is the study of the effect of language; semantics is the study of meaning of language; and syntax is the study of the logic or grammar of language. The methodology used in this paper involves a literature on the subject matter with a view to enhancing the understanding of the classification of accounting theory, by level (pragmatic, semantic and syntactic).

2. Literature Review

2.1 Definition of Accounting Theory

Accounting theory is seen as the aggregation of the entire accounting literature, postulates, principles, assumptions, statutes, standards etc, which guides the production and reporting of accounting information. Hendriksen and Van Breda (2001) define accounting theory as a coherent set of hypothetical, conceptual, and pragmatic principles forming a general frame of reference for inquiring into the nature of accounting. The definition is deliberately broad so as to encompass both the more traditional view of theory as a general frame of reference for the evaluation and development of sound accounting practices, and the more modern view of theory as a general frame of reference by which accounting practice can be explained and predicted. Wolk *et al* (2001) on their part, define accounting theory as the basic assumptions, definitions, principles and concepts — and how we derive them — and the reporting of accounting and financial information. From these definitions it can be deduced that accounting theory is a body of accounting literature which forms a general frame of reference for measuring and communicating economic information for the decision needs of various user groups.

2.2 Classification of Accounting Theory by level

The classification of accounting theory by levels relies on the nation that accounting is the language of business. Hendriksen and Van Breda (2001) highlight the classification of accounting theory by levels, as follows: Pragmatic; Semantic; Syntactic.

2.2.1 The Pragmatic Level

Pragmatics is the study of the effect of language. In accounting, like in any other language, pragmaticism is about looking at the effect of accounting vocabulary, which comes in form of financial information on the behaviour of users of the information in particular and the economy in general. Both the behavioural and economic approaches to accounting thoughts are primarily pragmatic in style.

Belkaoui (1980) posits that accounting can be viewed as a language, which embodies both lexical and grammatical characteristics. Within the linguistic relativity school, the role of language is emphasized as a mediator and shaper of the environment; this would imply that accounting language may predispose "users" to a given mode of perception and behaviour.

Accounting is, by and large, the language of business. It represents phenomena in the business world, just as language represents phenomena in the real world. Both linguistics and accounting have a great number of similarities. Adelberg (1979a, 1979b, 1982, 1986), Bean and Watanabe (1990), Baker and Kare (1992) for example, considered accounting rules as analogous to financial grammar and, based on this analogy, used the effect of grammatical structure on the perceptions of listeners to support the hypothesis that accounting methods affect decision making. However, as a language, accounting includes both lexical and grammatical characteristics, which play a role in our conception of the world. More explicitly, they shape the perception and thoughts of those who have assimilated the accounting information (Bedford and Beladouni, 1962; Barnett and Leoffler, 1979; Avard and White, 1986). Consequently, various decisions by users of accounting information emanate from the effect of accounting language, at varying degrees, from one geographical unit to another, based on cultural, socio-political and economic circumstances. This explains why Efficient Market Hypothesis operates at different levels in the world economies. While in the advanced world, investors rapidly respond to economic information in their stock dealings, in developing economies, like Nigeria, a lot of investors do not bother about that in stock dealings. This could be as a result of cultural or socio-economic factors, lack of understanding of the importance of accounting information and perhaps ignorance of how the capital markets operate.

2.2.2 The Semantic Level

This is defined as the study of meaning of language. Within the context of accounting, semantics refers to the study of meaning of accounting information. The FASB's Statement of Financial Accounting Concepts No. 1 (Objectives of Financial Reporting by Business Enterprises) as cited in Belkaoui (1995), posits that the information [presented in financial statements] should be comprehensible to those who have a reasonable understanding of business and economic activities, and are willing to study the information with reasonable diligence. The semantics of accounting language is enhanced through intervention by the regulatory authorities and standard setting bodies. For example, in Nigeria, the Nigerian Stock Exchange demands simplicity of presentation of accounting information in companies' annual reports and accounts and prospectus to enhance semantics to none accounting bias background.

Accounting numbers and classifications vary with respect to the degree of interpretation that can be inferred by the readers of accounting reports. For example the item "cash in hand" shown on a balance sheet is fairly well understood to mean what accountants intend it to mean. On the other hand, contingent liabilities or deferred charges have no specific interpretations apart from the structural processes that gave rise to each of them. Where expenditure is carried forward over a period of years, it is regarded as deferred revenue expenditure. For example, the cost of a special advertising campaign cannot equitably be charged against the revenue of the current year, as the benefit of the expenditure will be felt over a period of years. A contingent liability is one, which may or may not arise at some future date, and is caused by some transaction the result of which is not yet known. Such a transaction may or may not eventually create a liability. For example, where bills receivable have been discounted, it is not known definitely whether or not the bills will be met upon maturity, so that there is a contingent liability to repay to the banker the amount advanced if the bills are dishonoured. Other examples of contingent liabilities are damages in a pending legal action, or calls on partly paid shares held for investment purposes.

To provide a better understanding of accounting information by users of the information, items that do not seem to have clear interpretations are normally explained in the notes to the accounts, so that the reader can understand what is meant specifically, without any ambiguity.

Accounting is aimed at facilitating decision-making. One paramount characteristic of accounting language is its ability to facilitate the communication process. The development of accounting information is only part of the accounting function. A necessary companion aspect of the function is the development of the communication process so that information can be communicated to the various users, with clear meanings. Communication is a vital link in accounting activity. It is as important as the preparation of the information itself.

Readability is one of the qualities of information sought by users. For example, Laboury (1964) and Haried (1972) suggest that user perception of information had five basic dimensions: significance (usefulness); accuracy (reliability); timeliness; relevance and adequacy. For accounting information to have clear semantics, it should satisfy these qualities. These are being practicalised through the provision of information in the most simplistic way portraying true and fair view of the financial affairs of a firm. To ascertain that the information is not misleading, auditors are hired by members of companies, to help them ascertain the true and fair view of the information being presented to them.

2.2.3 The Syntactic Level

Syntax is the study of the logic or grammar of a language. In accounting, syntax has the same meaning as in other languages. It also refers to the study of logic and grammar of accounting. Explaining the syntax of accounting, Hawes as cited in Belkaoui (1995), posits that man's symbols are arranged in a systematic or patterned fashion with certain rules governing their usage. This arrangement of symbols is called a language and the rules which influence the patterning and usage of the symbols constitute the grammar of the language.

It is clear from the above explanations that there are two components to a language-namely, symbols and grammatical rules. Thus, the recognition of accounting as a language rests on the identification of these two components as the part of the levels of accounting.

The symbols or logical characteristics of a language are the "meaningful" units or words identifiable in any language. These symbols are linguistic objects used to identify particular concepts. Concerning this effect, Addams (1981) states that concepts are located in the world of thought rather than in the world of actual things referred to here as objects, including linguistic objects commonly referred to as terms. Symbolic representations do exist in accounting. For example, McDonald (1967) identifies debits and credits, as some of the symbols, accepted and unique to the accounting discipline. Other symbols and terms which have unique meaning in accounting are cash sales, cost unit, cost centre, qualified audit report, unqualified audit report, residual income, goodwill, etc.

The grammatical rules of a language refer to the syntactic arrangements existing in any given language. Such rules exist in accounting. They refer to the general set of procedures used for the preparation of all financial data. Holmes (1992) and Chomsky (1965) established that there are some similarities between grammatical rules and accounting rules. Ijiri (1966) explains that as the language of business, accounting has many things in common with other languages. The various business activities of a firm are reported in Balance sheet, income statement, cashflow statement, value added statement, etc. using accounting language, just as events are reported in newspapers in English, or in Hausa or in any other language. To express an event in accounting or in a language, we must follow certain rules of grammar. In accounting context in Nigeria, these rules are the accounting concepts and conventions, the Generally Accepted Accounting Principles (GAAP), Statement of Accounting Standards (SAS) issued to date by the Nigerian Accounting Standard Board (NASB), the relevant provisions of Companies and Allied Matters Act. (CAMA) 1990, etc. Without following certain rules diligently, not only does one run the risk of being misunderstood, but also risks a penalty for misrepresentation, lying, or perjury. Comparability of statements is essential to the effective functioning of a language whether it is in English or in accounting. Mills, as cited in Belkaoui (1995), notes that, the dependence of accounting on a specialized vocabulary and terminology is an important part of the practice of accounting, as a language, since every language has its own specialized vocabulary. Such specialized accounting vocabulary includes disclaimer of opinion, materiality, revenue centre, cost unit, carriage-in-wards, carriage-outwards, etc. Other scholars posit that the importance of accounting as a language is also very much evident in the proliferation of dictionaries of accounting (Bright, 1966; Fishman, 1972; Trudgill, 1983).

Conclusion and Recommendation

Accounting is a language. Its lexical characteristics and grammatical rules affect the behavior of users. Accounting terms and ideas are, therefore, used by people associated with business, whether they are managers, owners, investors, bankers, lawyers, or accountants. Pragmatics is important because accounting information has effects on users' behaviour and the overall economy. Semantics is also important because ideally financial information has different meanings to various users. Syntax is important in accounting because ideally one piece of financial information relates logically to another.

This paper concludes that the classification of accounting theory by levels helps firms in deciding the kind of information to be communicated to various user groups, the factors to be taken into account in the production and the transmission of the information as well as the nature of the presentation and reporting requirements.

Finally, the paper recommends greater simplicity in the presentation of accounting information by Nigerian firms to enhance the semantics to investors and other user groups with non-accounting background. Regulatory authorities, like the Nigerian Stock Exchange (NSE) and Securities and Exchange Commission (SEC) should continue to emphasize and reward simplicity of presentation by companies in Nigeria.

References

Addams, H. L. (1981), Should the Big 8 Teach Communication Skills?" *Management* Accounting. pp 37-40.

Adelberg, A. H. (1979a), Narrative Disclosures Contained in Financial Reports: Means of Communication or Manipulation? Accounting *and Business Research*. pp 179-190.

Adelberg, A. H. (1979b), A Methodology for Measuring the Understandability of Financial Report Messages." *Journal of* Accounting *Research*. pp 565-592.

Adelberg, A. H. (1982) An Empirical Evaluation of the Communication of Authoritative Pronouncements in Accounting." Accounting *and Finance*. pp 73-94.

Adelberg, A. H. and Farrelly, G. E. (1989), Measuring the Meaning of Financial Statement Terminology: A Psycholinguistic Approach." Accounting *and Finance*. pp

Andrews, J. D., and Koester R. J. (1979), Communication Difficulties as Perceived by the Accounting Profession and Professors of Accounting." *Journal of Business Communication*. Pp 33-42.

Anthony, R. N., and Reece, J. S. (1975) *Management* Accounting*: Text and Cases*. Homewood, IL: Irwin. United Kingdom.

Avard, S. L., and White, J. H. (1986), Readability Study of Principles of Financial Management Text Books." *Journal of Financial Education*. Pp 3-63.

Baker, H. E. III, and Kare, D. D. (1992), Relationship Between Annual Report Readability and Corporate Financial Performance. *Management Research News 4*. pp1-4.

Barnett, A., and Leoffler, K. (1979) "Readability of Accounting and Auditing Messages." *Journal of Business Communication. Pp49-59.*

Bean, V. L., and Watanabe. J. E. (1990), Techniques for Improvement of Communication Skills: accounting Students and Graduates Rate Effectiveness." accounting *Educators' Journal*. pp 36-45.

Bedford, N., and Baladouni, V. (1962) "A Communication Theory Approach to Accounting." Accounting *Review*. pp650-659.

Belkaoui, A. (1978), Linguistic Relativity in Accounting." Accounting, *Organizations and Society*. pp 97-104.

Belkaoui, A. (1980), The Professional Linguistic Communication of Accounting Concepts: An Experiment in Sociolinguistics. *Journal of Accounting Research*, volume 18, no. 2. PP362-374

Belkaoui, A. (1995), *The Linguistic Shaping of Accounting*, Connecticut, USA. Westport Quorum Books.

Bright, W., ed. (1966), *Sociolinguistics* In: Belkaoui, A. (1995), *The Linguistic Shaping of Accounting*, Connecticut, USA. Westport Quorum Books.

Chomsky, N. (1965), *Aspects of the Theory of Syntax.* In: Belkaoui, A. (1995), *The Linguistic Shaping of Accounting,* Connecticut, USA. Westport Quorum Books.

Fishman, J. A. (1972), *The Sociology of Language,* USA, Rowley, MA: Newbury House.

Haried, A. A. (1972), The Semantic Dimension of Financial Statements," *Journal of* Accounting *Research.*pp 376-391.

Henriksen, S.E. and Van Breda, M. (2001), *Accounting Theory,* McGraw-Hill Book Company, Singapore, 5th Edition.

Holmes, J. (1992), *An Introduction to Sociolinguistics,* Harlow Essex, United Kingdom: Longman Group UK Limited.

Ijiri, Y. and Robert, J. (1966), Reliability and Objectivity of Accounting Methods. In: Wolk, I. H., Tearney, M. G. & Dodd, J. L. (2001), *Accounting Theory: A Conceptual and Institutional Approach,* South Western College Publishing, Thomson Learning Centre, Cincinnati, Ohio, USA, 5th Edition.

Laboury, W. (1964), Phonological Correlates of Social Stratification. In: Belkaoui, A. (1995), *The Linguistic Shaping of Accounting,* Connecticut, USA. Westport Quorum Books.

McDonald, D. (1967), Feasibility Criteria for Accounting Measures, *In:* Wolk, I. H.,

Tearney, M. G. & Dodd, J. L. (2001), *Accounting Theory: A Conceptual and Institutional Approach,* South Western College Publishing, Thomson Learning Centre, Cincinnati, Ohio, USA, 5th Edition.

Trudgill, P. (1983) *Sociolinguistics: An Introduction to Language and Society* . In: Belkaoui, A. (1995), *The Linguistic Shaping of Accounting,* Connecticut, USA. Westport Quorum Books.

Wolk, I. H., Tearney, M. G. & Dodd, J. L. (2001), *Accounting Theory: A Conceptual and Institutional Approach,* South Western College Publishing, Thomson Learning Centre, Cincinnati, Ohio, USA, 5th Edition.

Chapter 5

An Examination of the Classification of Accounting Theory by Levels

Muhammad Aminu Isa

1. Introduction

The first classification of accounting theory, by levels, relies on the notion that accounting is a language of business and thus its primary role is measuring and communicating to stakeholders the rate of resources utilization and the result obtained there from. According to Mattessich (1964) the language of accounting is comprehensive enough to warrant the transmission of information to a great many potential users. It is a language that, though peculiar in dialect, but well proven. However, the major difficulty is to find the break through between the quest for simplicity of the language and diversity of its application.

The use of a language in accounting theory necessitates its classification by levels. This classification involves the study of syntactics, semantics and pragmatics theories as major components of the study of language. These components dwell on how contextual factors interact with linguistic meaning in the construction and interpretation of prepositions (information). However, Katz (1966) argue that for accounting purposes, only the syntactic and semantic aspects are relevant since accounting is primarily in written form. This view is also supported by Wikipedia (2007) when it states that pragmatics is interested predominantly in utterances, usually in the context of conversations. Conversely, Hendriksen and Van Breda (2001) observe that almost all current researches into accounting (see Clatworthy & Jones, 2006) are Pragmatics in orientation, while accounting reports and financial disclosures are syntactic and semantics in orientation.

Potts (2005) notes that pragmatic meaning is essential and inescapable in any discourse or text like accounting information. Though contemporary linguistic semantics generally abstracts away from the issue of language use; pragmatics, instead opting to focus on the context-invariant content of phrases, sentences, even discourses/texts, it is difficult to find an arena outside the field in which pragmatic enrichment is less central. Solan and Tiersma (2004) emphasis the use of Pragmatics when they posit that language cannot be interpreted outside context. The meaning of a word that appears ambiguous if viewed in isolation may become clear when the word is analyzed in light of the terms that surround it.

In accounting theory and practice, language use allows horizons to expand and connects meaning across time constructing meaningful totalities out of scattered data and financial events. It preserves meaning in time and transmits it to future generations. Because of its syntactics nature, accounting theory bridges different facets of economic events, and semantically integrates them into a meaningful financial position, and pragmatically transcends these dimensions by decoding and communicating meaning to users of financial information.

In accounting, as in modern history of pragmatics, it is common to find theorists setting up principled divisions between semantics and pragmatics, with tight controls on how information could be shared between the two subfields. However, it is essential to understand that the two are not alternative but semantics set inputs for pragmatics. If the study of accounting language should stop at semantics level only a lot of vital accounting information will be lost in context of text/discourse or disclosures.

This view is shared by Clatworthy & Jones (2006), when they state that accounting narratives are increasingly becoming important component of the contemporary annual report. Previous research demonstrates that such narratives are useful for the prediction of future financial performance (e.g. Beynon et al., 2004; Bryan, 1997) and bankruptcy (e.g. Tennyson et al., 1990; Smith and Taffler, 1995, 2000). For example, Smith and Taffler (1995) show that the chairman's statement is a significant indicator of financial performance, while Smith and Taffler (2000) show that both keywords and narrative themes in the chairman's statement are useful for discriminating between bankrupt and financially healthy firms. However, research also shows that accounting narratives may be used opportunistically by management to project a positive image of company performance.

This paper is aimed at examining the classification of accounting theory by levels, which involves the study of syntactics, semantics, and pragmatics- the aspects of language study as they are applied to accounting theory and practice. The remaining part of the paper is organize as follows: the methodology of the paper is presented in the next section; then followed by discussion on the prior literature on syntactics, semantics and pragmatics theories as they are apply in accounting theory; and lastly followed by conclusions and recommendations sections.

2. Methodology

This paper deployed an approach characterized as a method that uses a set of procedures to make valid inferences from documents already prepared for other uses. This implies that the sources of data to this study are purely secondary. Data have been collected from texts and research articles and other web pages on pragmatics, semantics and syntactics as they applied to accounting theory and practice and conclusions made there from.

3. Conceptual Framework and Literature Review

In this section, the paper tries to look at the conceptions of syntactics, semantics and pragmatics by scholars and the results of empirical studies on the application of these concepts in accounting theory.

3.1 The Concepts of Pragmatics, Semantics and Syntactics

According to Morris (1938) the logico-philosophical tradition divides semiotics (the study of signs, applicable to both natural and constructed languages) into syntax, semantics, and pragmatics. He mentions that Syntax (or "syntactics") examines the relationship between signs. Ullmann (1957) posits that syntactics appears to be a science of relations. Cherry (1961) also explains that syntactics is a component of language that must not be confused with the semantic component. Stalnaker (1972) notes that syntactics studies sentences. Postal (1973) explains that the rules of syntactics define the set of sentences of the language. They specify what sentences are and what they are not. The given circumstances result in the creation of new relationships (sentential structures), and the interpretations are dependent upon (created by) the new relationships. Partee (1999) indicates that syntactics concerns properties of expressions, such as well-formedness; semantics concerns relations between expressions and what they are "about" (typically "the world" or some model), such as reference; and pragmatics concerns relations between expressions and their uses in context. However, Salvary (2005) refers to syntax as the rules that abstractly represent an infinite number of possible constructions with a given set of signs. Wikipedia (2007) opines that syntactics is the study of the rules, or "patterned relations", which govern the way words, combine to form phrases and phrases combine to form sentences.

The consensus view of syntactics as forwarded is that it studies the appropriateness of words positioning in sentence construction. It ensures that the relationships among words, in a sentence, are cordial and logical and the rules of the language are not violated. In accounting syntactics is about the logics, procedures, relations, patterns and structures upon which economic events are constructed to give a meaningful accounting report.

Semantics according to Morris (1938) tends to focus on the actual objects or ideas to which a word refers. Stalnaker (1972) observes that semantics studies propositions. However, Kadmon (2001) mentions that Semantics covers truth-conditional interpretation and things that can't be called truth conditional. At any rate, roughly, semantics covers literal meaning. Also, Wikipedia (2007) notes that Semantics tells about the meaning of a language, code, or other form of representation and it is the literal meaning of an idea. Semantics provides a complete account of sentence meaning for the language, by recursively specifying the truth conditions of the sentences of the language (Kempson, 1988). The syntactic theory stops at the level of words while the semantic rules start with the meaning given by the syntactic structure. It is the foregoing condition which enables us to avail ourselves of the principle of compositionality, which is a traditional principle of semantics (Katz, 1966 & 1973). This compositionality principle states that the meaning of a syntactically complex constituent, including complete propositions, is essentially a compositional function of the meaning of its parts (Salvary, 2005).

Semantics, puts together, entails deriving the meaning of a sentence from the components of that sentence. As observed by Salvary (2005) the meaning of a sentence is generated from the meanings of the various constituents that form the sentence. In accounting the meanings of accounting prepositions are derived from scattered economic events within the framework of the concepts, postulates and conventions that are established to guide accounting theory and practice.

Pragmatics, according to Morris (1938), tries to understand the relationship between signs and interpretations. Gazdar (1979) posits that pragmatics has as its topic those aspects of the meaning of utterances which cannot be accounted for by straightforward reference to the truth conditions of the sentences uttered. Lycan (1995) views pragmatics studies as the use of language in context, and the context-dependence of various aspects of linguistic interpretation. Kadmon (2001) says pragmatics has to do with language use, and with going beyond the literal meaning. Wikipedia (2007a) notes that pragmatics is concerned with bridging the explanatory gap between sentence meaning and speaker's meaning. The study of how context influences the interpretation is hence crucial. In this setting, context refers to any factor — linguistic, objective, or subjective — that affects the actual interpretation of signs and expressions.

Pragmatics is the study of linguistic acts and the contexts in which they are performed. There are two major types of problems to be solved within pragmatics: first, to define interesting types of speech acts and speech products; second, to characterize the features of the speech context which help determine the proposition expressed by a given sentence (Stalnaker, 1972). Pragmatics provides an account of how sentences are used in utterances to convey information in context (Kempson, 1988). Pragmatics is interested predominantly in utterances, usually in the context of conversations. A distinction is made in pragmatics between sentence meaning and speaker meaning. Sentence meaning is the literal meaning of the sentence, while the speaker meaning is the piece of information (or proposition) that the speaker is trying to convey (Wikipedia, 2007b). The ability to understand another speaker's intended meaning is called pragmatic competence. Pragmatics is the implied meaning of the given idea.

Pragmatics provides an account of how sentence are used in utterances/text to convey information in context. In accounting, pragmatics revolves around the ability to use the accounting information or report to predict future economic events, such as, the use of earning per share and other financial indicators to predict strength or other wise of firms.

3.2 Application of Syntactics, Semantics and Pragmatics in Accounting Theory

Accounting as language of business is built on the principles that guide the construction of sentence in the study of language grammar and the meaning derived there from. As the classification of accounting theory by levels, it ensures that the rule of grammar is enforced in accounting communication processes.

According to Hendriksen and Van Breda (2001), syntactics theories are descriptive theories which have no empirical content. They are confirmed by logic alone. Many accounting propositions fall into this category and are true for syntactical reasons only. Bailey (1982) observes that only the syntactic and semantic theories are relevant since accounting is primarily in written form. The evidence is quite pervasive that with financial accounting the foregoing position is readily noticeable: "When an audit report is published, the market receives information set containing not only an audit opinion but also financial statements and notes... Investors do not receive isolated bits and pieces of audit reports". According to Cherry (1961) financial statements as a set of printed text are not merely a chain of individual words and numbers which have been picked one at a time; on the contrary, they constitute a whole.

Katz (1966) notes that four items must be specified by the syntactic description: (1) the set of words (symbols) comprising the representation of the situation (e.g. cash, inventories, accounts payable); (2) the order of the words, (e.g., short-term investment vs. long term investment) can contain the same set of words (e.g., marketable securities and cash in bank); (3) the specific group of words (e.g., cash restricted for plant expansion, deferred income tax payable); and (4) the syntactic categories to which each of the words and constituents belongs (e.g., assets - current assets, fixed assets; liabilities - current liabilities, long term liabilities). Given these four conditions, a structure assignment algorithm can be used. The algorithmic structure assignment is said to be a function of F, where F(i,j) is the distinguishing features of a financial relationship (in linguistic terms, the set of phrase markers of the sentence S) that are given by the syntactic rules (Rj) of accounting principles.

Hendriksen and Van Breda (2001) explain that measurement of income at syntactics level involves the recognition of earnings on the basis conventions and rules that should be logical and internally consistent. The conventions and rules are made logical and consistent by being based on premises and concepts that have been developed from existing practice. Such rules and convention are only defined in terms of precise rules, because they do not have real word counter part.

The implication of syntactics in accounting as observed by Salvary (2005) are: (1) Financial accounting, as a language, imposes a structure on observed phenomena and reduces the uncertainty about the environment; (2) The imposition of structure is critical, since the accountant would be frustrated were he/she attempt to relate empirical laws of accounting (continiuty, profitability) to specific commodities (shoes, drycleaning etc.); (3) Essentially, the accountant relates financial accounting laws to the simplest of constructed forms: a linear relation in binary oppositions (viz: assets and equities; revenues and expenses; fund sources and uses). Then, with the aid of the laws pertaining to these constructed forms, the accountant is in a position to simplify the complex: to decompose into suitable or workable elements, the complicated behavior of real organizations into communicable accounting information; (4) It is through this structural approach that explanation (description) and prediction (projection) in accounting are made possible.

This is to say that accounting information is prepared on syntactically structured procedures, patterns and relations developed on accounting principles. All the words in accounting reports are logically constructed and related to one another on the bases of accounting concepts and conventions to give the clear financial position of an organization, or convey the message of accounting research report, and/or communicate information for planning and control.

Hendriksen and Van Breda (2001) notes that semantics theories are descriptive theories which do not have empirical content. Since they are intended to say something the real world, however they truth depends on observation. Verification of semantics theories can be obtained from research studies which determine whether users of accounting information understand the information producers' intending meaning, within the context of relevant theory. Salvary (2005) mentions that semantics applies to accounting as: (1) the semantic component of financial accounting is embedded in the relationships of individual items (ratios, trends of events, etc.) as contained in financial statements. The meaning(s) of these relationships is (are) assigned by financial analysts; (2) The terminology of financial accounting constitutes the dictionary, and the interpretive rules for financial statements analysis constitute the projection rule; (3) Financial analysts, given the relationships considered important to their task, assign meaning to the relationships which are present in the financial statements under scrutiny; (4) The process, which underlies the purpose of analysis of financial statements, is the search for information.

However, the issue of ambiguity surfaces; this time, it is semantic ambiguity. Semantic ambiguity is the situation when multiple senses to the meaning of a statement or proposition occur as a result of an ambiguous word or words contained in the underlying structure (Katz, 1966).

Income, at the semantics level, is measured as an increase in well being, which involves entity's cash flow plus the change in the value of the enterprise. The objective of asset measurement, at this level, is to ensure that all measures used in accounting are representationally faithful- there should be correspondence or agreement between a measure or description and the phenomenon that its purported to represent (Hendriksen and Van Breda, 2001).

The application of semantics theory to accounting theory and practice is very crucial. This is because all accounting reports try to put across information which should be clearly understood by the end users. Impliedly, all accounting information should convey message whose meaning is adequately appreciated without ambiguity. The financial position shown by a balance sheet of an entity should adequately represented actual financial position of the reporting entity.

Pragmatic theories, according to Hendriksen and Van Breda (2001), are also descriptive theories with empirical content. Pragmatic theories emphasize the usefulness of accounting to investors and others. Their verification depends not so much on their truth as on their value to users. In other words, one does not verify a pragmatic accounting theory but rather use it. At the pragmatic level, income relate the decision process of investors and creditors, the reactions of security prices in organized markets to income reporting, the capital expenditure decision of management and the feedback reactions of management and accountants. Income is seen as predictive device for assessing the prospects for enterprise net cash inflows, evaluate earnings, or assess the risk of investing in or lending to the enterprise. In the same manner, Salvary (2005) mentions that the implications of pragmatics theory for accounting revolve around the term predictability.

Some accounting theorists have argued for current value financial accounting in order that financial accounting information would possess predictive value: the ability to project into or predict the future. However, financial accounting information can only satisfy the predictive criterion of being able to be decoded. Kaplan et al. (1990) find that individual expectations of future corporate performance and equity investment decisions were significantly influenced financial indicators.

Conclusions

The paper concludes that the use of this classification of accounting theory is important in enhancing the grammatical structure of accounting reports. All the three aspects of the classification are found to be useful and relevant to accounting theory and each of them has a specific importance. It is, therefore, recommended that scholars should be encourage to make sufficient contributions on each facet of this classification separately as applied to accounting theory, to enhance the understanding of these language structures in accounting theory.

References

Bailey, W.T. (1973), "The Realm of Meaning." *Communication, Language and Meaning: Psychological Perspectives.* Ed. by G.A. Miller. New York: Basic Books.

Bailey, W.T. (1982), "An Appraisal of Research Designs Used to Investigate the Information Content of Audit Reports." *Accounting Review* V.57:141-146.

Beynon, M.J., Clatworthy, M.A. and Jones, M.J. (2004), "The prediction of profitability using accounting narratives: a variable precision rough sets approach", *International Journal of Intelligent Systems in Accounting, Finance and Management,* Vol. 12, pp. 227-42.

Bryan, S.H. (1997), "Incremental information content of required disclosures contained in management discussion and analysis", *The Accounting Review,* Vol. 72 No. 2, pp. 285-301.

Cherry, C. (1961), *On Human Communication: A Review, A Survey and A Criticism*. New York: Science Editions, Inc.

Clatworthy, M. A. & Jones, M. J. (2006), "Differential patterns of textual characteristics and company performance in the chairman's statement" *Accounting, Auditing & Accountability Journal,* Vol. 19, No. 4, pp. 493-511

Gazdar, G. (1979), *Pragmatics: Implicature, Presupposition and Logical Form*. New York: Academic Press.

Hendriksen, E.S. & Van Breda, M (2001). *Accounting Theory,* McGraw-Hill

Kadmon, N. (2001), *Formal Pragmatics,* Oxford: Blackwell.

Katz, J.J. (1966), *The Philosophy of Language,* London, Harper & Row.

Kaplan, S.E., Pourciau, S. and Reckers, P.M.J. (1990), "An examination of the effect of the president's letter and stock advisory service information on financial decisions", *Behavioural Research in Accounting,* Vol. 2, pp. 63-92.

Kempson, R. (1988), Grammar and conversational principles. in Newmeyer, F. (ed.): Linguistics: *The Cambridge Survey, Vol. II. Cambridge,* Eng.: Cambridge University Press, pp. 139-163.

Lycan, W. (1995), Philosophy of language. In Robert Audi, ed., The Cambridge

Mattessich, R. (1964), *Accounting and Analytical Methods: Measurement and Projection of Income and Wealth in the Micro and Macro-Economy.* Homewood, Illinois: Richard D. Irwin, Inc.

Morris, C. W. (1938), 'Foundation of the theory of signs.' in *International Encyclopaedia of Unified Science* 1, No. 2, O. Neurath, R. Carnap, C. Morris, eds. Chicago: University of Chicago Press, pp. 1-59.

Partee, B. H. (1999), "Semantics" in R.A. Wilson and F.C. Keil, eds., *The MIT Encyclopedia of the Cognitive Sciences*. Cambridge, MA: The MIT Press.

Potts, C. (2005), Introduction to Pragmatics, UMass Amherst, http://homepage.mac.com/cgpotts/nyi05-pragmatics/

Smith, M. and Taffler, R.J. (2000), "The chairman's statement – a content analysis of discretionary narrative disclosures", *Accounting, Auditing & Accountability Journal,* Vol. 13 No. 5, pp. 624-46.

Smith, M. and Taffler, R.J. (1995), "The incremental effect of narrative accounting information in corporate annual reports", *Journal of Business Finance and Accounting,* Vol. 22 No. 8, pp. 1195-216.

Solan, L. M. and Tiersma, P. M. (2004), Speaking of Crime: The Language of *Criminal Justice*. Chicago, IL: University of Chicago Press.

Stalnaker, R. (1972), Pragmatics, In G. Harman and D. Davidson (eds.): Semantics of Natural Language. Dordrecht: Reidel, pp. 380-397.

Tennyson, B.M., Ingram, R.W. and Dugan, M.T. (1990), "Assessing the information content of narrative disclosures in explaining bankruptcy", *Journal of Business Finance and Accounting,* Vol. 17 No. 3, pp. 391-410.

Ullmann, S. (1957), *The Principles of Semantics.* Oxford: Basil Blackwell. Glasgow: Jackson, Son & Co.

Wikipedia (2007a), *Semantics-pragmatics-syntax trinity,* Wikimedia Foundation, Inc., http://en.wikipedia.org/wiki/Semantics-pragmatics-syntax_trinity

Wikipedia (2007b), *Pragmatics,* Wikimedia Foundation, Inc., http://en.wikipedia.org/wiki/Pragmatics

Chapter 6

History of Accounting Thought

Muhammad Liman Muhammad

Introduction

Though the practice of accounting has undergone several changes, its history can be traced to the history of civilization. Glautier & Underdown (1986) opine that stewardship accounting has its origin in the function which accounting served from the earliest times in the history of human society as a means of providing owners of resources with information on how their resources have been managed. The stewards (managers of resources) rendered periodic accounts of their stewardship as a demonstration of accountability. It is this practice that has metamorphosed into the preparation and presentation of financial statements by companies today.

Accounting thought is about accounting ideas or rules which may also be described as accounting theory, principles or standards that lay the foundation for the practice of accounting. Hendriksen (1982) in Glautier & Underdown (1986:27-28) defines accounting theory thus:

> ... a logical reasoning in the form of a set of principles that (1) provide a general frame of reference by which accounting practices can be evaluated, and (2) guide the development of new practices and procedures.

Accounting theory may also be used to explain existing practices to obtain a better understanding of them. But the most important goal of accounting theory should be to provide a coherent set of logical principles that form the general frame of reference for the evaluation and development of sound accounting practices.

A study of the history of accounting is important as it enhances the way in which we can understand our present and forecast or control our future (Haskins, 1904). This implies that knowledge of the history of accounting thought would enable us to identify the problems both in the accounting thought and practices, and assists us to put in place all necessary measures for a better future for accounting. In a similar manner, Littleton (1933) posits that a study of accounting history assists us to gain perspective. The Committee on Accounting History (1970) justifies accounting history which it described as both intellectual and utilitarian because it throws light on the origins of concepts, practices and institutions in use today, thereby providing insight for the solution of modern accounting problems.

This paper attempts to examine the history of accounting thoughts. To achieve this, the paper used the documentary source to obtain the required data for the study. Thus, relevant books, journals and conference proceedings were used for the study. Accordingly, the remainder of the paper is divided as follow: Section two covers the development of double entry bookkeeping. Section three is on the development of management accounting. Section four is about the approaches to the development of accounting theory. Section five is on the evolution of accounting thought. Section six deals with the development of accounting standards. Section seven covers accounting thought and accounting practice, while section eight presents the summary and conclusion of the work.

The Development of Double Entry Bookkeeping

The idea of double entry originated from the duality of every transaction. This is as a result of the fact that there are two sides to every transaction, which is commonly viewed to imply that for every giver, there is a receiver. Yamey & Littleton (1963) state that the practice of book-keeping had existed for several years but only achieved perfection in recent times. The practice of double entry book-keeping, according to Hendriksen and Van Breda (2001) began during the 13th and 14th centuries in several trading centres in Northern Italy. They report that the first codifier of accounting was a Franciscan Frias by name Father Luca Pacioli, who was a teacher and a scholar at Universities for most of his life. Luca Pacioli was a Mathematician, who published a book titled "Summa de Arithmetica, Geometrica, Proportioni et Proportionalita" (Everything about Arithmetic, Geometry and Proportions) as far back as 1494 in Venice. Though the book is essentially, on mathematics, it included a section on double entry book-keeping called "particularis de computis et scriptures" (Details of Accounting and Recording). Hatfield (1924) also traced the history of accounting leading from Pacioli's Summa to contemporary record keeping.

Yamey (1980) considers the introduction of double entry as the last significant historical event, that is, it marks the end of history. Similarly, Littleton (1993) also observes that accounting has never been static and it originated from a definite cause and also moves towards a definite destiny. However, as a result of the dynamism of accounting, being mostly influenced by the volatility of its environment, socio-cultural and otherwise, accounting history is a continuous exercise that seems to have no foreseeable end.

The Emergence of Management Accounting

The emergence of management accounting, according to Glautier & Underdown (1986), is associated with the advent of industrial capitalism as a result of the industrial revolution. The emergence is necessitated by the need to develop an accounting technique that could assist in the management of companies. Management needed much more detailed and timely accounting information than the summarized results often found in financial statement. As a result of mass production, it became imperative for management of corporations to device costing techniques that could be applied in determining cost of production which would serve as guides in decision making, particularly in the areas of pricing and cost control. Therefore, the goal of management accounting has been the provision of accounting information exclusively for consumption of management.

However, reputable surveys of accounting history, majority of which are not based on examination of business archives but rather on the published works on professional accountants traced the advent of meaningful cost accounting to the mid 1880s (Fleischman and Tyson, 1993). According to Fleischman and Tyson (1993), the practical applications of cost accounting for decision making are said to have developed from the United States as an innovation of scientific management movement by Fredrick Taylor. In their (Fleischman and Tyson, 1993) opinion, cost accounting practices measured up to the demands and complexities of the economic environment at a given time. They conclude that cost accounting procedures during the industrial revolution (1760-1850) were commensurate with the level of economic activity of the period and were far more developed, sophisticated and widely utilized than many renowned scholars have suggested.

Approaches to the Development of Accounting Theory

Glautier & Underdown (1986) identify four approaches to the development of accounting theory as follows:

(i) Descriptive

(ii) Normative general

(iii) Decision usefulness:

 (a) Empirical

 (b) Normative

(iv) Welfare

The descriptive approach is concerned essentially with what accountants do. It involves a process of inductive reasoning which consists of making observations and drawing general conclusions from those observations. This approach involves sampling from a population. Sterling (1970) opines that, probably, the most ancient and pervasive method of accounting theory construction is the observation of accountants' actions and rationalizing the actions by including them under generalized principles.

The normative general approach to theory construction is, according to Glautier and Underdown (1986), concerned with establishing "what should be" and thus less influenced by observations of "what is". In other words, accounting theories, or thoughts should be developed independently, and not from practice, and should be mainly concerned about the quality of information in terms of its relevance, objectivity, accuracy, understandability and timeliness etc. In support of the normative approach, Chambers (1955) argues that accountants do not seem to have any complete system of thought about accounting as there are unquestionably several systems of thought about the practice of accounting. Chambers (1955) believes that these systems attempt to categorize the kinds of things accountants do in practice, and also that the systems are almost all the subject can boast of in the way of a theory, and as a result, accounting lacks the sharpness, the progressiveness and vitality of other technology.

Normative theory largely employs deductive reasoning, which starts from a specific objective about accounting; proceeds to the making of basic propositions or assumptions about the subject of study; and eventually arrives at specific conclusions. Thus, deductive reasoning moves from the making of general statement to particular statements.

The decision usefulness approach to the development of accounting theory derives from the primary objective of providing accounting information, which is decision making. The American Accounting Association (AAA, 1971) identifies the objective of accounting thus:

> To state the matter concisely, the principal purpose of accounting reports is to influence action, that is, behaviour. Additionally, it can be hypothesized that the very process of accumulating information, as well as the behaviour of those who do the accounting, will affect the behaviour of others. In short, by its very nature, accounting is a behavioural process.

The two types of decision usefulness theories of accounting derived from this approach are the empirical and normative specific. Empirical approaches emerged as a result of the failure of the normative approach to produce the desired single and all encompassing framework for treating the problems of accounting theory. Caplan (1972) argues that those that adopted the normative approach neglected a fundamental aspect of scientific reasoning by providing no evidence to support their logic except the opinion of authors. He asserts that though these theory formulations often contain valuable insights about accounting, they represent only "armchair" theorizing that the reader can accept or reject depending on his own perceptions since they simply do not stand by themselves as convincing and compelling works or research. The empirical approach is thus concerned about the verifiability and reliability of accounting works that would produce accounting theories.

In the case of the normative specific approach, it presumes that there are several users of accounting information; and therefore, in developing accounting theories, the information needs of each category of users should provide the basis. This is consistent with the view of Zeff (1978), who considers economic consequences to represent a veritable revolution in accounting thought. Zeff describes economic consequences as the impact of accounting reports on the decision making behaviour of their various users. Since accounting information is largely used for economic decisions, the information requirements of the respective users should be the focus in formulating accounting theories.

The welfare approach to theory formulation is concerned with the effects of decision making on social welfare. Among other issues, this approach places emphasis on the comparability of financial statements between enterprises; fairness to all users in providing accounting information, and how financial information impacts on the allocation of resources. Financial statements provide investors with data which assist in establishing the price of a company's shares. Therefore, it is indisputable that accounting data play a significant role in share prices.

The Evolution of Accounting Thought

In the present day, financial statements prepared by companies are required to be accompanied by auditor's report testifying that they are prepared in accordance with the provisions of the Generally Accepted Accounting Principles (GAAP). According to the Accounting Principles Board (APB), GAAP incorporate the consensus at any time as to which economic resources and obligations should be recorded as assets and liabilities, which changes in them should be recorded, when these changes should be recorded; how the recorded assets and liabilities as well as changes in them should be measured; what information should be disclosed and how it should be disclosed; as well as which financial statements should be prepared. Generally Accepted Accounting Principles serve as guides to accounting practice and they constitute basic accounting thought.

Bryne (1973) describes principles as fundamental truths, while May (1973) argues that principles should not be seen just as fundamental truths. May believes that a more appropriate definition is that offered by the Oxford dictionary, which sees principles as a general law or rule adopted or professed as a guide to action or a settled ground or basis of conduct or practice. Gilman (1939) attempts to sort out the confusion in terminology caused by the introduction of the word principle to the audit report. He distinguishes between rules, which can be made, and principles that cannot and suggest that the term doctrine describes the "teachings" of accountants more accurately. He also points out that many books on accounting described as principles do not even have the word principles in their index. Chambers (1963) opines that if principles of accounting were actually just rules, it should be possible to deduce them from the more basic assumptions called postulates. The word principle was a slightly pretentious term in accounting since it is not a natural science (Nolan in Hendriksen & Van Breda, 2001). Nolan believes that there is no one way of doing things as far accounting is concerned, and considers what are referred to as principles in accounting as mere convenient ways of doing things.

According to McCullers & Schroeder (1987) and Hendriksen & Van Breda (2001), many individuals and groups started work as far back as in the 1930s to describe what they thought accounting principles are all about. Under the leadership of a Michigan Professor, William Paton, the first director of research for the American Accounting Association (AAA), the first publication, which covers a series of monographs on accounting principles, was made in 1936. This edition was titled "A tentative Statement of Accounting Principles Underlying Corporate Financial Statements". The edition emphasized on cost basis of accounting and sought to eliminate the revaluation of assets based on price level changes and random variation in accounting procedures.

Paton and Littleton published "An introduction to Corporate Accounting Standards" in 1940 with a view to presenting a framework of accounting conceived to be a coherent, coordinated, and consistent body of doctrine that would support the principles in the 1936 statement. Paton and Littleton (1940) replace the world principles by standards in their belief that principles suggest universality which cannot be obtained in a service institution like accounting. Their (Paton & Littleton) monograph was very popular because of the recognition of the concept of matching cost to revenues. Patron & Littleton define matching thus:

> The central problem of accounting is to bring into association, in the present, the revenues identified with the present and related costs, and to bring into association, in the future, the revenues identified with the future and their related costs. In solving this problem, those who use accounting are, in effect, matching enterprise efforts and accomplishments. Some efforts are effective in the present; they are measured by the costs (effort) currently deductible from revenue (accomplishment); they are the revenue and costs of the present. Other efforts are expected to be effective in the future; they are measured by the costs that are deferred as being revenue and costs of

> the future (assets). Some efforts prove ineffective in the present and are judged unlikely to be effective in the future; they are measured by the costs that must be currently deducted from revenue as recognized losses. The fundamental problem of accounting therefore is to cut through a continuing stream of costs and correctly assign portions to the present and to the future ...

Hendriksen & Van Breda opine that the matching concept view was to dominate accounting thought for several decades. Paton (1922) posits that it is only when the accountant sees clearly the foundation upon which he or she is standing that improper applications and erroneous general conclusions can be avoided. He (Paton), therefore, identifies six postulates of accounting as follows:

(i) Existence of a distinct business entity: This requires that the affairs of the business be separated from those of its owners and those of other business entities. This facilitates control and performance evaluation.

(ii) Continuity of the entity (going concern): This presupposes that the business should be seen as an entity that would last for an indefinite period of time and not on the verge of cessation unless there are circumstances that suggest otherwise.

(iii) Balanced sheet equation: This means that the total assets of a business should be equal to the sum of its capital and liabilities.

(iv) Monetary postulate: This means that accounting should be concerned about transactions, events and activities that can only be expressed in monetary terms. Though this postulate is still being applied, Paton (1922) describes it as an unfounded assumption which provides that a statement of assets and liabilities in dollars and cents is a complete representation of the financial condition of the enterprise on the date of the statement. Further, according to Kokubu & Sawabe (1996), Takatera argues that the monetary nature of accounting makes it not a reflective technique of reality but a distortion of it. Takatera, however, believes that the major weakness of monetary accounting is its inability to accurately account for social costs and benefits that do not have a market value and not the impact of fluctuations in the value of money on accounting information since this can be improved by introducing changing monetary value into accounting calculations

(v) Cost postulate: This is concerned about the values to be assigned to resources deployed to earn income. This postulate provides that the value of an asset be determined only by reference to its cost of acquisition (historical cost). In spite of its shortcomings, the historical cost accounting, according to Muhammad (2002) is still accepted and widely applied by organizations in Nigeria.

(vi) Revenue recognition postulate: This is about the time at which revenue can be considered earned and thus form part of the profit of an accounting year. The recognized revenue for an accounting period is matched with expenses for the same period in order to ascertain the profit realized from operations during the period. Commenting on revenue recognition by business enterprises, according to Kokubu & Sawabe (1996), Takatera argues that one reason why accrual accounting and the matching concept have the capacity for income smoothing is that managers can use their discretion to decide when certain revenues are to be recognized or certain expenses are to be accounted for.

According to Hendriksen & Van Breda (2001), in 1938, at the request of Haskins and Sells Foundation, Harvard Professor Thomas Henry Sanders, California Professor Henry Rand and Yale Law School Professor Moore, published 'A Statement of Accounting Principles' designed to provide the principles and rules of accounting which dictate what should appear in a balance sheet and income statement as well in the account from which they are compiled. The authors permitted companies to defer losses by treating them on the balance sheet as asset (fictitious) and amortize them over time. They also allow the treatment of discount on bond as assets. The historical basis for assets and going concern concept are considered as conventions by the authors, and described as "hardened practice" underlying the preparation of balance sheets. However, the Financial Accounting Standards Board was opposed to the idea of deferred liabilities and assets. But SAS 2 requires that deferred charges like pre-incorporation and formation expenses, pre production and re-organization expenses be treated as intangible assets.

As the search for a comprehensive accounting principles continued, in 1959, the American Institute of Accountants (AIA) was re-organized to advance the written expression of what constitutes the generally accepted accounting principles in order to guide its members and others. A major objective of the reorganization was to address the broad problems of financial accounting at four levels, namely: i) establishing postulates; ii) formulation of broad principles, iii) development of rules or other guides for the application of principles in a specific situation, and iv) conducting of research. According to Hendriksen & Van Breda (2001), the American Institute of Certified Public Accountants (AICPA) describes postulates as basic assumptions on which principles rest and are derived from the economic and political environment as well as from the modes of thought and customs of all segments of the business community. In 1975, the Auditing Standards Executive Committee issued its statement on Auditing Standards (SAS) No. 55 with the purpose of explaining the meaning of the phrase "present fairly" in conformity with GAAP as used in auditors report. The Committee explains that the auditor should be able to use his judgement as to whether:

a) the accounting principles selected and applied have general acceptance; (b) the accounting principles are appropriate in the circumstances; (c) the financial statements including related notes are informative of matters that may affect their use, understanding. and interpretations; (d) the information presented in the financial statements are as classified and summarized in a reasonable manner, that is, neither too detailed nor too condensed; and (e) the financial statements reflect the underlying events and transactions in a manner that presents the financial position, results of operations and changes in financial position stated within a range of acceptable limits, that is, limits that are reasonable and practicable to attain in financial statements

The Development of Accounting Standards

For accounting to qualify as a profession, just like any other profession, it needs standards or a kind of benchmarks to regulate its practice. Glautier & Underdown (1986) opine that the need for standards arose as a result of the lack of uniformity existing as to the manner in which periodic profit was measured and the financial position of the enterprise represented. It is this idea that informed the formation of bodies charged with the responsibilities of producing accounting standards by several countries of the world.

McCuller & Schroeder (1982) report that the AICPA established several committees and boards like the Committee on Accounting Procedure (CAP) in 1938, Accounting Principles Board (APB) in 1959, and the Financial Accounting Standards Board (FASB) in 1973 to deal with the need for development of accounting principles or standards.

The establishment of FASB led to the abolition of APB. Similarly, the United Kingdom established the Accounting Standards Committee (NASB) in 1970, while Nigeria established the Nigerian Accountings Standards Board (NASB) in 1982, all with similar objectives. Thus, Accounting bodies all over the world engage in the review of their conventions and standards in order to obtain qualitative practice; achieve high degree of uniformity and consistency as well as protect the interests of the stakeholders in the provision of accounting information.

The statement of Standard Accounting Practices (SSAP) No. 2 issued by the Accounting Standard Committee, addresses the issue of disclosure of accounting policies and states that there are four fundamental accounting concepts which should be regarded as established standard concepts. They are: the going concern, accruals, consistency, and prudence concepts. They are also referred to as the fundamental accounting concepts by the Statement of Accounting Standard (SAS 1). Before it was replaced by FASB, the APB issued several pronouncements, one of which is APB statement No.4 "Basic concepts and Accounting Principles underlying Financial Statements of Business Enterprise. This statement covers most of what are referred to today as accounting postulates, concepts and conventions and also identified the qualitative objectives of accounting to include relevance, understandability, verifiability, neutrality, timeliness, comparability and completeness. With the Abolition of APB, FASB, adopted these qualitative objectives almost completely, but renamed them as qualitative characteristics in its Statement of Financial Accounting Concepts (SFAC) 2. The terms conventions, postulates and concepts are found in many financial accounting text books, but more often than not, they are interchanged by authors. However, whichever ways the terms are used, the message they articulate are the same.

Accounting Thought and Accounting Practice

Accounting principles, conventions or standards are reflections of the system of thought that are expected to regulate accounting practice. However, since the principles, conventions or concepts are not laws, total compliance may be difficult to achieve. Even where there are laws governing the practice of a profession like the Companies and Allied Matters Act (CAMA), the Banks and Other Financial Institutions Act

(BOFIA) and the NASB Act 2003, among others, it is not impossible to notice deliberate contraventions of such laws.

In some Nigerian public sector organizations, some accounting items often lumped together as miscellaneous income or expenses can be split into several items as some of the components of such miscellaneous items can stand on their own because of the significance of the amount involved. This practice is not in conformity with the convention of materiality. In his work, Mainoma (2002), found that contrary to the provisions of section 335 (4) of CAMA, which requires that the value added statements prepared by any company shall report the wealth created by the company during the year and its distribution among various interest groups, like employees, government, creditors, proprietors and the company, in practice, the presentation of value added statement falls short of the statutory requirement both in terms of the wealth created and its eventual distribution.

Though the periodicity concept of accounting requires that financial statements be prepared at least once in every year as a means of demonstrating accountability, Muhammad (2002) observes that many companies in Nigeria operate for several years without preparing financial statements.. According to Odoh & Nwadialo (2004), Enron, a US-based energy giant company, which has collapsed, used creative accounting tricks to fool its investors. Among other accounting malpractices, Enron used to take credit for value of contracts yet to be executed contrary to the requirements of the realization concepts and the convention of prudence.

Summary and Conclusion

This paper has made a general overview of the history of accounting as a profession, which it traces to the history of civilization. The paper shows that a study of history of accounting is important in order to appreciate past and present events so as to be able to forecast or control future events. The paper also traces the development of double entry book-keeping, which emphasizes the dual nature of every transaction, to the period between 13th and 14th century in northern Italy, up to the publication of Luca Pacioli's Summa in 1494. The paper shows that though the practice of cost accounting predate the Industrial revolution of the 19th century, it was more widely used and developed during that period because of the expansion of businesses and the need for cost accounting information to guide in decision making. The approaches to the development of accounting theory such as the normative, descriptive, decision usefulness and welfare are identified and discussed in the paper. The paper also traces the evolution of accounting up to the formation of accounting bodies by countries to standardize the practice of accounting. Though it is found that accounting principles, concepts, conventions and standards reflect the systems of thought that are required to govern accounting practice, this appears not to be so, as many enterprises do not observe such rules.

Like in any other profession, the presence of standards and principles to regulate accounting practices are a fundamental requirement. It is, however, important to note that it is the commitment, integrity and objectivity demonstrated by accountants in the conduct of their affairs that underscore the success of any accounting system and not mere availability of accounting principles, concepts and standards. Therefore, the professional accounting and standards issuing bodies should consider it an obligation to put in place appropriate measures not only for monitoring but also for enforcing compliance to accounting concepts, principles and standards.

References

American Accounting Association (1971), Report of the Committee on the Behavioural Science Content of the Accounting Curriculum, Accounting Review Supplement, 46.

Bryne, G. (1937), "To what Extent can the practice of Accounting Be Reduced to Rules and Standards?" Journal of Accountancy

Caplan, E.H. (1972), "Accounting Research as an Information Source for Theory Construction", in Sterling, R.R.(ed), *Research Methodology in Accounting*, Scholars Books Co.

Chambers, R.J. (1955), "Blueprint for a Theory of Accounting", *Journal of Accounting Research,* Vol. 6, No. 1

Chambers, R.J. (1963), "Why Bothers with Postulates?" *Journal of Accounting Research,* Vol. 1, No. 1

Committee on Accounting of the American Accounting Association, report, 1970

Gilman, S. (1939), *Accounting Concepts of Profit,* New York: Ronal Press

Fleischman, R.K. & Tyson, T.N. (1993), "Cost Accounting the Industrial Revolution: The present State of Historical knowledge" *Economic History Review*, Vol. 46, No.3.

Glautier, M.W.E. & Underdown, B. (1986), *Accounting Theory and Practice,* London: Pitman Publishing

Haskins, C.W. (1904), *Business Education and Accountancy,* New York: Harper and Brothers

Hatfield, H.R. (1924), "A History Defense of Book-keeping" *The Journal of Accountancy,* Vol. 37, No.4

Hendriksen, E.S. (1982), *Accounting Theory,* Homewood: Richard D. Irwin Inc

Hendriksen, E.S. & Van Breda, M.F. (2001), *Accounting Theory: Text and Reading,* New York: McGraw Hill, 2nd edn

Kokubu, K & Sawabe, N. (1996), "The Past, Present and Future of Accounting: A Review Essay of Accounting, Organizations and Society: the Inside and Outside of Accounting by Sadao Taketera". *Accounting Organizations and Society,* Vol.21

Littleton, A.C. (1933), *Accounting Revolution to 1900,* New York: American Institute Publishing Co. 2nd edn.

Mainoma, M.A. (2002), "Adequacy of Accounting Information to Users" in Ezejelue, A.C. & Okoye A.E. (eds), *Accounting: The Nigerian Perspective,* Nigerian Accounting Association

May, O.G. (1927), "Principles of Accounting", *Journal of Accountancy,* November

McCullers, I.D. & Schroeder, R.G. (1982), *Accounting Theory,* New York: John Wiley Son.

Muhammad, L. M. (2002), "Valuation of Fixed Assets by Business Enterprises in Nigeria" in Ezejelue, A.C. & Okoye, A.E. (eds), *Accounting: The Nigerian Perspective,* Nigerian Accounting Association.

Nolan, J. (1972), "Wheat Study Members Assess Product". *The Journal of Accountancy,* June, in Hendriksen, E.S. & Van Breda, M.F. (2001), *Accounting Theory: Text and Reading,* New York: McGraw Hill, 2nd edn

Odoh, C.M. & Nwadialo, E.O. (2004), "Auditor's Liability to the Third Party: A Landmine for Nigerian Auditors", in Dandago, K.I. & Tanko, A.I. (eds), Prudence, Transparency and Accountability, proceedings of the Second national Conference of Ethical Issues organized by the Department of Accounting, Bayero University, Kano, Nigeria.

Paton, W.A. (1922), *Accounting Theory,* New York: Accounting Studies Press

Paton, W.A. & Littleton, A.C. (1940), "An Introduction to Corporate Accounting Standards," Fla: American Accounting Association.

Sterling, R.R. (1970), "Theory Construction and Verification", *Accounting Review,* Vol. 45

Yamey, B.S. & Littleton, A.C. (1956), *Studies into the History of Accounting,* London: Sweet & Maxwell.

Yamey, B.S (1980), "Early Views on the Origins and Development of Book-keeping and Accounting," *Accounting and Business Research,* Special accounting History, Vol. 10. No. 37A

Zeff, A.S. (1978), "the Rise of Economic Consequences," in McCullers, I.D. & Schroeder, R.G. (eds) (1982), *Accounting Theory,* New York: John Wiley Son.

Chapter 7

Ethical Thoughts in Accounting

Ibrahim Magaji Barde

1. Introduction

Ethics refers to conduct, action or practice that is acceptable to an individual, an organisation or a society. The issue of ethics was, and still is an issue of concern among professionals including accountants. It is not quite clear or obvious why ethics is persued vigorously nowadays, and is increasingly becoming an issue of discourse as observed by Gambling and Karim, (1991) and recently by Bello (2004).

Perhaps the nature of accounting as means of reflecting reality, makes ethics a necessity in the accounting arena since it differentiates between right and wrong, good and bad, and justice and injustice. This was observed by Iwan and Gaffikin, (2000) which made Bello (2004) to conclude that accounting must be based on sound ethical foundation or else the reality that accounting is meant to reflect and report may be lost, and if that happens, accounting would end up misleading its users rather than guiding them,.

An issue of concern then becomes the basic derivatives of ethics and what constitutes ethics. It should be noted that ethics is basically derived from values that an individual, an organisation or a society holds true and most revered. Therefore, ethical conduct may vary from one community to another, as what is ethical in one community may be unethical in another. This is because, the perception of ethics depends on the values held and respected by an individual or society which makes societal ethics to vary but ethics tends to be similar or uniform among professional bodies .Despite this however, the constituent of ethics are not subject to differences in opinion as there is usually a consensus on what constitute ethics.

This paper presents some thoughts on ethics in accounting. Specifically, the paper examines the foundations or bedrocks of ethics, as well as what constitutes ethics in Accounting.

2. Methodology

The paper is concerned with a study of various issues on ethics as carried out in the past and therefore is principally adopting a secondary data source.

3. Literature Review

3.1 Ethical Systems

Efforts have been made to describe ethical systems that try to explain the sources and, perhaps, perspectives of ethics in the accounting practice. Cottell and Perlin (1990) identified two main systems that provide the bedrock foundation upon which ethics is based. These systems are Utilitarianism and Deontologism.

Utilitarianism

Utilitarianism is a system which tries to shape ethics from the perspective of consequences of actions. This system of thought considers ethics to be guided by consequences of our activities or behaviour. Therefore, Utilitarianism seeks to promote the best long term interest of every one concerned. Hence Utilitarianists look to consequences of acts for their moral justification, and therefore an action is ethical if it will bring overall positive result. They attempt to maximize good (or pleasure, or right) over harm (or evil, or wrong). Utilitarianism claims that rights and duties have no independent standing; that they derive from the goal of maximizing the overall good.

Utilitarianism manifests itself in two major forms. The stronger of the two is called Act-utilitarianism. Under this system, the moral agent considers the consequences of only the action under consideration. The second system is called rule-utilitarianism. Here the moral agent considers a set of rules by which life should be lived. The basis of accepting or rejecting a rule is whether the consequences of everyone following the rule will result in the maximum probable good consequences.

Rule-utilitarianism may be regarded as a weaker form of utilitarianism than act-utilitarianism. A rule-utilitarian, when confronted with a situation in which he believes that abiding by the rule will not in the present case be most beneficial, will simply modify the rule. Ultimately, this would end logically in one rule, "maximize probable benefit," which is the position of the act-utilitarian.

Most accountants are already familiar with a system that acts very much like utilitarianism: cost/benefit analysis. In the cost/benefit system the accountant/manager attempts to balance the probable costs of taking a particular course of action with the probable benefits to be derived. Most realize that cost/benefit analysis becomes more and stickier as the analysis moves away from measurability in terms of the naira. Measurement of benefits has been particularly problematic.

Nevertheless, cost/benefit analysis appeared prominently in the accounting literature in arguments about an ethical issue of interest to the profession: social responsibility accounting. There is the need to balance the costs of companies reporting on their adherence to social responsibility with the costs of not doing so.

Critics of utilitarianism have pointed out many flaws. One is the apparent ability of utilitarianism to justify the imposition of great suffering on a few people as long as benefit is derived by many people. A second, more practical criticism centers around the difficulty of defining the probable benefits, called "utility," and somehow summing them. Great disagreement may be generated over which consequences are in fact "good," which consequences should receive greater or lesser weight, and what probability should be assigned to different future consequences. Modern critics of utilitarianism also note that ultimately utilitarianism must seek non-utilitarian answers on assigning boundaries and values around the measurement of activities and values associated with the calculation of utilitarian systems. All these matters serve to cause what appears to be an exceptionally practical system to become less and less practical.

3.1.2 Deontologism

The second major system of ethics found in modern society is deontologism. The term stems from the Greek word *Deon*, which means duty. In contrast with the utilitarian ethical system, deontologism holds that right action is independent of consequences. Deontological theories focus instead upon the correctness of the action itself. The assumption is that there are duties, rules, and principles that are inherently valuable and should never be violated. We respect the law, for example, because it is correct to do so, not because it smoothes the way in which the courts or the police operate. Deontological theory is anti-utilitarian: it states that an action is morally correct if it is rooted in a true moral principle. A moral (ethical) person has a duty to take the right action regardless of consequences.

While much deontologism comes from religious directive, for example, "thou shalt not kill" as a strict moral rule, strong philosophical support also exists. The premier deontologist was Immanuel Kant (1724-1804), as cited by Cottell and Perlin (1990) who prescribed a just society that could come about only if all persons based moral decisions upon the "categorical imperative":

The categorical imperative means that one should take that action which he or she would wishes everyone to take in all circumstances, irrespective of the consequences of the single, individual action. For example, Kant believed the moral choice to be truth telling irrespective of the consequences, since if no one told the truth we would have chaos in society because communication would be meaningless. To the categorical imperative Kant added the "practical imperative," that in considering actions one must treat all persons, including oneself, as an end and never as a means.

Many people who have reflectively considered Kant's suggestions have found his categorical imperative too rigid. More flexibility was given to deontological ethics by W. D. Ross, a premier Kantian scholar who wrote during the middle of the 20th century. Ross identified seven prima facie duties that he believed to be intuitive. They are fidelity, reparation, gratitude, justice, beneficence, self-improvement, and non-malfeasances. Ross contended that adherence to these duties was the preferred moral course of action irrespective of the consequences foreseen in a particular circumstance.

Brief consideration should be given to the most prominent modern major ethicist who has written from the deontological view, John Rawls. He calls his theory "justice as fairness." The viewpoint is complex but may briefly be described as stepping away from a situation mentally and pretending that you will predetermine right action in a particular society without knowing what role you would have in that society. Without the benefit of knowing one's role in society, an ethical agent can make a judgment about justice that is fair, since it is untainted by the self-interest of that agent.

3.2 Ethical components

Though the base or perception of ethics may vary depending on the ethical system one is using, there is however an understanding of what ethics should be, which includes the question of vital issues like honesty, prudence, transparency, accountability and integrity. This is supported strongly by the view of Herbert (1978) for to him, ethics simply means moral philosophy or practical morality. The application of moral principles of honesty, integrity, prudence, transparency and accountability clearly specifies what is good and what is bad (Ahmad, 2003).

The basic components of ethics have received attention for a relatively long period of time. In effect, various scholars have tried to shed light on what should be the basic components of ethics. Adams, (2001) enumerated some basic universal values of ethics as identified by Michael Josephson, one of the most widely quoted American spokesman on ethics. Such values, according to Ahmad (2003) must be present in any person (business executives, accountants, politicians, professionals etc) who is serious about ethics. These values include honesty, integrity, promise keeping, fidelity, fairness, care, respect, responsibility, excellence, and accountability. However, current discussions on ethics make us to add two more values or components which are prudence and transparency.

3.2.1 Honesty

This is the condition of being sincere, truthful, fair and straightforward in conduct (Ahmad, 2003). It is mandatory, for ethics to be present in an individual, that sincererity and truthfulness be his watchwords as well as be fair and straightforward in his dealings with people. Auditors in the discharge of their audit task need to exercise high level of honesty in expressing opinion on the financial statements they audited. Obviously, reliance can not be placed by the users of the statements if the honesty of auditors is doubtful.

3.2.2 Integrity

This is the second element of ethics identified by Adams (2003) as stated by Michael Josephson. Ahmad (2003) believes that integrity is the core value of ethics and is measured in terms of what is RIGHT and

JUST .This means decisions must be carried out in the best interest of all, and such decisions must be carried out with utmost honesty. For instance, creative accounting entails manipulation of accounting policies to suppress an unfavorable situation or result. It is also known as income smoothing, earnings management, earning smoothing, financial engineering and cosmetic accounting. Whatever the name, creative accounting is seen as deceitful and an undesirable practice, and questions the integrity of accountants and should be avoided in the spirit of being 'RIGHT' and 'JUST'.

3.2.3 Promise Keeping

This is an ex-post issue as it deals with what comes after a particular promise or decision has been taken. This is because, it is possible to take a decision with utmost honesty but to implement that decision depends on the extent to which an individual keeps promises. Ethics demands that promises must be kept which, according to Ahmad (2003) requires moral courage, honesty of purpose, integrity and commitment. In the audit practice, the letter of engagement drafted by the auditor and signed by the client covering the nature, extent and the responsibilities of the auditor is more or less just like a promise that the auditor made to the client and it would be unethical of the auditor if he fails to execute the audit job that he earlier promised.

3.2.4 Fidelity

Fidelity is in other word, known as loyalty. Ethics demands that one should show a reasonable level of loyalty to those it is due. But Ahmad (2003) observed that this is one of the most difficult aspects of ethics as loyalty can take many forms. In most cases, it is difficult to decide on where ones' loyalty is to be .For instance, an auditor may have to decide and act on to whom is his loyalty going to be? Is it to the Share holders (who appointed him?) or to the Management (with whom he works directly) as the interests of shareholders and management may often be at conflict. How would such loyalty affect the auditor himself?

3.2.5 Fairness

Fairness implies not allowing ones' own feelings, desire, interest and prejudices to affect his decision, judgment or expression of his opinion on a particular issue. Therefore, Ethics entails one to be fair in all his judgments as without being fair, our decisions may be questionable and therefore not acceptable to the people. The expressing of an auditors opinion on whether financial statements of an organisation shows a true and fair view very much rests on the ethical component of fairness. The feelings, desire or interest of the auditor should not affect the opinion he expresses.

3.2.6 Care

It is a golden principle of ethics that one must care for others just as he would like other people to care for him. Accounting ethics demands that accountants care for their colleagues as well as their accounting environment – the companies they work for, their clients, the government and the country they operate in. All the interests of the aforementioned must be depended in their best interest.

3.2.7 Respect

Ahmad (2003) holds that respect is all about recognizing the autonomy of others and considering the nature of the Accounting profession, it is just natural that respect should be part of ethics. Since accounting is made up of several branches like financial accounting, management accounting, auditing function, taxation, treasury management, investment analyses, financial management, etc, the profession will only excel if due respect is accorded to various parts. Lack of respect will results in chaos and confusion and certainly, a house divided against itself falls!

3.2.8 Responsibility

Responsibility means that an individual must discharge tasks or schedules required of him. Accounting ethics therefore requires accountants and practicing professionals to carry out tasks (jobs) assigned to them to the best of their ability. Practicing accountants should only sign contracts that they are capable of executing.

3.2.9 Excellence

Excellence demands that jobs or tasks be carried out very well. It is an ethical obligation for someone to be excellent in his job. If jobs are not executed properly, errors may occur due to neglect and the fame, reputation and integrity of accountants may be affected.

3.2.10 Accountability

In the view of Lonsdale (1986), Johnson (1996), Orjioke (2002) and Muhammad (2004), accountability means the obligation to answer for a responsibility that has been conferred on someone. Accountability is found where rulers readily delegate authority, where subordinates confidently exercise their discretions, and where abuse of power is defined and punished under the rule of law. Ethics demands that one should give explanations for actions taken.

3.2.11 Transparency

Greuning and Koen (1999) defined transparency as the principle of creating an environment where information on existing conditions, decisions and actions are made accessible, visible and understandable to all participants through disclosure. Iyayi (2001) opined that transparency is the ability to act in such away that one is not only honest but also seen to be honest. He explained that transparency entails the ability to discharge ones obligation in a way that leaves no blames on ones character, name or reputation.

Transparency is the twin brother of Accountability and in fact Muhammad (2004) and Anyafo (2004) opined that the duo cannot be separated because any accounting report that lacks transparency will be misleading and fraudulent. This made Hamid (2004) to conclude that a transparent person is open and has nothing to hide.

The inseparability of transparency and accountability has to do with their origin since both are based on the same premise. Baffa (2004) opined that transparency and accountability are based on the following principles, which includes:

(i) Rule of Law: Transparency and accountability seek to check abuse, inequity and injustice and therefore must be legitimated by law for it to be practiced effectively.

(ii) Public Interest: Everything must be aimed at promoting public good.

(iii) Consultation and Communication: For transparency and accountability to prevail, there must be due consultation and effective communication so that all nooks and corners of activities are covered.

(iv) Mutual Participation and Decision Making: Information needed for decisions should be adequate and decision making should be approached collectively. This would ensure good policy formulation and their effective implementation.

(v) Professionalism and Merit: Transparency and accountability need good adherence to professionalism and technical competence.

(vi) Equal Opportunity: All must be guaranteed equal access to opportunities in every respect without discrimination or bias from what ever perspective.

(vii) Pluralism and Minority Rights: Marginalisation of the weak and the disadvantaged should be avoided and their rights should be guaranteed.

(viii) Trust and Confidence Building: The trust and confidence of the citizens must be obtained for transparency and accountability to prevail. This can only be achieved through rewarding of honesty, integrity and selfless service.

(ix) Deterrence: There is the need for prompt execution of justice not to only penalize erring subjects but also to deter others from learning from bad examples.

(x) Check and Balance: A system that is complete and devoid of any loopholes should be in place to correct and guide actions.

3.2.12 Prudence

Ideally, prudence is an accounting convention which prohibits over statement of profits, mostly by way of anticipation of future profits, and therefore allows and encourages the provisions and incorporation of anticipated loss in to accounting records. However, to the Non-Accounting professionals, prudence simply means being miserly where no penny is spent unless extremely necessary. In either case, it is not ethical for an accountant to give misleading information on profits or for an officer (public or otherwise) to embezzle funds entrusted to his custody. The technique of value for money audit needs to be emphasized upon by auditors and those in authority to ensure efficiency and effectiveness of expenditures, particularly in the government sector, where funds misappropriation is more pronounced. Efficiency means expenditures are incurred only where necessary and in the best way while effectiveness means the target/purpose of the expenditure is achieved and the expenditure itself is not derailed.

The above are the components parts of ethics which formed the basic building blocks of Ethics in both the Accounting and Non-Accounting profession. It is quite an acceptable fact that the above may form, on general bases, the constituents of ethics but professional differences may expand and redefine ethics in their own perspectives.

Ethics in the Accounting Profession

Accounting profession relies on the trust placed by the public on Accountants which means accountants must exercise high a level performance to win and maintain the trust and confidence of the general public. This can be achieved only through ethical practices in the discharge of professional duties. Consequently, professional accounting bodies at local (e.g. ICAN, ANAN etc) and international (e.g. ACCA, IMA etc) levels have developed ethical codes to guide their members in discharging professional responsibilities. Though such codes may vary in their context, they have a common target and stem from the principles of competence, confidentiality, integrity and objectivity.

i) Competence:

Accountants must maintain an appropriate level of professional competence by continuous development of their knowledge and skills. In addition, professional duties should be discharged in accordance with relevant laws, regulations, and technical standards. Relevant and reliable information should be analysed appropriately, based on which complete and clear reports and recommendations should be prepared.

ii) Confidentiality:

Information obtained by accountants in the discharge of their duties should be treated with a high level of confidentiality and should only be disclosed when authorized or legally compelled to do so. Subordinates must also be sensitized, encouraged and monitored to safeguard the confidentiality of information. In addition, accountants must refrain from using confidential information in unethical way to gain illegal advantage either personally or by proxy.

iii) Integrity:

Integrity requests that Accountants must develop an unquestionable ability to discharge their professional responsibilities. Therefore, they must refuse any gift, favor, or hospitality to avoid being influenced in their actions. In addition, conflict of interest must be avoided as well and all parties must be advised as such. They must show an active or passive participation in the attainment of the organizational objectives. Integrity also demands that Accountants must communicate unfavorable as well as favorable information and use same to pass professional judgment.

iv) Objectivity:

Accounting is basically about information dissemination to enable users of the information make informed judgment about an entity. Accountants must disclose information that is fair and highly objective. Users of Accounting information must be supplied with all relevant information that could reasonably be expected to influence their understanding of the reports, comments and recommendations presented.

Factors affecting ethical judgment

The codes of conduct developed by professional accounting bodies aim at ensuring high ethical practice among their members in the discharge of professional accounting responsibilities. Thus ethical code of conduct seems to be an important factor affecting ethical perception or judgment of accounting professionals and financial executives. However, the works of Martinson and Ziegenfus (2000) and Aras and Muslomov (nd) indicated that the ethical perception and judgment of an accountant is generally affected by the following factors:

i) Professional code of conduct: This has to do with regulations set up by statutorily established professional bodies, which governs the conduct of accountants in the discharge of their responsibilities. Professional accounting bodies like ACCA, ICAN, ANAN, etc have rules that must be followed by their members and therefore affect the ethical perception and judgment of their members. However, Aras and Muslomov opined that the impact is limited by the level of the professional institution's development, obligatory status of the professional ethical standards and professional consciousness.

ii) Corporate ethical values: This has to do with the seriousness of an organisation towards its internal ethical behaviour. For instance, consideration is given to whether or not company's management is involved in unethical practices, whether it is necessary to compromise ethics for an employee to succeed, the extent to which management tolerates unethical behaviour, whether or not unethical behaviour that results in benefit (personal or corporate) is reprimanded, whether employment is done on merit or not, and whether previous unethical behaviour affects the decision of the company.

iii) Environmental Variables: Just like the way business activities of an enterprise is affected by its environment, so also is ethics affected by the environment in which a business operates. It is simply a matter of the relationship of the company with its environment. Ethical consideration given in this respect include whether the company has to give gifts to facilitate its business (PR), whether personal relationships influence bank credits and whether receivables can be collected in exceptional ways.

iv) Demographic Variables: Demographic variables refer to how factors like age, education and experience affect the ethical judgment of accounting professionals and financial executives. The level of one's age, educational qualification and working experience is capable of influencing ethical judgment.

Conclusions and Recommendations

The paper carried out a study of ethics generally and discussed the basic systems that try to explain the source or foundation of ethics. It was established that Ethics usually sprouted from either of the 2 systems of Utilitarianism or Deontologism. It was similarly discussed in the paper, the basic components of ethics which includes honesty, integrity, prudence, and transparency to mention but a few. It is on the bases of the above discussions that the paper concludes that ethics is mostly a product of beliefs that an individual is holding. Consequently, ethics can have a strong support and therefore a strong fellowship among people with religious inclination if and only if, they follow their religions deligently. This is strongly based on the Deontologist system of ethics. However, one also notices high level of ethics among non religious followers which further suggests and makes the paper to conclude that the Utilitarian system of ethics is equally being followed and is inspiring many.

Based on the above conclusions, the paper suggests the following recommendations:

- Since ethics is inmost cases dependent on values, the paper is recommending that ethical principles must be inculcated and developed by all concerned. This means religious leaders, community leaders as well as professional organisations must strive hard to instill and encourage ethical conducts among their subjects.
- In addition, adequate rewards and appropriate punitive measures must be mated on those that observe ethical practices as well as breakers of ethical code of conduct.
- There is the need for accountants to continuously be involved in training and retraining programmes to improve their professional competence which will assist them in the discharge of their accounting responsibilities. This shall apply to both accountants in the academics and in practice.
- In line with above, professional accounting bodies need to be updating their professional code of conduct regularly, to capture recent phenomenon that are ethical challenges. Recently, the collapse of Enron was largely attributed to cosmetics accounting and hence, professional accounting bodies need to issue anti-accounting engineering pronouncements in their professional codes of conduct.
- The government needs to pass a statutory law compelling accountants in practice to totally comply with practicing guidelines contained in their institutes' professional code of conducts. Appropriate punitive measures with full legal consequences should await practitioners who violated professional accounting code of conducts. This will

strengthen accounting professional bodies and enable them to breaths an air of ethical practice in the accounting arena.

References

Abdel-Magid, M. F. (1981). The theory of Islamic banking: Accounting Implications. *The International Journal of Accounting Education and Research* 17 (1): 79-102.

Adams, R.A. (2001).*Public Sector Accounting and Finance made Simple.* Corporate Publishers Ventures Lagos.

Ahmad, H.A (2003).A review of Ethical Concepts in relation to the work of State Accountant General. A case Study of Kano State. In: *Proceedings of the 1st National Conference on Ethical Issues in Accounting,* Organised by the Department of Accounting, Bayero University, Kano, Edited by K.I. Dandago and Tanko I.A.

Anyafo, A.M. (2004).Transparency and Accountability in Intergovernmental Financial Relations: A Literary Essay on State-Local Governments Joint Account Operation in Nigeria. *Bayero International Journal of Accounting Research.*1(1), 24-35.

Aras, G. and Muslomov, A. (2007) : The analysis of factors affecting ethical judgments: The Turkish evidence, @ www.ssrn.com

Baffa, A.U (2004): Issues on Principles of Transparency and Accountability in Nigeria. *Bayero International Journal of Accounting and Research. Vol. 1 Number 1.* 81 – 86. Gidan Dabino Publishers, Kano-Nigeria.

Bello, M.S (2004) .Usury as an Ethical Problem: The Islamic Banking Perspective.In:*Proceedinds of the 2nd National Conference on Ethical Issues in Accounting,* Organized by the Department of Accounting, Bayero University, Kano, Edited by K.I. Dandago and Tanko I.A.

Blumer, Herbert. (1969). *Symbolic Interactionism: Perspective and Method.* Englewood Cliffs, N. J.: Prentice-Hall, Inc.

Cottell, P.G. and Perlin T.M. (1990).*Accounting Ethics.*Qourum Books. London.

Charon, J. M. (1979). *Symbolic Interactionism: An Introduction, an Interpretation, Integration*. Englewood Cliffs, N.J: Prentice-Hall, Inc.

Davis, S. W., Krishnagopal M. and Gareth M.. (1982). The images that have shaped accounting theory. *Accounting, Organizations and Society* 7 (4): 307-18.

Devitt, M. (1984). *Realism and Truth.* New Jersey: Princeton University Press.

Dillard, J. F. (1991). Accounting as a critical social science. *Accounting, Auditing and Accountability Journal* 4 (1): 8-27.

Gambling, T. and Karim, R.A. A.(1991). *Business and Accounting Ethics in Islam.* Mansell Publishing Limited. London.

Greuning H.V. & Koen, M, (1999): Transparency in Financial statements. CAR Newsletter-July 1999.@www.icar.org.

Hamid, K.T. (2004).Prudence Transparency and Accountability in The Nigerian Banking Industry: A Means for Building Customer Confidence. In: *Proceedings of the 2nd National Conference on Ethical Issues in Accounting,* Organised by the Department of Accounting, Bayero University, Kano. Edited by K.I. Dandago and Tanko I.A.

Herbert, W.E. (1978).*Pragmatism Versus Ethical Conduct.*Qourum Books, USA.

Idris, J. S. (1987). The Islamization of the sciences: its philosophy and methodology. *The American Journal of Islamic Social Sciences* 4 (2): 201-8.International Institute of Islamic Thought (IIIT). 1988.

Iwan, T. and M. Gaffikin (2000) .The Shariate Accounting: An Ethical construction of Accounting Knowledge, *IBFNET*

Iyayi, P. (2001). *The Principles of ASUU.*Ibadan Printing Press, Nigeria.

Johnson, I.E (1996).Public Sector Accounting and Financial Control, Surulere Financial Training. Nigeria.

Martinson, O. B. and Ziegenfus, D. E. (2000): Looking at what influences ethical perception and judgment. *Management Accounting Quarterly,* Fall, pp 41-47.

Morgan, G. and Linda S.(1980). The case for qualitative research. *Academy of Management* 5 (4): 491-500.

Muhammad, L.M. (2004). The Impact of Internal Audit on Accountability in Nigerian Organisations.In: *Proceedings of the 2nd National Conference on Ethical Issues in Accounting*, Organised by the Department of Accounting, Bayero University, Kano. Edited by K.I. Dandago and Tanko I.A.

Muhammad, L.M.(2005).The Status of Prudence, Accountability and Transparency in Nigerian Companies. *Bayero International Journal of Accounting Research.*1 (2), 176-189.

Orijioke, B.A.M (2002). Corporate Governance in Nigeria, a paper presented at Mandatory Continuing Professional Development (MCPD) of the Association of the National Accountants of Nigeria (ANAN)

Ragab, I. A. (1993). Islamic perspectives on theory building in the social sciences. *The American Journal of Islamic Social Sciences* 10 (1): 1-22.

Chapter 8

Ethical Considerations in Accounting

Ahmed Bawa Bello

1.1 Introduction

The concept of ethics is broad, its application in accounting is complex, and its necessity is on the increase as unethical behaviour of some accountants threatens the integrity of the profession and undermines the relevance of accounting information and audit opinion. Ethics means different things to different people. There can be cultural ethics, social ethics, religious ethics, business ethics, professional ethics, research ethics, and financial ethics among others. Ethics may be viewed to be associated with morality, religion and or rationality. However, morality, religion and rationality are considered to be futility to some school of thought. David (2004:3) states that:

> Deceit is the Cinderella of human nature; essential to our humanity but discovered by its perpetrators at every turn. It is normal, natural, and pervasive. It is not, as popular opinion would have it, reducible to mental illness or moral failure. Human societies are a network of lies and deceptions that would collapse under the weight of too much honesty. From the fairy of tales our parents told us to the propaganda our government feeds us with, human beings spend their lives surrounded by pretense

Recent financial scandals in large and small corporations both at national and international levels have generated unwarranted and adverse publicity for the accounting profession. This brings to question the integrity of accountants in practice and in the academics. The issue of ethics in accounting has now become a contemporary matter.

Similarly, it has created doubt in the minds of many people regarding the validity of profits declared by most organisations. This is more particularly in Nigeria where banks (service industry) declare profits in tens of billions while the manufacturing companies (real sector) report much lower profits.

In Nigeria, many view ethics as an elitist idea and thinking while others see it as means of blocking the less privileged from the "national cake". That is why many people condone corruption because of the expectation that they would have the opportunity of misappropriating public funds.

Rationality and objectivity are virtues meant to guarantee ethical compliance. However, because the society attaches more value to material wealth than any other virtue, people tend to ignore the need to be rational and objective. This influences the behaviour of accountants within and outside practice. This is because the environment influences behaviour.

This paper aims at discussing ethical thoughts in Accounting with a view to identifying the major attributes required for ethical behaviour, the consequences of unethical behaviour, and the challenges that affect ethical issues in accounting.

2. Conceptual Framework and Literature Review

2.1 Conceptual Framework

Ethical thoughts in accounting started receiving serious attention in the early 1930's. However the concept got prominence in the 1990's when companies, particularly, banks began to collapse within and outside the country. Up to date most attention is on financial accounting. But in real life (practice), the impact of ethics is on the whole accounting system. Cooper and Hopper (1990), states that accounting is a formal system with structural and behavioural characteristics whose terms are expressed in fundamentally financial forms, whose meaning is derived from the organization of which it is an integral part. Although Cooper and Hopper's statement made reference to financial forms which accounting system is broader, yet is explains that accounting is more than financial accounting, as he also made reference to structural and behavioural characteristics. This is more evident when one looks at the work of Davis, Menon and Morgan (1982:307) where accounting is seen to consist of four distinct images. "They are those which treat accounting as historical records, as a descriptor of current economic reality, as an information system, and as a commodity".

Generally, thought may be referred to as meaningful concept and reasoning. The concept of ethical thought under discussion is on the accounting profession. Therefore reference is made to the two broad classifications of accounting, that is financial and management accounting.

Ethical code is imperative for every professional body. Adhering to accounting ethics is central to the survival of any organisation. A fall in accounting ethics will jeopardize the existence of any sector (private or public). This is supported by Asaolu, Oladele and Oladoyin (2005:17) where they stated that: "The accounting profession is intimately intertwined with the ethical virtue of integrity. Once an accounting profession falls short of this virtue, whatever remains is a ruse: a mere shadow of the practice".

2.2 Literature Review

Scholars have viewed ethics differently; the views that are often expressed include the combination of feeling of wrong and right, morality, complying with rules and regulations, religious belief and societal acceptance of behaviour.

It should be stated that ethics goes beyond doing the right or wrong thing, complying with rules and regulations, obeying laws, religious belief, doing what is acceptable to society and/or morality.

Ethics can not be said to stop at being moral in the strict sense of it, yet, morality stand to be a very good character every professional should maintain. Swanda (1990:62) states that while morality as a resource cannot be considered in the same context as tangible assets or goods, it can be considered, however, as a highly valuable but volatile asset, one which reflects the perception of the community.

One would, however, say that ethical behaviour depends on accountability. Where accounting officers are accountable there is high probability they would behave ethically. Kantudu (2004:98) states that "Management's accountability could be judged in terms of its ability to handle and account for the use of resources entrusted unto it (by the owners or those who can claim interest on the resources) with honesty, commitment, trust and probity".

This implies that the need for integrity is necessary for any professional ethics. This is so because all accountants are required to be accountable as decisions by different users will be based on information provided by the accountant. Dandago (2005:57) states that "auditors are expected to be as independent as possible, and demonstrate a high degree of honesty and competence for their opinion to be shared by interested parties"

2.2.1 Dispositional Ethical Realism (DER)

Brower (1993) observes that the imperialist have left many with the impression that we have only two choices regarding ethical truth: either realism is true, in which case there are ethical acts and properties that are independent of our attitudes, or non-realism is true, in which case what appear to be ethical facts and properties are mere "projections" or mere "expressions" of a "non-cognitive attitude". Brower (1993:246) justifies why DER should be accepted since dispositional ethical realism holds that we have a moral responsibility, molded by nature and culture. It treats moral truth as determined by the empirically discoverable output of this sensibility. The proponent of DER went further to state the DER will not appeal to kantians because it treats moral truth as a contingent and does not pretend to argue that the nature of practical reason requires that all rational agents be moral. Hobbesian, according to David (1986:46), suggests that ethics begin with a severe moral skepticism and then treat morality as the result of an agreement between self interested individuals seeking mutual advantage.

2.2.2 Education for Professional Accounting

The challenges being faced by the accountant on ethical issues are enormous, particularly in the educational institution (academic and professional) as they are seen to be responsible for inculcating ethics. Mautz (1965:308) states that accounting education is under pressure from a number of directions. It is caught in the current criticism of all undergraduate schools of business that education for business generally is not sufficiently rigorous, that it neglects the basics of being descriptive, that it is too specified, that it emphasizes procedure and descriptions rather than being analytical in nature, and that all in all it has forsaken the liberal approach and ought to be raised.

His argument may be only in the context of lack of proper inclusion of ethics in the educational curriculum. However, the argument that the scope is too specialized may not be accepted as professionalism is about specialization. It is only with specialization that an ethical code can be enforced.

2.2.3 Rationality and Ethics

While ethics may be linked to the level of ones rationality; in Accounting, rationality could be said to be a function of conscience which may be natural or learned. It can be argued that to achieve a professional status in accounting requires some degree of rationality which makes compliance with an ethical code almost natural. Madsen (1995:452) states that the classical view of rationality hold that a judgment is rational only when it displays the properties of being universal, necessary and rule-governed. He went ahead to proffer what might be called a more reasonable account of rationality. In place of the classical view, he sees rationality as having three completely different features. He holds that;

(i) Rationality is not a matter of following some set of rules

(ii) Rational Judgments can be rational without also being necessary judgments.

(iii) Rational judgments are produced against a backdrop of two kinds of information – "a body of background knowledge" and 'information relevant to the case at hand'

In this context, it can be stated that ethics in accounting may not be only about following a set of ethical codes, but also requires a high degree of rational judgment. For example the concept of objectivity in the profession may be viewed differently by different people; to satisfy all stakeholders requires a high skill and rational judgment. Rationality would surely be a useful attitude to professionals in order to be successful in practice and to live a good life. William and Murphy (1990:68) notes that the perspective of an ethical system is that all rules and regulations are, at root, an attempt to preserve a human way of life; thus our fundamental task in ethics today is not primarily concerned with analyzing situations so that one can make the right decisions, but rather with reflecting on what constitutes a good life.

2.2.4 Ethics and Gender Difference

The level of compliance with an ethical code would vary with age and gender. The younger professional may be more tempted to compromise ethics for self interest than the older professional who might have built a strong reputation, and for whom consequences of unethical behaviour may be viewed serious. The female accountant may respond to ethical codes more than the male. Gilligan (1982) attributes differences in resolving ethical dilemmas between men and women to differences in the socialization. Because women have been taught to be reserved and relationship oriented, they tend to develop a caring ethic. Men on the other hand, having been socialized to be tough and achievement oriented, tend to develop an ethic of justice and fairness. The gender differences in ethical decision making are thought to have implications for adults' business attitudes and interactions. Men are more likely to break rules given their competitive orientation; women on the other hand, are more likely to abide by rules and be less tolerant of rule breakers because of their concern for relationships.

3. Methodology

This paper reviewed the work of some scholars in the area of accounting ethics and other related disciplines with a view to making some conclusions and recommendations. There is, however, dearth of material (particularly empirical studies in the area – ethical thoughts in accounting). There are no theories on accounting ethics.

It is also found that the bulk of discussion on ethics is mainly on financial accounting, although, ethics in accounting goes beyond Financial Accounting but also includes Management Accounting.

The source of data for this paper is secondary. Various sites were visited on the internet; textbooks, newspaper, journals and conference proceedings were also consulted in order to come out with a considered opinion.

Ethics is broad and complex and therefore attention is focused on professional ethics and most particularly, accounting ethics.

4. Discussion of Findings

The complexities of business environment all over the world necessitate the need for objectivity in accounting because stakeholders in accounting information often do not have the same interest. The discipline (accounting) requires great skills and competence that must be augmented with a basic ethical code. Accounting profession like any other profession has its own set of ethical codes that vary slightly from country to country, and from one professional body to another even within the same country. The need for an ethical code in accounting is high for the multiplicity of accounting policies that may tempt accountants to manipulate an account for a particular interest.

4.1 Accounting Ethics

Ethical thoughts in accounting date back to early 1930s, when businesses were not as complex as they are today. Ethics cannot be easily defined. However, in accounting one can view it to be standard set of code of behaviour intended to control the conduct of members to discharge their duties with diligence, objectivity and to guarantee the integrity of the profession.

Accounting is aimed at providing useful information which can be quantitative and/or qualitative, that can be expressed in monetary terms in the case of quantitative information, and non-monetary terms in the case of qualitative information for the purpose of decision making. There are various users of accounting information for decision making. They are commonly referred to as internal and external users. However, Dandago (2007) classifies them as primary and secondary users. Each user depends on the quality of information provided by the accountant to make a decision. Therefore the accountant owes the users the obligation to be objective and observe due diligence in providing dependable information because of the requirement for analysis of risk and returns. Burton, Palmer and Kay (1981) state that investors and lenders are concerned with amount, timing and the risk associated with a return on investment. The unique role of financial reporting is to furnish some of the information useful in the assessment of risk and return and thereby to contribute to the maintenance of healthy capital markets.

In most of the literatures consulted, attention is given to financial accounting. However, when discussing ethical thoughts in accounting, there is need to consider the two broad classifications of Accounting (Financial and Management Accounting) as emphasized by Dandago (2007).

4.1.1 Financial Accounting

Information generated by financial accountants can be used by different people that may be classified as follows:

Primary users:

(i) Investors

(ii) Creditors (long and short term)

Secondary users:

(i) Employers

(ii) Governments: Local and International

(iii) General Public

(iv) Competitors

(v) Trade Unions

(vi) Academic Institutions, etc.

Each category of users has its specific needs for the information to which an accountant/auditor owes some responsibilities. In this instance, ethics is required for objective reporting.

4.1.2 Management Accounting

When it comes to ethical matters, management accounting is often kept hidden. Although the information generated by management accountants may strictly be for internal consumption, yet there are ethical responsibilities on the part of the Management Accountant to provide correct information. As it can be seen in the subsequent sections, ethics requires the maximization of shareholders wealth (arguable). Therefore, if for example a management accountant provides a wrong information on the cost of producing an item then that may lead to under- or over-pricing of the item and ultimately put the company at a disadvantage, and may lead to the collapse of the company.

4.2 The Aim of Ethics

The primary purpose of an ethical code is to protect clients and third parties from any possible loss as result of professional negligence and incompetence. Behaving ethically is also aimed at maintaining the image of the profession. The purpose of ethics in accounting is to direct accountants to abide by a code of conduct that facilitates and encourages public confidence in their service. The need for public confidence dates back to the 1930's when Richardson in Flory, Phillips, Reidenbach, and Robin (1992:2) state that many of the early discussions of accounting ethics focused on the need to establish public confidence in the accounting profession through ethical codes such as those governing practice in the legal and medical professions.

4.3 Attributes of Professional Ethics

Ethical thoughtS in accounting can only be practicable when members possess certain qualities which can be referred to as the attributes of professional ethics, that is conditions necessary for ensuring compliance with ethical codes. These attributes are (1) independence (2) integrity (3) rationality (4) objectivity (5) competence (6) morality (7) honesty (8) confidentiality (9) time consciousness. Others include prudence, transparency, accountability and commitment.

4.4 Consequences of Unethical Act

The consequences of unethical behaviour are colossal; the worse is the closure of a business outfit. Unethical behaviour may lead to loss of public confidence (goodwill), which may eventually lead to loss of demand (market). For example the sale of substandard products could lead to various litigations and the eventual collapse of an entity. Therefore unethical behaviour would lead to the following effects:

(i) Investors: loss of profit and in some instance complete loss of capital

(ii) Creditors: when an accountant behaves unethically; creditors (long and short term) would be reluctant to allow further credit facilities, and in some instances request the payment of outstanding liabilities, which would lead to liquidity problems and eventually lead to liquidation.

(iii) Employee: the employees will lose confidence in the company and begin to look for alternative employment. That is, labour turnover may be high which will result in a high cost of training and waste in the learning process.

(iv) Government: government may impose a fine on the company or ban the company from carrying out its activities. Alternatively the company may not have any government incentive.

4.5 Professional Bodies

Specific responsibilities of the accounting profession are expressed in the various codes of ethics promulgated by major professional organisations. A profession is formed on the basis of:

(i) Generally accepted body of knowledge.

(ii) A widely recognized standard attainment.

(iii) An enforceable code of ethics.

The following are the major accounting related professional bodies recognized by law in Nigeria:

(i) Institute of Chartered Accountants of Nigeria (ICAN)

(ii) Chartered Institute of Taxation of Nigeria (CITN)

(iii) Association of National Accountants of Nigeria (ANAN)

(iv) Institute of Certified Public Accountants of Nigeria (ICPAN)

(v) Chartered Institute of Stock Brokers (CIS)

(vi) Chartered Institute of Bankers of Nigeria (CIBN)

Some of the bodies came up of recent, and there are many more struggling for recognition. The ethical code of some of these bodies may be abused in the short run for their quest for more membership, establishment, and survival; but in the long run it may be good for the economy.

4.6 Challenges of Accountants and Professional Bodies in Nigeria

There are various challenges being faced by accountants and their professional bodies in Nigeria. These problems to some extent undermine the independence of members and supervisory roles of professional bodies which lead to some compromises. This in fact affects the ethical conduct of members, and in some instances even the professional bodies. Some of the problems identified include:

a. Corruption: Nigeria was rated in 2005 by Transparency International as the second most corrupt country in the world. This suggests that the society is highly corrupt and accountants are part of the society. Therefore in some instances accountants may have to lobby to secure employment, consultancy or audit job.

b. Fear of Losing Clients: Where a client behaves unethically, the accountants would have some reservations in questioning the client for fear of losing the client or his job. The need for objectivity may then be jeopardized.

c. Poor remuneration: Salary paid to accountants is generally low, particularly in the public sector.

d. Lack of action on auditors report and accountants' advice: Many audit firms do report wrong acts in their management report, but no action is often taken. This is more common in the public sector. In some organisations, they do not base their decision on the advice of accountants, in that they see accountants merely as bookkeepers.

e. Wrong Perception of the Accounting Profession: Recent scandals in the finances of many institutions have negatively polluted the minds of the public on the integrity of accountants. This reduces their confidence on accounting information. Beside, some people are not aware of the extent or scope of auditing and accounting responsibilities.

f. Lack of Monitoring Committees: Most professional bodies do not have a monitoring committee to monitor the activities of their members. In fact, some do not even have a disciplinary committee. For some that have, they take a long time to deal with a reported case and the outcome of the committee's activities is not properly publicized.

g. Curriculum of Accounting Courses: Ethical issues are not adequately integrated in accounting courses at the undergraduate, postgraduate and professional levels.

h. Stakeholders are ignorant on how to report cases of abuse of ethical codes. For those that know, the procedure of laying complaints is not convenient.

i. Inadequate Continuous Education on ethical issues.

j. Proliferation of accounting professional bodies: Professional bodies are coming up day by day, and this makes the bodies to admit incompetent members who have not read accounting with a view of getting recognition.

Conclusion

Ethics in accounting is very crucial in producing reliable and complete information for rational decision making. Ethics would also guarantee public confidence and provide a podium for consistency and uniformity.

Ethical codes may be contradicting, but the influence of the interest of a client supersedes the influence of the interest of a third party. The consequences of unethical acts are enormous and may lead to the collapse of a company or subject it to undue and negative publicity.

Recommendations

On the basis of the findings from the literature consulted and observations made, the following recommendations are made with a view to strengthening the compliance with ethical codes of the accountancy profession.

(i) Integrate ethics into existing undergraduate courses through case studies. This will help students to appreciate the need for ethics in any matter, analyze ethical issues, handle uncertainty and prepare the minds of students towards ethics.

(ii) Professionals should assess the ethical environment found within clients and business partners before accepting any offer.

(iii) Recognized professional bodies should have a monitoring committee to monitor the activities of accountants.

(iv) Recognized professional bodies should provide dedicated telephone lines to enable clients and third parties to report unethical matters (cases).

(v) Disciplinary Committees should act fast on any disciplinary matter, and the outcome should be known to the general public. The Committee should not only be objective but should also be seen to be objective.

(vi) Seminars/Conferences on ethical conduct should be organized at least twice a year for accountants and all stakeholders. It should be a participatory seminar.

(vii) Professional accounting bodies should create public awareness by sponsoring newspaper articles, granting interviews, and organizing public lectures. These should educate people on the scope of the profession, the challenges, the rights of clients and third parties and also the responsibilities of all stakeholders.

(viii) Professional bodies should draw out a minimum salary table for Accountants in the public and private sectors, as ICAN does for its practicing auditors.

References

Asaolu T.O. Oladele, P.O. and Oladoyin, A.M. (2005), "An assessment of the ethical values of honesty and integrity in accounting establishments. The case of Obafemi Awolowo University (O.A.U)"; in Dandago K.I and K.T. Hamid (eds) Honesty and Integrity Department of Accounting, Bayero University, Kano Nigeria, Gidan Dabino Publishers.

Brower, B. W. (1993), "Dispositional Ethical Realism" Ethics, Vol. 103, No. 2; Chicago, University of Chicago Press

Burton, J. C., Palmer R. E. and Kay R. S. (1981), A Hand book of Accounting and Auditing, London: Warren, Gorham and Lamont

Cooper, D. J. and Hopper, T. M. (1990), Critical Account, London: The Macmillan Press

Dandago, K.I. (2005), The role of internal auditors in establishing honesty and integrity. Are the watch dogs asleep?, in Dandago K.I and K.T Hamid (2005), Honesty and Integrity, Department of Accounting, BUK, Kano; Gidan Dabino Publishers,

Dandago, K.I. (2007), Advanced Accounting Theory and Practice, Department of Accountant, BUK, PhD Lecture Note.

David, G. (1986), Morals by Agreement, Oxford; Oxford University Press

David, L. S. (2004), WHY WE LIE, "The evolutionary Roots of Deception and the Unconscious Mind" http://mww.issafrica.org

Davis, S. W., Menon K. and Morgan, G. (1982), "The Images of that have Shaped Accounting Theory" London: Accounting, Organizations and Society

Duska, R. F. (1992) "Why be a Loyal Agent? "A systematic Ethical Analysis" in Bowie N. E. and R. E. Freeman (eds) (1995), Ethics and Agency Theory, New York: Oxford University Press

Flory, S. M.; Phillips, T. J. Reidenbach, E. R. and Robin, D. P. (1992), "A multidimensional Analysis of Selected Ethical Issues in Accounting ". The Accounting Review; Vol. 67 No. 2 http://www.jstor.-org/journals/aaasoc.html

Gilligan, C. 1982 in Adebayo, D. O (2005), "Gender and Attitudes towards Professional Ethics: A Nigeria Police Perspective" African Security Review Vol. 14 No. 2 http://www.issafrica.org

Kantudu, A.S. (2004), "The Relevance Of Auditors Report In Enhancing Management Accountability In Nigeria", in Dandago K.I. and A.I. Tanko. Prudence, Transparency and Accountability. Department of Accounting, BUK, Kano; Gidan Dabino Publishers.

King, J. B. (1989), "Confronting Chaos", Journal of Business Ethics - January

Madsen, P. (1995), "A Theoretical Ground for the Practice of Business Ethics; A Commentary". Business Ethics Quality, Vol. 5, No. 3 http://www.jstor.org/journals/pdc.html

Mautz, R. K. (1965), "Challenges to Accounting profession". The Accounting Review, Vol. 40 No. 2 http://www.jstor.org/journals/aaasoc.html

Romal, J. B. and Hibschweiler, M. A. (2002), "Improving Professional ethics: Steps for Implementing Change, the CPA Journals, New York, New York State Society of CPAs

Swanda, J. R. (1990),"Goodwill, Going Concern, Stocks and Flows: A Prescription for Moral Analysis" Journal of Business Ethics Vol. 9 No. 9

William, O. E and Murphy, P. E. (1990), "The Ethics of Virtue: A Moral Theory of Marketing", Journal of Macro Marketing; http://www.-jstor org/journals/aaasoc.html

Chapter 9

Approaches to Accounting Thoughts

Kabir Tahir Hamid

1. Introduction

Financial statements are the basis for a wide range of business analysis. Managers use them to monitor and judge their firm's performance relative to competitors, to communicate with external investors, to help judge what financial policies they should pursue, and evaluate potential new business to acquire as part of their investment strategy. Securities analysts use financial statements to rate and value companies they recommend to clients. Bankers use them in deciding whether to extend a loan to a client and how to determine the loan's terms. Investment bankers use them as a basis for valuing and analyzing prospective buyouts, mergers and acquisitions. And consultants use them as a basis for competitive analysis for their clients. Other user groups also require the financial statements and use them for some other purposes (Palepu, 2000).

An organization may be involved in making some accounting decisions, on issues that have not been addressed by accounting authorities. As Financial Accounting Standard Board (FASB) put it, in its Statement of Financial Accounting Concepts No. 2, accounting choices are made at two levels at least. At one level they are made by the Board (FASB) or other agencies (SEC, NASB, IASC, IFAC, etc.) that have the power to require business enterprises to report in some particular way or, if exercised negatively, to prohibit a method that those agencies consider undesirable. Accounting choices are also made at the level of the individual enterprise. As more Accounting Standards are issued, the scope for individual choice inevitably becomes circumscribed. But there are now, and will always be, many accounting decisions to be made by reporting enterprises involving a choice between alternatives for which no standard has been promulgated or a choice between ways of complying with the standards (Hendriksen and Van Breda, 2001).

Accountants have tried numerous approaches to solving various accounting problems. Six approaches are discussed in this paper. These approaches are tax approach, legal approach, ethical approach, economic approach, behavioural approach, and structural approach. The methodology used in this paper involves a review of various write-ups on the subject matter to understand the various approaches that are used in resolving problems in accounting, with a view to ascertain their continued relevance, in theory, and practice

2. Conceptual Framework and Literature Review

2.1 Definition of Accounting Theory

Accounting theory comprises the entire concepts, conventions, principles, rules and standards that guide decision making in the accounting profession. Drawing on the definition of theory as found in Webster's dictionary, Hendriksen and Van Breda (2001) define accounting theory as a coherent set of hypothetical, conceptual, and pragmatic principles forming a general frame of reference for inquiring into the nature of accounting. The definition is deliberately broad so as to encompass both the more traditional view of theory as a general frame of reference for the evaluation and development of sound accounting practices, and the more modern view of theory as a general frame of reference by which accounting practice can be explained and predicted.

Wolk, Tearney, and Dodd (2001) on their part, define accounting theory as the basic assumptions, definitions, principles and concepts and the reporting of accounting and financial information. From these definitions, it is clear that accounting theory is the entire accounting literature that guides decision making by accountants, the treatment of business transactions in the books of accounts and the conduct of accounting responsibilities.

2.2 Approaches to Accounting Theory

There are numerous approaches that are used in solving problems and in taking decision in accounting. Some of these approaches as highlighted by Hendriksen and Van Breda (2001) include the following:

- Tax Approach
- Legal Approach
- Ethical Approach
- Economic Approach
- Behavioural Approach
- Structural Approach

Each of these approaches is relevant, and can be used individually or in conjunction with another approach, in taking a decision to solve an accounting problem.

2.2.1 The Tax Approach

Although tax accounting has different objectives from financial accounting, various income tax Acts have had a major impact on accounting practice in many areas. They were important in bringing the average accounting practices up to the required standard. Even firms that do not produce financial statements are usually motivated to do so, so as to conform to the requirements of the tax authorities. This created an improvement in general accounting practices and in maintaining consistency.

Businesses are assessed a variety of taxes (including company income tax, excise duties, Value Added Tax (VAT) and capital gains tax) all of which require the preparation of periodic financial reports to taxing agencies (FIRS and SBIR). Although financial reports prepared by businesses are general purpose in nature, they are adjusted for income tax purposes, using the tax approach. This is done by reflecting the provisions of the tax laws on the general purpose statements so as to conform to the requirements of the tax authorities. For example in deciding on expenses allowable and those not allowable, relieves and allowances, capital allowance, tax rate etc. reference is made to the relevant provisions of tax laws. From these discussions, it can be said that the tax approach to accounting thought is more relevant in taking decision on issues bordering on tax accounting.

2.2.2 The Legal Approach

The usual question asks here is what is the position of the law or decisions of judges regarding an item or its treatment in the account. In establishing a conceptual framework for accounting, the FASB (FASB Memorandum, 1976), as reported by Henriksen and Van Breda (2001), investigated the use of law to establish accounting principles. They noted that, in many situations there are economic as well as legal issues. For example companies listed on the Nigerian Stock Exchange, would have to consider the laws relating to the standards for financial reports established by the Exchange, in addition to the relevant provisions of Companies and Allied Matters Act (CAMA) 1990, Banks and Other Financial Institutions Act (BOFIA) 1991, Central Bank of Nigeria (CBN) circulars, Generally Accepted Accounting Principles (GAAP) etc in their reports.

In practice, this approach is applied by businesses. Although there may be instances where there is conflict between the legal form and financial reality of a transaction. In such situations, the financial reality takes precedence over the legal form, in compliance with the concept of substance over form. For example in hire purchase transaction, the hire purchaser would have to bring the assets into his books and depreciates it, as if it belongs to him, even though the property in the good still lies with the vendor, until the hire purchaser pays the last installment, and exercise the option to buy the asset.

From the above discussion, it can be said that in practice the legal provisions (CAMA 1990, BOFIA 1991 etc) have greatly enhanced the quality of financial statements by ensuring the disclosure of minimum information, which is considered necessary in taking informed decisions by various user groups.

2.2.3 The Ethical Approach

A third approach to accounting thought asks the question whether there is an ethical solution to an accounting problem. Is there something management ought to be doing? Is this something more than following a set of Generally Accepted Accounting Principles (GAAP)? In asking these questions, it does not imply that other approaches have no ethical content, nor does it imply that ethical theories necessarily ignore all other concepts. As James (1965) points out, ethical questions are at the heart of all modern theory.

The ethical approach to accounting theory places emphasis on the concepts of justice, truth, and fairness of decisions relating to the treatment of items in the account and its presentation to various users. Information should not be bias or coloured to influence behaviour in a particular direction. Rather, information presented should show a true and fair view of the state of affairs of the business. For example, the recognition of a gain at the time of sale of an asset is reporting of "true" condition, where as reporting an appraisal increase in the value of an asset, prior to sale as income, lacks truthfulness.

Dalhat and Barnabas (2003), found that a sizeable number of Nigerian accountants do not comply with ethical standards in the discharge of their responsibilities leading to the misrepresentation of financial information. In a similar vein, Bello (2003), found that some organizations, especially banks, are involved in accounting income smoothing (i.e. earnings management), reporting earnings other than actual earning to their shareholders, so as to show at all times, as if all is well with their operations. This practice is clearly unethical because, it is an aspect of creative accounting.

In practice, studies (Dalhat & Barnabas, 2003 and Bello, 2003) have shown that the approach is not respected at all times, as more often than not, some company managements deliberately opt for methods that are clearly unethical, which colours financial information. The cases of Enron, Savannah bank, etc are good examples.

From the discussions above, it can be deduced that the ethical approach emphasized on the need for accountants to show truthfulness, honesty, integrity and follow due process in the treatment of business transactions in the books of accounts and the discharge of their responsibilities in its entirety.

2.2.4 The Economic Approach

Accountants have long attempted to interpret accounting concepts in terms of economics. In recent years, there have been veritable explorations of research investigating the correspondence between economic interpretations and accounting data. Henriksen and Van Breda (2001), highlight the three avenues in adopting an economic approach to accounting. These are the macroeconomic approach, the microeconomic approach, and corporate social accounting approach.

i. Macroeconomics

A macroeconomic approach attempts to explain the effect of alternative reporting procedures on economic measurements and economic activities at a level broader than the firm, such as an industry or national economy. This is done on the argument that one of the objectives of accounting is to direct the behaviour of firms and individuals towards the implementation of specific national economic policies. As such, national economic objectives require accounting reports that will permit and even encourage higher dividend and larger capital investments during periods of inflation. Henriksen and Van Breda (2001), report that some countries, notably Sweden, attempt to base accounting concepts and practices on macroeconomic goals. One of the objectives of this approach is to report stable earnings from year to year to legitimize the use of reserve and flexible depreciation policies. The most important question to ask is how ethical is this approach? Where it is unethical, accountants should never indulge in it.

Bello (2003) has found that there is some element of accounting income smoothing (earnings management) in practice in Nigeria, which reports stable earnings from year to year, although the firm was the point of consideration, rather than the economy, by those who practice the system. But the question still lingering is how ethical is the practice?

ii. Microeconomics

A microeconomic approach to accounting theory attempts to explain the effect of alternative reporting procedures on economic measurements and economic activities at the level of the enterprise and the firm. Modern accounting theory, which is founded in microeconomics, focuses attention on the enterprise as an economic entity with its main activities affecting the economy through its operations in the markets. As reported by Wolk *et al* (2001), this view is also adopted by the FASB in its fundamental premise that financial information has inevitable economic consequences. The exact form these consequences take is not always easy to determine and is subject to some dispute. This approach is used by firms in Nigeria, more especially those that are required to render reports to the (Nigerian Stock Exchange) NSE. Firms weigh the implications and consequences of all items to be disclose on the financial statements, on its activities and operations, before deciding on the nature and the need for disclosure (more especially where the disclosure is not sanction by the law). It can therefore be said that this approach is the basis for reporting only the activities of the firm on the financial statement, excluding the activities of the owner(s) or the shareholders.

iii. Corporate Social Accounting

The microeconomics view of accounting does not necessarily encompass all the effects companies have on society. The costs of environmental pollution, unhealthy working conditions and other social problems are not normally reported by firms. Proponents of stakeholder analysis argue, with some justification, that traditional accounting with its emphasis on shareholders is really a subset of a social accounting with its emphasis on the broader group of stakeholders. The enterprise theory considers the corporation as a social institution operated for the benefit of many interest groups (Hendriksen and Van Breda, 2001). The FASB formally recognized in its conceptual framework that there are many parties other than present owners interested in financial information. In the broadest form these groups include, in addition to the stockholders and creditors, the employees, customers, the government as a taxing authority, the regulatory agencies, and the general public. From an accounting point of view, this means that the responsibility of corporate reporting extends not only to stockholders and creditors, but also to many other groups and to the general public.

Corporations can no longer operate solely in the interest of stockholders, and it cannot be assumed that the forces of competition will necessarily protect the interests of other groups. From a study of thirty firms quoted on the Nigerian Stock Exchange (NSE), Mamman (2004) found that 83% of the firms present corporate social responsibility performance information on their financial statements in different formats, but that does not result in a systematic measurement of externalities (social costs and benefits). This has reaffirmed what Idoko (1998) found some years ago. In practice in Nigeria, only big firms see themselves as socially responsible to the society in which they operate, but small firms and business enterprises do not see themselves as such. This is in view of the fact that there are in adequate laws which ensure that all business outfits are environmentally friendly and socially responsible. This is evident from the level of environmental pollution through reckless dumping of waste, pure water polythene bags, and other refuse by business firms throughout the Country.

2.2.5 Behavioural Approach

This approach relies on the insights of psychology and sociology in the development of accounting theories. The focus in this approach is on the relevance of information being communicated to decision makers and the behaviour of different individuals or groups as a result of the presentation of accounting information (Ijiri and Robert, 1966). Behavioural theories take into consideration the effect of the actions of accountants and auditors on the behaviour, reactions and decisions of users of the accounting information. The most important outside users of accounting information include stockholders, investors, creditors and government authorities.

Thus, behavioural theories attempt to measure and evaluate the economic, psychological, and sociological effects of accounting information on the various users of such information. Thus, where auditors or reporting accountants (in case of public offer of shares), give their professional opinion on the financial statements, the behaviour and decision of users is influenced. For example, if an auditor gives his report, the behaviour of users is influenced as whether to divest, invest, resign his appointment, look for job, supply goods, extend credit facilities etc.

The behavioural approach to accounting theory has stimulated a search among both academics and practicing accountants for the basic objectives of accounting and for answers to questions such as: Who are the users of published financial statements? What is the nature of the specific information wanted by the several user groups? Can common needs be found for the presentation of general-purpose statements or should specific statements be presented? How do investors, creditors, and managers react to different accounting information and presentation? In practice, search to answers on the above questions are continuously made through research undertakings by both academics and practicing accountants. But there is the need to sponsor more researches through funding by private organizations and results published for the benefits of all and sundry.

2.2.6 Structural Approach

Most reasoning in this approach is by analogy (comparison), which attempts to treat like with like. Using this approach, accountants attempt to classify similar transactions or, more formally, to seek consistency in recording and reporting transactions. It is only when they encounter a transaction which does not fit into a previous mold that they are forced back to more basic principles (McDonald, 1967; Sterling and Raymond, 1969; Larson, 1996). For example treatment of payment for patent right, contingent liabilities, deferred advertisement expenditure, import duties on raw materials, charges for delivery of items purchase on the internet, etc. can all be made using this approach.

This process of classifying like data with like, and summarizing them in specific groupings (accounts and ledgers) and further summarizing the groupings into reports and statements has been called "compacting" (i.e. compilation of accounting information) (Hendriksen and Van Breda, 2001). It is this compacting process that has made the American Institute of Accountants (AIA) in 1941 to define accounting as the art of identifying, measuring, recording, classifying, and summarizing in a significant way and in terms of money, transactions, and events, which are in part, at least, of financial character, and interpreting the results thereto (Most, 1982; Kam, 1986). Broader definitions of accounting are given today by various authorities, but the process of "recording, classifying, and summarizing" is still the heart of accounting, because its nature has virtually remain the same. In practice, this is what is obtained in Nigeria, especially on recording of business transactions and presentation of information on financial statements.

Conclusion and Recommendations

Six approaches to developing accounting theory have been discussed in this paper. These are tax, legal, ethical, economic, behavioural, and structural approach. Each of these approaches has some merit in helping to establish and evaluate accounting principles and procedures. Economic and behavioural approaches help set the stage for explaining the environment within which accounting operates and for selecting what data should be reported. The ethical approach provides fundamental objectives in establishing accounting standards.

The social and macroeconomic approaches help to resolve the controversies of theory development and application. The tax and legal approaches help to determine acceptable presentation or treatment of items on the financial statements from the point of view of tax authorities, laws and regulatory authorities. Structural approach explains how items are identified, classified and summarized. Each of the approaches discussed in this paper has its place in accounting theory and is use in inquiring into the nature of accounting, providing a framework for evaluating, developing, explaining and predicting practice.

Theoretical issues are not just matters of "theory". They have practical implications for both management and other users of financial statements. Accounting theory is often a matter of professional judgements made by individuals involved with specific cases. It is clear from the above discussion that it is not only members of the FASB, NASB, SEC, etc who are obliged to theorize, practicing accountants are often required to exercise their own judgements and discretions on theoretical issues. This is because there are now, and will always be many accounting decisions to be made by reporting enterprises, involving a choice between alternatives for which no standard has been issued or a choice between ways of complying with a standard.

Finally, the paper recommends that accountants in all walks of life should acquaint themselves with the approaches in view of their continuous relevance in solving issues in the accounting profession. The IASC, NASB, FASB, CAC, etc. should give due regard to the approaches in issuing standards and enacting laws. This would make the standards and laws to stand the test of time.

References

Bello, M.S. (2003) How Ethical is Accounting Income Smoothing? An Empirical Investigation. *In: Proceedings of the First National Conference on Ethical Issues in Accounting,* organized by the Department of Accounting BUK From 6-10 January 2003, pp.113-129

Belkaou, A. (1993), *Accounting Theory,* Dryden Press, Britain, 3nd Edition.

Dalhat, B.S. and Barnabas, A.O. (2003), The Effects of Low Adherence to Ethical Standards of Accountants in Nigeria. *In: Proceedings of the First National Conference on Ethical Issues in Accounting,* organized by the Department of Accounting BUK From 6-10 January 2003, pp.102-112

FASB Memorandum (1976), An Analysis of Issues Related to Conceptual Framework for Financial Accounting and Reporting: Elements of Financial Statement and Their Measurement. *In*: Henriksen, S.E. and Breda, M.V. (2001), *Accounting Theory,* McGraw-Hill Book Company, Singapore, 5th Edition.

Henriksen, S.E. and Breda, M.V. (2001), *Accounting Theory,* McGraw-Hill Book Company, Singapore, 5th Edition.

Idoko, O.G. (1998), *Corporate Social Responsibility Accounting Practice.* Unpublished M.Sc. Accounting Thesis, ABU Zaria.

Ijiri, Y. and Robert, J. (1966), Reliability and Objectivity of Accounting Methods. *In:* Wolk, I. H., Tearney, M. G. & Dodd, J. L. (2001), *Accounting Theory: A Conceptual and Institutional Approach,* South Western College Publishing, Thomson Learning Centre, Cincinnati, Ohio, USA, 5th Edition.

James, W.P. (1965), *The Foundation of Financial Accounting,* Baton Rouge: Louisiana State University Press, USA.

Kam, V. (1986), *Accounting Theory,* John Wiley and Sons, New York, USA.

Larson, K. (1996), Implications of Measurement Theory on Accounting Concept Formulation. *In*: Wolk, I. H., Tearney, M. G. & Dodd, J. L. (2001), *Accounting Theory: A Conceptual and Institutional Approach,* South Western College Publishing, Thomson Learning Centre, Cincinnati, Ohio, USA, 5th Edition.

Mamman, S. (2004), Disclosure of Corporate Social Responsibility Performance in Accounting Reports. *The Nigerian Journal of Accounting Research,* Dept. of Accounting, ABU, Zaria, Vol.1 No. 1, pp 14-21

McDonald, D. (1967), Feasibility Criteria for Accounting Measures, *In:* Wolk, I. H., Tearney, M. G. & Dodd, J. L. (2001), *Accounting Theory: A Conceptual and Institutional Approach,* South Western College Publishing, Thomson Learning Centre, Cincinnati, Ohio, USA, 5th Edition.

Most, K.S. (1982), *Accounting Theory,* Grid Publishing Inc., Columbus USA, 2nd Edition.

Palepu, K.G., Healy, P.M. and Bernard V.L. (2000), *Business Analysis and Valuation,* South-Western College Publishing, Ohio, USA.

Sterling, R. R. & Raymond, R. (1969), A Valuation Experiment. *In:* Wolk, I. H., Tearney, M. G. & Dodd, J. L. (2001), *Accounting Theory: A Conceptual and Institutional Approach,* South Western College Publishing, Thomson Learning Centre, Cincinnati, Ohio, USA, 5th Edition.

Wolk, I. H., Tearney, M. G. & Dodd, J. L. (2001), *Accounting Theory: A Conceptual and Institutional Approach,* South Western College Publishing, Thomson Learning Centre, Cincinnati, Ohio, USA, 5th Edition.

Chapter 10

An Alternative Approach to Accounting Theory

Y. M. Salaudeen

1. Introduction

A theory is a systematic statement of rules and principles. It may be viewed as a framework which permits the organization of ideas, the explanation of phenomena and the prediction of future behaviour (Kerlinger (1964). Accounting Theory is that branch of accounting, which consists of systematic statements of principles and methodologies as distinct from practice. Accounting theory is conceptual framework for accounting profession. It provides a set of rules and regulations for what accountants do or are supposed to be doing (Glautier and Underdawn, 1977).

Accounting theory is made-up of generally accepted accounting principles (GAAP) that have won acceptance by the accounting profession because of their perceived usefulness and logic. GAAPs represent guides to accountants in the choice of accounting techniques applicable in particular accounting situation and in the preparation of financial statements (Belkoui,1981).

In the construction of accounting theories various approaches have been adopted depending on individual perception about the approach the accounting profession should take to solve accounting problems (Kieso and Weygandt 1983). Notable amongst writers who attempts to classify approaches to accounting theory formulation are Bekaoui (1981) Kieso and Wegyandt (1983) Statement of Accounting Theory and Theory Acceptance (1977). Other are Whittington (1986) Chua (1986), Valayutham and Rahman(1992) etc. The objectives of this paper, therefore, is to establish the approaches that have been adopted by accounting theorists in the formulation of Accounting Theory.

The remainder of this paper is divided into four sections. The next section reviews the available literature in the area of approaches to formulation of accounting theory and related issues. This second section presents the methodology adopted in writing the paper, the third section presents an evaluation of alternative approaches while the last section concludes the paper and makes recommendations.

2. Literature Review

2.1 Nature of Accounting Theory

Theories generally, especially in the nature sciences, involve making assertions, predictions or explanations (theorizing) about phenomena and the verification or validation of these assertions etc to confirm or reject the assertions etc. The occurrence of the predicted phenomenon confirms the theory while the occurrence of a phenomenon that negates the prediction will call for a re-examination of the assertion (theory), which will lead to a new assertion (theory) Machlup (1955). The theory process therefore involves construction and verification. The process of theory verification albeit accepted is non-existence in accounting theories especially with the traditional theorists who consider theory construction and verification as synonymous (Belkoui,1981).

"Modern" accounting theorists however argue that the process of verification is possible with accounting theory or that accounting theory actually conform to construction and verification processes. For example Hendricksen (1977:1) defined accounting theory to encompass the two aspect of a theory. He defines accounting theory as "a set of broad principles that (i) provides a general frame of reference by which accounting practices can be evaluated and (ii) guides the development of new practices and procedures". While McDonald (1972) on his own identified three elements of any theory, which he opined are found in accounting theory:

(i) Representation of phenomena by symbols; here he says accounting employs symbolic representation, which are unique to it for example "debit" and "credit".

(ii) Manipulation or combination according to rules, accounting employs translation rules; and the symbolic representation of economic events and transactions.

(iii) Translation back to real world phenomena; the accounting output in the form of balance sheet, profit and loss account and other financial statements are translation back to real world.

Classification of Accounting Theory

Many attempts have been made to formulate accounting theory, each attempt using different assumptions and methodologies (AAA,1977) based on these divergence in opinions, assumptions, approaches, values especially noticeable between accounting professionals and accounting teachers and researchers accounting theory can be classified as descriptive (positive) and normative (prescriptive) (Wolk et al,2001).

Belkaoui(1981) holds the opinion that the accounting professionals see accounting as an art, which cannot be codified or formalized. They, therefore the use descriptive accounting theory. Descriptive Accounting is an attempt to justify "what is" by a codification of existing accounting practices.

On the other hand, Normative Accounting Theory tries to formulate accounting theory based on a justification what ought to be. Normative theories are based on making a judgement of what is good and what is bad.

Both categories of theory are related. For a normative statement starts from a belief of what really is (descriptive) for the accounting profession to progress attention must be turned to the normative by the descriptive, moreso, normative theory presents a testing of the validity of accounting practice (Glautier and Underdown,1970).

2.3 Approaches to Formulation of Accounting Theory

Bolkaoui (1981), appears to have provided the most comprehensive approaches to accounting theory formulation. He classifies approaches into traditional and new approaches.

2.3.1.1 The Traditional Approaches

Traditional approaches are mainly descriptive in nature and they are: practical (non theoretical) and theoretical.

2.3.1.1.2 Non Theoretical Approaches

The non-theoretical approaches to setting accounting standards, which are; pragmatic (practical) and authoritarian approaches are hinged on providing practical solutions to accounting problems as they emerge.

Pragmatic approach to accounting theory is based on construction accounting theory that will confirm with real world situation and which will be useful as practical solutions to accounting problems. According to this approach, the choice of accounting techniques and principles is based on how useful the accounting information is and their relevance in the decision making process.

Authoritarian Approach to formulation of accounting theory consists of the issue, by mostly professional bodies and organizations, pronouncements for the regulation of accounting practice. This approach linked accounting theory to accounting practice.

2.3.1.2 Theoretical Approaches

This is the other aspect of traditional approaches to formulation of accounting theory and it includes:

Deductive Approach

Deductive approach to constructing accounting theory is based on deductive logic or reasoning. Deductive logic starts with a general proposition, which by deduction may be applied to specific or particular case. Applied to accounting theory, the deductive approach begins with basic general accounting proposition and proceed to derive by logical means accounting of principles that serve as guides and bases for the development of accounting techniques. (Glautier and Underdown, 1977).The ensuring theory thereby becoming a yardstick for which accounting practice can be evaluated.

The followings are the steps in deductive theory settings:

- Specification of objectives of financial statements.
- Selection of accounting postulates
- Derivation of accounting principles and
- Development of accounting techniques,(Belkoui,1981).
- Inductive Approach

The inductive theory employs inductive logic or reasoning. Inductive logic is a process of reasoning which allows a general proposition to be made from a particular case. (Glautier and Underdown,1977) Applied to accounting theory, the inductive approach starts with observations of financial information of business enterprises and proceed to draw, on the basis of recurring relationships observed, generalizations and principles of accounting. Inductive approach to accounting theory relies on a particular proposition as a basis for making general statement.

The four steps involved in inductive theory are:

(i) Observation and recording of all observations made.

(ii) Analyzing and classifying the observations to identify any recurring relationship.

(iii) Inductive derivation of generalization and principles of accounting from the observations that show recurring relationship.

(iv) Testing the generation (Belkouyi, 1981).

Ethical Approach

This approach originated from Scott (1941), he identified four ethical issues (fairness, justice, equity and truth) which must be considered in any attempt to construct accounting theory. Scott (1941) equates fairness to being unbiased and impartial in presentation, justice as being equitable and giving equal treatment to all users of accounting information and truth to accurate accounting reporting (without misrepresentation). Writers after Scott (1941), for example Yu (1976) considers justice and fairness as the only ethical issues; while other like Patilo (1965) considers fairness as the only ethical issue for all other attributes are inherent in fairness.

Sociological Approach

While Ethical Approach based accounting theory on fairness, sociological based it on social welfare. Sociological approach to the formulation of accounting theory emphasizes the social effect of accounting techniques. According to sociological approach, for any accounting theory to be accepted it must be evaluated on the basis of effects on the society as a whole. This approach presupposes the existence of established social values that will be used as criteria for the determination of accounting theoryand measurement criteria. Writers on sociological approach include Gambling (1974), Ladd (1983) and Mobley (1974).

Economic Approach

Sociological approach emphasis social welfare, economic approach emphasis the general economic wellbeing and effect of particular accounting technique on it. Economic approach focuses on the general economic welfare hence the choice of an accounting technique depends on its impact on the national economic good.

To construct an accounting theory therefore the economic reality and economic consequence of it must be considered. Proponents of this approach include; Enthoven(1973), Mueller(1962) and Zeff(1978).

Here the choice of accounting techniques will depend on the particular economic situation.

2.4.2 New Approaches To Formulation Of AccountingTheory

The new approaches to the formulation of an accounting theory according to Belkoui(1981:34) "represents new streams of accounting research that use both empirical reasoning to formulate and verify a conceptual accounting framework". They include: events, behavioural predictive approaches.

Events Approach

Sorter (1969) proposes the Events Approach as a dissenting opinion from other members of the American Accounting Association`s Committee Statement of Basic Accounting Theory. Other members favoured value approach to the preparation of financial statement. Event and value approaches differ on what in their opinion, is the responsibility of accountants with respect to financial reporting, or put another way, what should accountants be reporting?

Value approach considered the needs of users of accounting statements being known sufficiently to allow a deduction of accounting theory that provides optimal input to specified decision models. So accountants should report information for use in users' decision models.

Event approach on the other hand opined that accountants should provide all information about relevant economic events, not just the monetary aspects, thereby allowing users to generate their own information input to their decision models. The accountants provide information about events and leave the users to fit events into their decision models. Users against accountants should transform events into accounting information.

The event of approach suggests a tremendous increase of accounting data presented in financial reports. The effects of events approach on conventional financial statements are:

- On the balance sheet, the balance sheet will be constructed in such a way that will allow reconstructability of the events to be generated. The intention is to show, as far as most practice, all events that have occurred since the inception of the company.
- The events in the profit and loss account should be described in such a way that facilitates the forecasting of the same events in future; as against the current (values) approach of summing the result of operations for a particular period.
- On the events approach the statement of cash flow should reflect an expression of financial and investment events during the period.

Behavoiural Approach

Accounting is seen as action oriented, it purpose is to influence the behaviours of users of accounting information (AAA,1971). In the design of accounting theory, the behavioural approach opined that two main criteria must be considered, the relevance of accounting information communicated to decision making and the effect on the individual and group behaviour of the information communicated. Behavioural approach to accounting theory applies behavioural science to accounting, the ultimate objective of which is to understand, explain and predict human behaviour in all possible accounting contexts (AAA,1971). Proponents of behavioural approach include Devine (1960) and Bringerg and Nath (1971) and Bradish (1965).

The Predictive Approach

This approach to accounting theory believes that the accounting technique that enable users of financial statement to predict events of interest to them should be chosen amongst different accounting options. The choice of different accounting technique should therefore depend on its predictive ability. Beaver et al (1968:675) say "the measure with the greatest predictive power with respect to given event is considered to be the best method for a particular purpose.

Proponents of this approach include Abdelkhalik and Ayjinka (1979) Gonedes (1972) Belkoui (1989)

2.3.2Statement of Accounting Theory and Theory Acceptance (SATTA)

The American Accounting Association Committee on Concepts and Standards for External Reporting issued the Statement of Accounting Theory and Theory Acceptance. The statement classified approaches to accounting theory into:

- Classical-inductive and true income
- Decision usefulness and
- Information economics

"The true income and inductive theories arose from the 'classical approach to theory of development". Hameed and Ibrahim (2005). The true income approach is further divided into normative-deductive and inductive approaches. Hatfield (1939), Paton (1922) are notable writers in this regard.

Decision usefulness Approach aims to provide uses with information useful to their decision making process, the committee further identified decision makers and decision model approaches under this category. The decision model approach models decision making problems of users and hopes that accounting will provide the necessary information to fit into these models. Decision Model Approach focuses on the behaviour of individual or group to accounting information.

Information Approach sees accounting information as a resource to be used efficiently in the management of other resources, efficient use entails the cost of such information should not exceed the benefit from the use of such information.

2.3.3 Kieso and Weygandt (1983)

Other writer have identified accounting theory foundation approaches differently from the one presented above. For example Kieso and Weygandt (1983) identified the following approaches to accounting theory; true income approaches, decision-making approach, individual user approach, aggregate user approach and information economics approach. Their ideas seem to follow on the classification by SATTA.

True Income Approach

Currently we can say that there is no one method in accounting to account for various business transactions. The true income approach proponed are of the opinion that is if research long enough it is possible that we find the proper method to account by various business transactions so research should continue. This implies that there is a single accounting method that will correctly identified the economic substance of business transaction. Writers like Canning (1923) Sweeney (1936) and MacNeal (1939) could identified as True Income Approaches.

Decision-model Approach

This approach establishes assumptions about what the goals, decisions, and information needs of users ought to be and even this assumptions, drives the account method that best suit his perceived needs. This approach attempt to develop appropriate decision models to meet users need. Revsine (1973) Sterling (1970) and Staubus (1961) are some of the proponent of this approach.

Individual Users Approach

In setting accounting theories the effect of the information communicated on the individual user of such information must be considered.

Aggregate User (Efficient Market) Approach: holds that all publicly available information about the company is reflected in the stock price and that if the information is publicly disclosed the market as a whole cannot be deceived. Therefore the market should determine what cost to use in preparing financial statement Beaver (1978)

Information Economic Approach: Maintains that all accounting information should be evaluated using the cost benefit framework. Kieso and Weygandt (1983) opine that to say simply that reporting method reflects the economic substance of a transaction and therefore should be used is equally inappropriate what must be considered are the cost and benefit of using this approach – Demsai (1974)

2.3.4 Other Approaches

Whittington (1986) classified approaches to accounting theory according to historical periods with each approach representing a stage in historical development of accounting theory. His approach consist of empirical inductive, deductive and new empiricism.

Empirical inductive belongs to the earliest period or accounting when theory of accounting is a rationalization of what accountants do (accounting practice). The next period is made up of theories that are logically derived from assumptions – the deductive approach, the later stage is characterized by theories which are testable against empirical evidence-new empirical theory.

Velayutham and Rahman (1992) classified accounting theory construction according to purpose, approaches, underlying assumptions and level of development.

The purpose of constructing accounting theory will enable us to typify them as either descriptive or normative, while the approach to theory formation could be deductive, inductive or eclectical. Economic, sociological, ethical, human behaviour and communication theory are identified under underlying assumptions. And the following levels of development were identified.

Level I: According to common sense, credit are not subject to empirical testing.

Level II: A scientific level in which hypothesis are tested empirically.

Level III: Hypothesis subject to different sets of experimental testing.

Level IV: Series of facts, principles form a structured body of knowledge.

Level V: More general ideas about reality, existence, knowledge etc i.e. ontology and epistemology.

The various approaches by other authors were thereafter put under each level to example Biekoui(1981)`s pragmatic and authoritarian approaches were identified under level I.

Chua (1986) in the work Radical Development in Accounting ThoughtS took classification of Accounting Theory to a meta-theoretical level (hammed and Ibrahim, 2005). She classified all accounting theories approaches before her work, which albeit, are based on divergent assumptions share common scientific world view, as functionalists, because of their common assumptions on society and social science. Her classification is based on two assumptions of society and social science. The assumption in respect to the society is whether the society is orderly and stable or unstable and in a state conflict, the assumption of social science is based on belief on ontology of empirical world, epistemology, human nature and methodology. These sets of assumptions lead to four paradigms in accounting; radical humanist, radical structuralist interpretive and functionalist. She concluded by introducing two approaches to accounting - the interpretive and critical approaches (in line with social science research methodology (Neuman, 2003), which she believes will provide a different insight of accounting.

3. Methodology

The library research method has been adopted in order to produce this paper. The data collected are secondly and qualitative in nature and mainly from textbooks, journals and internet. In analyzing qualitative data, unlike quantitative data, which are amenable to statistical tools and techniques, content analysis was employed to find patterns among the mass of literature describing the subject matter to reach logical conclusions.

4. Evaluation of Approaches

The non-theoretical approaches of Belkoui (1981), (pragmatic and authoritarian) though attempt to provide solutions to accounting techniques problems as they emerge have failed to achieved uniformity in the treatment of accounting issues. Kohler (1939) is of the opinion that though good accounting principles emerge from these approaches alternative approaches continued to flourish and this was (and still is) because there was no underlying theory. Wolk et al (2001) saw them as leaving much to be desired. The main criticism against these approaches is their lack of theoretical bases.

The sociological approach suffers from its assumptions that there exists an acceptable social value which is general to all, which can be used for the determination of accounting theory. Human social values are as varied as human race and there can not be an established social value, additionally, it is difficult to identify the information need of those who make social welfare judgement and who make this judgement. However, this approach to accounting theory can be said to be partly responsible for the birth of social responsibility accounting or social accounting.

The Events Approach of Professor Sorter if adopted to prepare accounting statement may result in information "over-dose" and users may be confused on the use of such information. In his original work Sorter (1969) failed to provide accounting norms about the approach neither did it specify the form and content of events based financial statements. We can say that this approach favoured a multi-dimensional measuring ways and measuring nature where the choice of measuring way and nature becomes difficult. An adoption of event approach will lead to high cost of producing financial statement, it is left to be seen whether the benefit derivable from such approach will justify the high cost that may be involved.

With so many events that can be predicted and so many decisions models of users the failure of the predictive approach is its inability to specify the decision model of users or the event to be predicted.

The committee of American Accounting Association that issued the Statement of Accounting Theory and Theory Acceptance (SATTA) discovered, during their work, different accounting theories which were propounded depending on the perception of both the users of accounting and the environment in which the user and preparer of accounting data are supposed to behave or operate (Hameed and Ibrahim (2005). These divergences led to the conclusion that no single governing theory of financial accounting is rich enough to encompass the full range of user-environment specification effectively. The committee sought to explain the divergence in theories as evolutionary stages of science in accounting and saw the various theories as paradigm. Making accounting a multi-paradigm subject, each paradigm specifying its domain of accounting and approaches to accounting theory formulation – Belloni (1981).

The term paradigm was made popular by Kuhn (1970) and aptly defined by Ritzer (1975) as the fundamental image of a subject matter within a science which defines what to study, what question to ask, how to ask the question and how to interpret the answers given. The paradigm nature given to accounting by SATTA is an attempt to make accounting a science. It is contestable to say that accounting has reached a science stage because accounting is a multi-paradigm (Belkoni (1981) identified seven paradigms in which accounting can be divided while Chua (1986) identified four) where no particular paradigm is dominant and therefore generally accepted. And as Hammed and Rahman (2005) concluded accounting is still at the pre-science stage.

The true income approach of Kieso and Weygandt (1983) cannot be said to be an approach. The AAA through it SATTA concluded that it is not possible to have a comprehensive accounting method suitable for every accounting problem, but this approach believes it is possible only it has not been found, hence the search should continue. The Decision Model Approach is equivalent to the users need Approach discussed under Belkoui's even approach; while the individual and aggregate users approach is similar to his (Belkoui, 1981) behavioural approach. The information Economic Approach is in line with that of SATTA`s which seems to agree with the information theory basis of accounting Theory (Glautier and Underdown, 1970).

Chua (1986) based her work on the sociological work of Burel and Morgan (1979) which portends China as a Sociological Accountant. This belief is further enhanced by her suggestion of interpretive and critical approaches to accounting theory construction, interpretive and critical are social science research methodologies (Neuman, 2003). Interpretive Approach may be equated with descriptive approach, as interpretatives observe people in their natural domain to gain an understanding of them and interpret their meaningful social actions. Critical approaches equals prescriptive (normative) approach, the critical, unearth underlying real situations of the material world in order to help people change their conditions and better their lots (Neuman, 2003).

Velayutham and Rahman (1992) did not seem to introduce any new approaches into the accounting theory formulation literature, what they did was a classification of all approaches in the literature under various headings; purpose (descriptive or prescriptive); approach (deductive, indicatives etc) underlying assumptions (economic, sociological, etc) and levels these levels of development was based on the original work of Smith (1968).

It is necessary to point out at this juncture, that this paper does not claim to be exhaustive of all appellations given to approaches to accounting theory construction.

Conclusion and Recommendation

A discussion of the various approaches to formulation of accounting theory has been offered in the preceeding pages from where we can conclude as follows:

(i) Same approaches are tending to be given the difference appellations by different authors. For instance the individual users and aggregates users approaches by Kieso and Wegyandt (1983) meant he same thing with the behavioural approach of Belkoui (1981).

(ii) The formulation of accounting theory and the development of accounting techniques and procedures have not be found to follow any particular approach rather what we have in use is a combination of approaches. This combination of approaches is referred to as eclectic approach (Belloni, 1981).

(iii) The divergence in approaches has its root in the difference between the perception of what accounting theory should be by accounting practitioners and accounting teachers and researchers noticeable in the United States where most of the literature in accounting theory formulation emanates.

(iv) Approaches and their respective paradigm will continue to be modified while some will likely be replaced in future by other approaches and paradigm (that is the end of approaches to accounting theory formulation may not be insight.

Directly following from this it is hereby recommended that efforts should be geared towards finding a common ground for agreement within the accounting community (professionals, teachers and researchers and users) on the users and environments of accounting and therefore a common approach to accounting theory formulation.

References

Abdel Khalik, A. R. and Ajyinka, B. B. (974), Empirical Research in Accounting: A Methodological View Point., Sarasota: AAA.

American Accounting Association (1977), Statement of Accounting Theory and Theory Acceptance.

Bearer, W. H. Kennelly, J. W and Voss W. M (1968), "The Predictive Ability as a Criterion for Evaluation of Accounting Data" Accounting Review, Sarasota: AAA

Belkauoi; A. (1981), Accounting Theory, New York: Harcourt Brace Javonvich.

________(1989) Behavioural Accounting, Westpert: Greenwood Press.

Bradish, R. D. (1965) "Corporate Reporting and the Financial Analyst" The Accounting Review (Oct) Sarasota:AAA.

Bringerg, J. G and Nath, B. (1975), "Implications of Behavioural Science for Managerial Accounting" Accounting Review (Jan) Sarasolu AAA.

Canning, J. B. (1923) Tax Economics of Accounting, New York: The Ronald Press.

Chua, W. F. (1986) "Radical Development in Accounting Thoughts" Accounting Review (021) Sarasota AAA.

Committee on Concepts and Standards for External Financial Reporting (1977): Statement of Accounting Theory and Theory Acceptance: Sarasota:AAA.

Devine, C. T. (1960), "Research Methodology and Accounting Theory Formation". The Accounting Review (July) Sarosota: AAA.

Enthoven, A. J. H. (1973), Accountancy and Economic Development Policy, New York: American Elseir.

Gambling, T. (1974), Societal Accounting, London: George Allen and Unwin.

Glautier, M. W and Underdown B. (1970) Accounting Theory and Practice, Great Britain: Pitman Publishing Ltd.

Gonedes, N. J. (1972) "Efficient Capital Markets and External Accounting" The Accounting Review (Jan) Sarasota:AAA

Hameed; H. J. S. and Ibrahim, M. (2005), Financial Reporting: Assignment Essay<http:/www.accountant.org.cn/doc./acc2005 12/acc 2005,1202>

Hatfield; H. R. (1927): I, New York: D. Appleton & Co.

Hendriksen, E. S. (1977); Accounting Theory, Homewood: R. D. Inwin 3rd Edition.

Johnson, O. (1970) "Towards An Event Theory of Accounting`, (Oct) Sarasota; AAA.

Kelinger, F. N, (1964), Foundations of Behavioural Research, New York: Holt, Rinhart & Winston.

Kieso, D. E; and Weygandt, J. J. (1983), Intermediate Accounting, New York: Wiley & Son Inc. 4th Ed.

Kohler, E. L. (1936) "Theories and Practice" The Accounting Review (Sept) Sarota: AAA.

Kuhn, T. S. (1970), "The Structure of Scientific Revolution" International Encyclopedia of Unified Science, Chicago: University of Chicago Press. 2nd Enlarged Ed.

Ladd, D. R. (1963), Contemporary Corporate Accounting and Public, Honewood: Richard D. Irwin.

Machlup, F. (1955), "The Problem of Verification in Economics". The Southern Economic Journal.

MacNeal, k. (1939) Truth in Accounting, Philadelphia: University Pennyslvania Press.

McDonald, D. L. (1972), Comparative Accounting Theory, Reading: Addison-Wesley.

Mobley, S. C, (1970) "The challenges of socioeconomic Accounting" Accounting Review, Sarosota: AAA.

Mueller, G. G. (1967) "Accounting within a Macroeconomic Framework", International Accounting, New York: Macmillan.

Neuman, W.L. (2003), Social Research Methods: Qualitative and Quantitative Approaches, International Student Edition, USA: Pearson Education Inc.

Patilo, J. W. (1965), The Foundation of Financial Accounting, Balton Ruge: Louiscana State University Press.

Paton, W. A. (1922); Accounting Theory, New York: The Ronald Press.

Revsine L. (1973), Replacement Cost Accounting, Englewood Cliffs, N. S.

Prentice Hall.

Ritzer, G. (1975) "Sociology: A Multiparadigm Science", The American Sociologist.

Scott, D. R. (1941). "The Basis for Accounting Principles". Accounting Review (Dec) Sarosota:AAA.

Sorter, G. H. 91941), "An Event Approach to Basic Accounting Theory", Accounting Review, Sarosota:AAA.

Staubus, G. I. (1961) A Theory of Accounting to Investors, Berkeley, California: University of California Press.

Sterling, R. R. (1970) "On Theory Construction and Verification" The Accounting Review, Sarosota: AAA.

Sweeney, H. W. (1936), Truth in Accounting, Philadelphia: University of Pennsylvania Press.

Velayutham and Rahman (1992) cited in Hameed, H.J.S and Ibrahim M (2005), Financial Reporting Theory Assignment.

Whiltington A. (1986) cited in Hameed, H. J. S and Ibrahim M.

(2005) Financial Reporting Theory Assignment <http://www.accountant.org.cn/doc>.

Zetf, A. S. (1978) "The Rise of Economic Consequences", Journal of Accountancy New York. AICPA

Chapter 11

Classification of Accounting Theory by Stance

Junaidu Muhammad Kurawa

1. Introduction

The origin of record keeping is traced to the Babylonian merchants (who kept records on clay tablets) since around 3500 B.C. However, the history of accounting stretches back to when the first organized society existed although the development of accounting theory (accounting thoughts, principles, and standards) is mainly a child of the 20th Century. Several scholars believe that the debate about accounting principles did not start seriously before the 20th century. Up to the late 19th century accounting practice was primarily concerned with the development of bookkeeping techniques stretching into the beginning of the 20th century. They based their arguments on the evidence that, early bookkeeping books seem to have been concerned with the methods of making bookkeeping entries only. Scholars argued further that, the early books did not mention even such basic issues as the use and calculation of depreciation or income recognition. On these premises, they contend that accounting theory development started as a result of the contribution of accounting academics and the participation of the accounting profession in trying to establish acceptable accounting procedures, principles and standards to guide accounting practice. These contributions were more noticeable in the 20th century.

It has been documented by several scholars including: Littleton (1953), Ijiri (1975), Hendriksen (1982), Most (1982), and Hendriksen and Van Breda (2001); that accounting theory is about accounting ideas or rules which may be described as accounting thoughts, principles or standards that set the foundation for the practice of accounting. It follows, therefore, that one of the hallmarks of a profession is the need for a body of knowledge or theory as a rationale for the existence of the profession.

This has been partly responsible for the agitations of the development of accounting theory, principles, rules and standards to guide accounting practice right from the early part of the 19th Century to the present day.

Mathews and Parera (1996), argued that, for accountants to aspire to be professionals in search of social acceptance of their profession as equal to that of Medicine, Law and Engineering, "the search for a theory was necessary". If there is a need for a theory, then there should be the purpose and/or objective for which the theory should serve. This is where accounting scholars are divided amongst different paradigmatic views.

Scholars are divided amongst three fundamental groups; namely, the descriptive accounting theorists; the prescriptive accounting theorists and positive accounting theorists. Even though, they seek to establish and achieve the same goal, their approaches are fundamentally different.

The descriptive scholars were more concerned with what accountants do (their action), they were preoccupied with the interpretation of the accountants actions over time. These actions later metamorphosed into an accounting norm. These norms (actions) were rationalized and included under generalized accounting principles. The prescriptive scholars are more concerned with what accounting theory should be. What accounting ought to be or what accountants ought to do. They are objective and logical in their attempt to forecast the future. The positivist scholars on the other hand view the other groups as 'unscientific'. They believe that, accounting theory should be used to describe a value-free, unbiased and neutral reality. The purpose here is for the theory to explain and predict accounting practice as it is. They strongly emphasize the ability of accounting theory to provide a basis for the prediction and explanation of accounting behavior and events. This position is the more recent development within the search and the establishment of accounting theory.

In the light of the discussion above, this paper examines the classification of accounting theory according to the descriptive, prescriptive and positive approaches. The objective is to determine whether this classification and development have any relationship with the development of accounting rules and standards in Nigeria. The paper adopts content analysis of documentary secondary data as its methodology. The paper is divided into five sections including the introduction. The next section reviews the search for accounting theories and the major issues surrounding their emergence. Section three addresses the methodology of the study. Section four addresses results and discussions. And the last section concludes the paper and offered some recommendations.

2. Conceptual Framework and Literature Review

2.1 Definition of Accounting Theory

A popular working definition of accounting theory was offered by Hendriksen and Van Breda (2001); In their view, accounting theory represents a coherent set of hypothetical, conceptual, and pragmatic principles forming a general frame of reference for inquiring into the nature of accounting. This definition is all encompassing, since both the prescriptive and the predictive theories can be accommodated. It is not surprising that, the positivist scholars challenged the normative scholars as a result of the argued shortcoming of some of the normative theories. A fundamental flaw of which is that, normative theories do not stand the test of time, in other words most normative theories out lived their usefulness and are therefore subject to review from time to time.

2.2 The development of Accounting Theory

Although accounting dates back to the Babylonian times and much earlier according to Most (1982), accountancy as a discipline and profession really took off in the late 19th Century. Whereas accounting was mainly an 'internal matter' where the proprietors were close to the business, the growth of limited liability companies and the consequent separation of owners from managers led to the requirement of stewardship accounting. Furthermore, industrial development, emergence and impact of railroad companies in the United States, introduction of companies and tax legislation plus audit requirements and the establishment of professional accountancy bodies led to the increase importance of accounting in modern society.

Matthews and Perera (1996) lists three main features of development of Anglo-American accounting in the twentieth century viz:

(i) The search for accounting principles.

(ii) The development of the institutional structure of accounting and

(iii) Consideration of accounting as a social phenomenon.

These stages are considered in detail in order to note the major contributors both at institutional and individual levels.

(a) The search for accounting principles

The search for 'principles' on which accounting is based began around the 1920's led by individual researchers like Patton (1922) and Hatfield (1924) amongst others. One of the first works on accounting theory was Patton's Accounting Theory: With Special Reference to the Corporate Enterprise in 1922, in which he identified eleven accounting postulates. Sanders, Hatfield and Moore (1938) produced more positive empirically tested principles using interviews of preparers and users of financial statements. Patton and Littleton (1940) produced a number of basic concepts or assumptions of accounting including business entity, continuity (the predecessor of going concern), matching and periodicity concepts. Other notable works in this period include Hatfield (1924) who explored accounting history in order to defend the double entry bookkeeping practice invented by Luca Pacioli; and MacNeal (1939) who was seen as a revolutionary, attacked the bases upon which accounting practice operates. He argues that the function of accounting is to report economic truth, but financial statements do not present truth. They are misleading to the investors and creditors. In particular, he believe that the historical cost principle and the conservatism convention prevent financial statements from presenting true financial position and the operating results of the firm. These early writers had an economics background which was easily discernable in their works. The American Accounting Association (1977) classifies Patton, Sweeney and MacNeal as advocates because they argued for the primacy of new theories or approaches to accounting practice, whereas Canning and Alexander are labelled as explicators (individuals who are explicit in analysis) who analysed and assessed what accountants did and seek to do, explained economic models to accountants and tried to adapt these models to suit practice.

In addition to the efforts of these individual academics there were the collective efforts of the various professional bodies. The most important attempt to research and document practice was that of the

American Accounting Association formed in 1916 consisting of US academics and professionals. The American Accounting Association published a series of statements in accounting theory beginning with the Tentative Statement of Accounting Principles in 1936 (AAA, 1936). This marked a new phase in the development of accounting theory as it was the first attempt at collective research by a committee of academics and professionals. This statement was revised in 1941, 1948, 1951 and 1952. In 1966, the AAA issued A Statement of Basic Accounting Theory ASOBAT (Shahul, 1998).

ASOBAT redefined accounting in the decision usefulness framework as the communication of economic information to permit informed decisions and judgment by users. In 1977, the AAA published the Statement on Accounting Theory and Theory Acceptance (SOATATA). In this statement the association gave up trying to arrive at a universally acceptable theory of accounting, and instead reviewed the various conflicting theories on accounting and suggested reasons for failing to arrive at a universal theory.

(b) The Development of Institutional Structures of Accounting

The industrial revolution, tax legislation and companies' legislation led to the birth of accounting as a profession in the late 19th Century in the United Kingdom (UK). For example the Society of Accountants was established in Edinburgh in 1853 which later became the Institute of Chartered Accountants of Scotland. In 1880, the Institute of Chartered Accountants in England and Wales was established in London. In the United State, American Association of Public Accountants was established in 1887 which later merged into the American Institute of Certified Public Accountants (Shahul, 1998). Despite the establishment of these bodies, the accounting bodies were not strong numerically or politically in the beginning of the 20th Century. From the 1920's however, accounting profession in America increased its influence due to the growing economic strength of the country, the entry of university students and a body of academics who conducted research in accounting added greater might.

The development of stock exchanges and increased corporate activity created the need for standardization and basic guiding principles on which accounting reports should be based. This search for objectives, principles and a conceptual framework was spearheaded by the professional bodies through developing standards which allowed a wide variety of alternative accounting practices. This situation was accentuated according to Most (1982: 99) by "the new financing techniques and procedures like conglomerate acquisitions, equipment leasing, convertible securities and leaseback agreements" which created problems that could not be solved from precedents and the then existing standards. This situation led to the search for a conceptual framework, objectives and postulates of accounting.

(c) Consideration of accounting as a social phenomenon

In recent years, it has been recognized that accounting itself has social (mostly undesirable) consequences i.e. accounting itself constructs social reality. Consequently, there has been calls for measures to redress especially the social (behavioural) problems, hence the consideration of accounting as a social phenomenon. These calls and agitations have been advanced by a new group of radical theorists who have challenged mainstream accounting thought using marxists perspective and critical thought approaches. These scholars include Tinker, Merino, and Neimark (1982), Cooper and Sherer (1984), Hopper and Powell (1985), Chua (1986), Hines (1988) and Lehman (1992). Although these radical theorists have not prevailed in changing the profession or management of companies, they received increasing academic support because of some of the inadequacies of the accounting principles in providing adequate protection against behavioral problems. To date behavioral problems have defied or eluded the impact of any accounting theory, rule or standard.

The positivists scholars like Watts and Zimmerman (1978, 1986), Christenson (1983), Belkaoui and Karpik (1989), Ness and Mirza (1991), Panchapakesan and McKinnon (1992) and Lemon and Cahan (1997) viewed accounting theory in the context of its ability to explain and predict observed accounting practices. This has contrasted with the normative view that focuses on prescribing 'optimal' accounting practices and or describing accounting norms. This (positivist) position is associated with the contractual view of the firm as developed by Coase (1937), and Jensen and Meckling (1986). In their views the firm is seen as a chain for a set of contracting relationships among parties, and accounting is seen as a language to facilitate the writing of such contracts. They argued that accounting practices evolve to mitigate contracting costs by addressing potential conflicts of interests between types of contracting parties. For example, positive accounting postulates that conservatism in accounting has evolve mainly in response to compensation contracts between shareholders and managers. In the absence of conservatism, a firm's manager can receive compensation for what is later recognized as losses to the firm, and recovering this prepaid compensation will be difficult (Wikipedia, 2006).

From these arguments, it is apparent that accounting theory has evolved through the efforts of individuals and institutions. While the individuals (scholars and practitioners) are divided amongst different ideologies resulting from background and environmental circumstances, the institutions were simply trying to justify the existence and continuity of the accounting profession from the 19th century to date. As it is the case with any profession accounting inclusive, the dynamic nature of organizations has continued to pose and create new accounting problems that require new solutions. These solutions could only be evolved through a dynamic system of accounting principles, standards, rules and theories. Hence the position of scholars like Ijiri (1975) who in trying to justify historical cost accounting as the most appropriate method of income measurement argued that accounting theory could best be built from observing the practice of accounting. In other words accounting theory should be used to justify the long-standing practice. This scholar is simply emphasizing the dynamic nature of accounting practice and encouraging that accounting theories should also be flexible enough to survive with existing practice. The development of accounting standards and their revision from time to time is a testimony to his line reasoning.

3. Methodology

The present paper adopt documentary descriptive research method with particular emphasis on the corporate accounting laws and standards in Nigeria. For the classification of these theories, the following modified assumptions are adopted from the work of Jensen (http://www.trinity.edu/rjensen/theory.htm):

1. *Descriptive Accounting Theories*

Assumes that optimal accounting standards and reporting rules can be derived by deduction much in the way that Pythagoras derived the rule for measuring the hypotenuse of a triangle based upon the square root of the summed squares of the other two sides. Descriptive theorists tend to advocate their opinions on accounting based upon subjective opinion, deductive logic, and inductive methods.

Generally conclude that some accounting rule is better or worse than its alternatives.

2. *Prescriptive Accounting Theories*

Assumes accounting standards are somewhat like the evolution of a species in nature (survival of the fittest). Theories rely heavily upon controlled experimentation and statistical testing.

3. *Positive Accounting Theories*

Positive theorists tend to explain why some accounting practices are more popular than others. They tend to support their conclusions with inductive theory and empirical evidence.

Positivists avoid advocacy of one accounting rule as being better or worse than its alternatives.

Three specific documents were used, [(CAMA 90, SASs and World Bank Report (ROSC, 2005)] as secondary sources of data. Therefore, the paper relies more on secondary data. The data analysis method used is qualitative in nature.

4. Results and Discussion

Recently, in many developing countries like Nigeria, financial reporting practices of corporate entities have come under severe criticism arising from the financial crisis of the 1990s. These criticisms have attracted the attention of both international investors and international financial regulators like the World Bank and The International Monetary Fund (IMF), especially after the financial crisis of the 90's (relevant to Nigeria). It was not surprising therefore, that the World Bank and the IMF in their effort to ensure adequate and standardized financial reporting practices, and to encourage foreign direct investments (FDIs) into Nigeria, called for the preparation of a

"Report on the Observance of Standards and Codes" (ROSC) of accounting practice in 2005. This was intended to assess the degree to which an economy observes internally recognized accounting standards, principles and codes of accounting practice. The review was specifically aimed at (a) assessing the strengths and weaknesses of the existing institutional framework that underpins financial accounting and auditing practices and (b) examines the degree of compliance with national accounting and auditing standards among others. We found a part of this report relevant for discussion in this paper in relation to the major accounting rules and standards in Nigeria.

4.1 The Companies and Allied Matters Act (CAMA,1990)

This is the main legal framework for corporate accounting and auditing practice in Nigeria. It contains provisions that include requirements for disclosures, and preparation, presentation and publication of financial statements. This law is classified as a descriptive theory within the context of this paper, because of its general characteristics and the nature of its evolvement, content and intent. We have already indicated that descriptive theories (normative deductive) evolve mainly through the intent to justify existing practice. The following reasons are submitted to buttress our claim:

- CAMA represents an improvement and/ or adaptation of the UK Companies Act (1948), which was the earlier law upon which reporting practices were based. World Bank Report, (ROSC, 2005). This is indicative of the fact that, the Act is a reflection of the long standing practice of accounting in the UK.
- CAMA is descriptive in content and its intent is to regularize acceptable practices existing at a particular time period. This is why the provision requiring a profit and loss account, statement of sources and application of funds is now stale because of the changing need of the accounting environment. What we have in practice today is the provision for an income statement and cash flow statement. It also does not contain provision of changes in equity position. In short the staleness of some of the provisions within the document is a clear evidence of its non dynamic nature and hence our classification of these rules as descriptive accounting theory.

4.2 Statement of Accounting Standards (SASs)

Accounting standards in Nigeria have resulted from a complex interaction among numerous parties including agencies of the Federal Government (notably, The Securities and Exchange Commission, Central Bank of Nigeria and the Nigerian Deposit Insurance Corporation), public accountants (ICAN and ANAN) and public tax consultants (CITN) and host of other bodies. These bodies and institutions constitute the council membership of the Nigerian Accounting Standard Board (NASB). At present the board had issued 21 standards and 4 exposure drafts. All the accounting standards issued are recognized and categorized as descriptive theories because of the following reasons:

According to Dandago (2006), "the responsibility and authority of issuing and developing Accounting Standards in Nigeria is bestowed in the hands of Nigerian Accounting Standard Board (NASB)" and in trying to address their significance, he stated that, "standards are set after due consideration is given to *Nigerian laws, customs, business culture* and level of economic development (emphasis added). This position is in support of Horngren (1973), who argued that, "the setting of accounting standards is as much a product of political action as of flawless logic or empirical findings". In other words Nigerian accounting standards are neither a logical deductions nor empirical findings. They are simply an answer to political pressures in line with customs and culture, thus they are descriptive theories.

There are many areas of accounting issues covered by International Accounting Standards (IASs) and the International Financial Reporting Standards (IFRSs) that are not yet addressed by Statement of Accounting Standards (SASs) in Nigeria. The Nigerian SASs seems incomplete as an authoritative guide to the preparation of financial statements. About 20 active IASs have not been reflected in the SASs. (World Bank Report, [ROSC, 2005]). We have argued that descriptive theories fail the test of time and in some instances become inadequate. These theories must be reviewed, withdrawn or become stale with the changing needs of existing accounting practice and the needs of accounting information users.

Conclusion and Recommendations

In the discussions above, some important attributes of accounting theories were analyzed in an effort to identify the nature and type of accounting theories we have locally. We have been able establish that, accounting theories have an important role in determining the content of financial statements. These accounting theories could either be descriptive, prescriptive or positive. The two major theories considered in our analysis have descriptive features due to their origin (Nigerian laws, customs, and business culture) intent (to regularize long standing practice) and content (descriptive provision devoid of dynamism). We have also established that CAMA represents an adaptation of the UK Companies Act (1948). It has failed to reflect the changing need of the Nigerian business environment. And as a guiding rule it has not kept phase with changing needs on accounting information of users of financial reports. The document does not contain provision of changes in equity position or the provision of an income statement and cash flow statement. The accounting standards on the other hand have not covered about 20 active IASs. Their contents are descriptive and their intent is to regularize existing practice. We established that they are neither logical deductions nor a product of empirical findings. They fail the test of time and must be reviewed from time to time to keep abreast with the changing needs of the accounting environment.

On the basis of these conclusions, the following recommendations are proffered:

- It is imperative to consider the changing needs of information users from time to time in developing accounting standards and rules. In other words NASB should enhance the standard setting framework to accommodate some dynamism so as to elongate the life span and utility of our local standards.
- The number of our issued accounting standards should be increased to cover all the other aspects covered by the IASs and the standards should be reviewed to reflect current practice and information needs of users
- Given the present level of contributions in the prescriptive and positive accounting theories domain, it would be desirable to consider future development of accounting standards using the prescriptive framework to enable them stand the test of time.

- CAMA should be reviewed to accommodate all the observed lapses and changes that had taken place since its creation. In fact a provision should be made within to mandate its periodic review in line with global changes in accounting practice.
- The present state of stale and less effective laws /standards must be reviewed in line with the IAS, or the complete adoption of all the relevant IAS should be encouraged.

References

American Accounting Association (1977), Committee on Concepts and Standards for External Financial Reports, Statement on Accounting Theory and Theory Acceptance, American Accounting Association.

Beaver, W.H. (1989), Financial Reporting: An Accounting Revolution, second edition (EagleWood Cliff, N.J: Prentice-Hall Inc.)

Chambers, R. J., (1993), "Positive Accounting Theory and the PA Cult", *Abacus*, Vol. 29, No. 1, pp. 1-29.

Christenson, C. (1983), "The Methodology of Positive Accounting" The Accounting Review (January), pp1-22.

Chua, W.F. (1986), "Radical Developments in Accounting Theory", The Accounting Review, Vol.LXI, No. 4 October 1986.

Coase, R. (1937), "The Nature of the Firm," Economica 4, pp386-405.

Cooper, D.J. and Sherer, M.J. (1984), "The Value of Corporate Accounting Reports: Arguments for a Political Economy of Accounting," Accounting, Organizations and Society, Vol. 9, No. ¾, pp 207-232.

Dandago, K.I. (2006), Advanced Accounting Theory, Environmental Factors that Influence Accounting: ACC 9301 Lecture Notes.

Glautier, M.W.E. and Underdown, B; (1986) Accounting Theory and Practice, London: Pitman Publishing.

Gray.R., Kouhy.R. and Lavers.S., (1995), "Corporate Social and Environmental Reporting: A Review of the Literature and a Longitudinal Study of UK Disclosure", *Accounting, Auditing and Accountability*, Vol. 8, No 2, pp.47-77.

Hatfield, H.R. (1924), "An historical defense of bookkeeping", *The Journal of Accountancy*, Vol. 37 No.4, pp.241-53.

Hendriksen, E.S. (1982), Accounting Theory, fourth edition (Homewood, III,: Richard D Irwin)

Hendriksen, E.S. and Van Breda, M.F. (2001), Accounting Theory, New York: MacGraw Hill, 2nd edition.

Hines, R (1988), "Financial Accounting: In Communicating Reality, We Construct Reality" Accounting, Organizations and Society, No. 3

Hopper, T. and Powell, A. (1985), "Making sense of research into the organizational and social aspects of management accounting: A review of its underlying assumptions", Journal of Management Studies, Vol. 22, No. 5, September 1985.

Ijiri, Y (1975), Theory of Accounting Measurement, SAR N10 (Sarasota: American Accounting Association)

Jensen, M., and W. Meckling (1986), "Theory of the Firm: Managerial Behavior, Agency Costs and Ownership Structure," Journal of Financial Economics, 3(4), pp305-360.

Lehman, C.R. (1992), Accounting's Changing Roles in Social Conflict, New York: Markus Weiner Publishing, Inc. 1992.

Lemon, A.J., and Cahan, S.F., (1997), "Environmental Legislation and Environmental Disclosures: Some Evidence From New Zealand", *Asian Review of Accounting*, Vol. 5, No. 1, pp. 78-105.

Littleton, A. C., (1953). Structure of Accounting Theory. Monograph No. 5. Sarasota, Florida. American Accounting Association

MacNeal, K. (1970, [1939]), Truth in Accounting, Lawrence, Kansas: Scholars Book Co.

Matthews, M. R. and Parera, M. H. B. (1996), Accounting Theory and Development, London: Chapman and Hall.

Most, K. S. (1982), Accounting Theory, second edition (Columbus: Grid Publishing)

Ness, K.E., & Mirza, A.M., (1991), "Corporate Social Disclosure: A Note on a Test of Agency Theory", *British Accounting Review*, Vol. 23, No. 3, pp. 211-217.

Panchapakesan, S., & McKinnon, J., (1992), "Proxies for Political Visibility: A Preliminary Examination of the Relation Among Some Potential Proxies", *Accounting Research Journal*, Spring, pp. 71-80.

Paton, W.A. and Littleton, A.C. (1940), "An Introduction to Corporate Accounting Standards," Sarasota, Fla: American Accounting Association.

Shahul, J. (1998), "Critical Financial Analysis and Accounting for Stakeholders", Critical Perspective on Accounting, Vol. 9, No. 2, pp 235-249

Sterling, R.R., (1970), "Theory Construction and Verification", Accounting Review, July 1970.

Sweeney, H. W. (1936), *Stabilized Accounting*. New York: Harper & Brothers.

Taffler, R., "Z Scores: An Approach to Recession," Accountancy, July 1991

Tinker, A.M., Merino, B.D., and Neimark, M.D., (1982), "The Normative Origins of Positive Theories: Ideology and Accounting Thought", *Accounting, Organisations and Society*, Vol. 7, pp. 167-200.

Watts. R.L. & Zimmerman. J.L., (1979), "The Demand for and Supply of Accounting Theories: The Market for Excuses", *The Accounting Review*, Vol. 54, No 2, pp. 273-305.

Watts. R.L. & Zimmerman. J.L., (1986), *Positive Accounting Theory*, Prentice-Hall, London.

Watts. R.L. & Zimmerman. J.L., (1990), "Positive Accounting Theory: A Ten Year Perspective", *TheAccounting Review*, Vol. 65, No 1, pp. 131-156.

Whittington, G., (1987), "Positive Accounting: A Review Article", *Accounting and Business Research*, Vol. 18, Autumn, pp. 327-336.

Wikipedia, (2006), "http://en.wikipedia.org/wiki/positive-accounting"

World Bank Report, (ROSC, 2005), http://www.worldbank.org/ifa/rosc-aa.html

Chapter 12

Accounting Theory by Reasoning

Ibrahim Magaji Barde

1. Introduction

Prior to the 20th century, accounting practice was primarily concerned with the development of bookkeeping techniques. The major concern then was the basic task of finding methods of making bookkeeping entries and attention was not given even to basic issues like calculation of depreciation, something that was at that time, unheard of. Being in its early stage, the main concern of accounting was the development of basic rudiments necessary to capture records of money received and money paid out. The merchants of Venice formed the Charge and Discharge System which effectively satisfied that requirement. This system was later refined by an Italian monk and the father of present day accounting, Luca Pacioli, into the double entry rule of bookkeeping.

However, the industrial revolution in the early 20th century resulted in the formation of large joint stock companies with multitudes of owners. The numerous owners necessitated the separation of ownership and control and managers had to be employed to run the companies on behalf of the owners. Stewardship accounting was then used, where managers report to the owners of the business through the preparation and the presentation of financial statements.

With more development in the business world, the financial statements became desirable to several other parties such as potential investors, creditors, tax authorities, financial institutions, financial analysts and many more. The reports therefore needed to satisfy the individual requirements of the users, and in doing that, the method, the manner, the process, the form and sometimes even the reporting preferences varied from one company to another. In most cases, the reports instead of showing what is expected, it rather ended up showing what the Chairmen of the companies wanted to be shown.

This was observed by Brigham (1996) who criticized the reports for lacking uniformity and authenticity.

To overcome these problems, efforts were made which led to the development of a framework of statutory and regulatory pronouncements within which accounting reporting must operate. This was done to ensure authenticity, orderliness, consistency and uniformity not only in financial reporting practices but in the entire accounting profession. Thus, the early part of the 20th century saw the need for accounting theorists to develop/construct accounting principles. The primary concern of the principles has been recognition and measurement issues. Several theories had been adopted, but the concern of this paper shall be the development of accounting theory through the normative approach which comes in 2 forms – deductive and inductive reasoning.

This paper is aimed at studying accounting theory as reasoning (deductive and inductive) and particularly how accounting practice is shaped using principles or rules developed through deductive or inductive reasoning. The methodology used by this paper is purely secondary data on deductive and inductive methods of accounting theory.

2. Conceptual framework and literature review

2.1 Meaning of Accounting Theory

Accounting theory has been a very controversial issue as there have been many attempts to define it. Watts and Zimmerman (1986) posit that accounting theory seeks to explain and predict accounting practice. They describe their version of accounting theory as a positivist theory but even though they study situation and discover problems, they seldom suggest remedy to these problems. This position was observed and attacked by Sterling (1990). In the view of Littleton (1953), the business of accounting theory is to examine beliefs and customs critically, to clarify and extend the best from experience, and to direct attention to the genesis and outcome of accounting work. This definition is more acceptable because it accommodates different strands of accounting research such as research in normative accounting and empirical accounting, as well as research in interpretive accounting.

Wolk et al (2001) see accounting theory as basic assumptions, definitions principles and concept (including how they are derived) that underlie accounting rule making by a legislative body and the reporting of accounting and financial information. If observed closely, one can see accounting theory as encompassing things like drafting of conceptual framework that provides guiding principles for making accounting rules, analyzing rules to see how they conform to conceptual framework, as well as understanding reason for a choice between principles, where choice exist. Since accounting theory deals largely with assumptions, definitions, concepts and principles, then there will be continues discussion and arguments on what these assumptions and definitions should be. The premise makes accounting theory to be a continuously dynamic issue and never a finished product.

From a synopsis of the above definition, it is obvious that accounting theory will always be faced with one problem or another, the most spectacular and crisis generating being the issue of revenue recognition and measurement. This point was affirmed by Hendrieksen and Van Breda (2001). When should one recognize revenue from transactions like hire purchase, conditional sales and credit sales with large deposits or, sales made through subsidiaries? Various approaches adopted often results in varying consequences, which creates conflicts between parties. Consequently, accounting theory has a continuous role to play particularly in providing premises for accounting rules. This supports the position earlier on adopted by Anthony and Reese (1983).

The relative importance of accounting theory led to its development using different perspectives. Such perspectives or approaches are classified as either accounting theory as a language, as a script or as reasoning. Accounting theory as a language posits that accounting is a language and therefore studies the effect of language (pragmatics), the meaning of language (semantics) and the logic or grammar of language (syntactics). Accounting theory as a script is concerned with the presentation of financial information and can be either descriptive (positive) or prescriptive (normative). Descriptive theories attempt to explain how and what financial information is presented while normative theories prescribe what data ought to be communicated and how they ought to be presented. Accounting theory as a reasoning basically studies accounting theory as either deductive or inductive. In deductive reasoning, arguments flow from generalization to specifics while in inductive reasoning, arguments flows from specifics to generalizations.

Accounting is a discipline that is guided by a body of rules and principles, which according to Wolk et al (2001) makes it highly analytical, and which provides bases for accounting's practical applications (Hendrieksen and Van Breda, 2001). But an important issue is the source of these rules or principles. Do they flow from generalizations to specifics (deductive) or from specifics to generalizations (inductive)? These rules are made up of postulates and principles, and they serve as the bases for practical applications.

Deductive theories

Deductive accounting theories seek to prescribe some basis of accounting measurement, particular accounting procedures and the contents of financial reports by starting with some goal assumptions and deduce some accounting procedures therefrom. Two important elements in deductive theories are (i) goal assumption and (ii) deduction. This position is maintained by Ijiri (1975) and Watts and Zimmerman (1986). Chambers (1966) supports this view and even holds that a deductive theorist may set his own goals that are not inherent to current accounting practice.

In deductive reasoning, emphasis is not placed on the status-quo, (i.e. the current accounting practice), but rather objectives or goals are set which predetermine how things should be. Hendrieksen and Van Breda (2001) opine that objectives play an important role in deductive reasoning. This objective-based nature of deductive reasoning makes it to require different structures, which often results in different principles. For instance, the objectives of tax accounting are different than those of financial accounting. This explains differences in the rules used to determine taxable income and the rules used to determine financial income. The reason simply is that the objectives of tax accounting and financial accounting are basically different.

In diagrammatic form, deductive reasoning can be shown as follows:

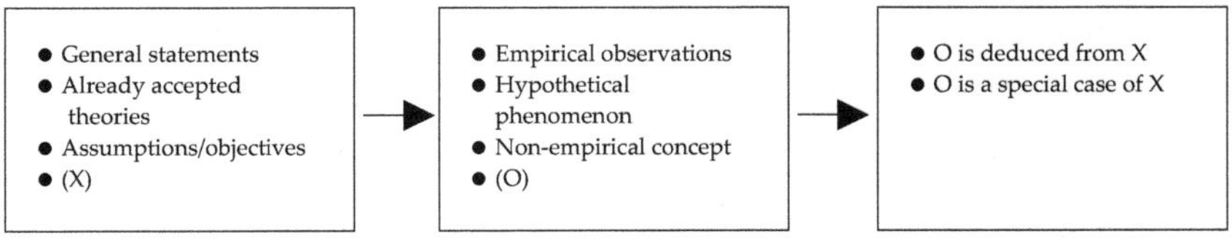

In deductive model, X is a set of theories or assumptions that have already been accepted from which O can be deduced. Consequently, O is a special case of X. For instance, historical cost is an existing accounting principle or assumption (X) and from its study or observation overtime, deductivists deduced a hypothetical phenomenon of current cost accounting (O), as an alternative to the existing historical cost accounting and suggest new bases of accounting measurement by advocating current cost or values, instead of historical cost. Consequently, current cost accounting (O) is deduced from (X) the existing accepted accounting assumptions but the goal is not limited to the current accounting practice.

Deductivists are basically reformers because they suggest new bases of accounting measurements (e.g. current cost accounting). Deductive accounting theory doesn't limit itself to the study of existing accounting practice for the fear of being pro-establishment or promoting the maintenance of the status qou. Deductivists such as Paton (1922), Cunning (1929), Sweeney (1936), MacNeal (1939) and Chambers (1966) developed accounting models using deductive reasoning, and made generalized conclusions meant for general application. Since deductive reasoning is concerned with how things should be, their models (like current cost accounting) did not consider the decision requirements of specific classes of users. Instead, they assume that their model would be equally useful for all type of users. The deductive camp comprised of many writers but this paper only will review the work of MacNeal (1939).

MacNeal, Kenneth (1939)

Kenneth MacNeal, (1939) is a leading deductivist whose work depicted him as a revolutionary, or at best, a reformist. MacNeal seriously attacked the current accounting practice because, as he opined, it doesn't report economic truth, which is the main purpose of accounting. MacNeal particularly attacked the historical cost principle and the conservatism convention and argued that they prevent financial statements from reporting the truth and therefore end up misleading creditors and investors alike.

MacNeal's theory is shown below:

Environmental Postulate	• Numerous small uninformed security holders • Existence of free and competitive markets • Continuity of entity operations.
Objectives	The objective of accounting is to provide information about the entity that is useful to the stockholders and creditors in making investment and credit decisions.
Information needs	Managers, creditors and stockholders are interested in knowing the present net worth of the business and having information regarding all types of profits and loses made by the business entity.
Accounting Measurement and recognition.	• Balance sheet should report present economic values of assets and liabilities. • The income statement should report both realized and unrealized current and capital profits and losses. • The realization principle is abandoned.

MacNeal's theory, as shown above, comprised of environmental postulates, objectives, information needs and accounting measurement and recognition.

Environmental Postulate

The environmental postulate of MacNeal assesses the environment in which a business operates. The environment is made up of numerous small-uninformed security/shareholders. These investors are ignorant of the state of affairs of the firm and must rely on the information supplied by the management. In addition, the business also operates in an environment of a free and competitive, market. This free market is regulated by the forces of demand and supply, which affects the price or value of assets. Now, since the entity's operation is continuous, MacNeal argued that the altered value of the business's assets become unknown to the shareholders and therefore the uninformed shareholders may not place appropriate claim on the business assets by their shares.

The basic argument of MacNeal here is that since ownership of corporate firms changes frequently and shares involve a claim against the assets, then equitable ownership changes with change in ownership. MacNeal asserted that equity and fairness to the changing shareholders can only be ensured if the values of assets are reported at their actual market price. This obviously goes against the historical cost concept but MacNeal felt that historical cost method does not report unrealized market prices and this prevents shareholders from assessing the true value of their shareholding and is thus, an obstacle to ensuring equity.

To overcome this, MacNeal further argued that fixed assets must be revalued at year-end to provide present economic values that are useful to investors and creditors in making investment and credit decisions. Therefore, the premise upon which he based his model openly rejects the historical cost concept and the conservatism convention, thus departing, albeit partially, from the conventional accounting system.

Objectives

According to MacNeal, the objective of accounting is to provide information about the business entity to assist investors and creditors in taking investment and financing decisions. Accounting can only serve this purpose if the information reported in the financial statement is relevant. To MacNeal, information can only be relevant if it reflects true market prices. However, conventional accounting reporting is based on historical cost concept, and the conservatism principle. The historical cost concept shows assets at their entry prices and the conservatism principle depletes earnings and the net worth of the firm. Thus, financial statement does not report the economic reality that will assist investors and creditors in taking good and informed investment and credit decisions. The MacNeal model of accounting theory asserts that the main objective of accounting is to provide current and relevant information for investors and creditors, and consequently discards the historical cost concept, the realization principle and conservatism convention, since these concepts hinders the achievement of the model's objective.

Information Needs

The information that financial statements should report should be the one needed by managers, creditors and stockholders which according to his deduction, should disclose the present networth of the entity. Creditors need this information to assess the probability of being repaid. Investors need this information to assess profitability of the firm. Financial statements can serve these information needs if they report present economic values (market prices or exit price) that are established through interplay of demand and supply in a market that is free and competitive. Replacements cost should be used if present economic values cannot be established through demand and supply, like in the case of work in progress and specialized buildings and equipments that lack broad and active market. MacNeal however, accepts that historical cost can be used in the case of non-marketable assets, like intangibles.

Accounting Measurement and Recognition

MacNeal's deductive accounting theory model as discussed above definitely has impacted on accounting measurement and recognition. It has brought about changes on what the income statement reports on profit or loss, and what the balance sheet measures in the context of assets and liabilities.

Profit and Loss: In MacNeal's model, the profit and loss should report all types of profit. The income statement should include both realized and unrealized current (operating) and capital profits and losses. He therefore suggests that an income statement should have 2 major sections. One section is to report current profit and loss, i.e. profit from business operations, and the other section to report capital profit which arises from changes in economic value of fixed assets, apart from depreciation, amortization or depletion. Both realized and unrealized value changes are to be included in capital profit and losses. Similarly, changes in the value of marketable securities should be included in the capital profit and losses, unless the entity is in the security trading business. Since the income statement has two sections, the current profit and losses section should show the earned surplus/loss while the capital profits section should show the capital surplus/loss. The summation of the profits reported in the 2 sections would be the total net profit from all sources. This way, all profits from whatever sources are recaptured.

Balance Sheet: Just as the model changed the measurement practice in income statement, it also deviates in the balance sheet reporting practice. According to the theory, the balance sheet should report the present economic value of assets and liabilities. The assets are to be shown at their economic value determined by free interaction of market forces or demand and supply. The liabilities are to be shown at amounts representing their legal claim on the assets of the entity. Money value liabilities (claims for definite sums of money, e.g. bonds) should be shown at their face values. Real value liabilities (obligations to deliver goods or services regardless of what the cost of performance may be) are to be shown at their present economic values at the balance sheet date.

MacNeal argued that financial statements drawn using this model have immense benefits to the users of accounting information. Firstly, since fixed assets are reported at their economic value or market price, then a prospective mortgager can decide on whether to lend money on a particular asset or not, since its market price is known. In addition, the safety of an existing loan (mortgaged on the asset) can easily be evaluated. Secondly, current asset and current liabilities can be effectively compared since they are all shown at their economic values and therefore current ratios and acid ratios calculated can be used with confidence. Thirdly, the balance sheet will not understate or overstate owner's equity, as assets are shown at their true market value. This avoids the case of watered stocks and secret reserves. Fourthly, the productivity of the management can be made clearer by separating showing capital profits separately as it doesn't resulted form management's performance. Fifthly, the efficiency of management can be correctly determined because the balance sheet reveals the amount of present capital employed that can be compared with current earnings. Lastly, readers of financial statements will be made aware of assets values caused by booms and depressions.

Criticisms of MacNeal's Theory

If MacNeal's deductive accounting theory is subjected to a critical examination, the following shortcomings would be observed:

(i) The purpose of the model proposed by MacNeal is to enable accounting reporting to show the true value of an entity by showing the economic value of its assets and liabilities. To do this, he suggested that assets should be shown at market prices determined by the forces of demand and supply. In some cases, however, replacement costs or even the dreaded historical cost can be used. The problem with this approach is that reporting the market prices of assets is prone to subjective judgment and opens a way for distorting financial statements to serve managers' self interest. Thus, the reliability of financial statements is hampered.

(ii) theory seems to concentrate most on the informational needs of investors and creditors, who seem to be the foremost beneficiaries when assets are shown at their economic value. The theory seems to be investor-creditor centered and neglects other users of accounting information, who also have stake in the entity.

(iii) The insistence that investors and creditors need economic value of an entity's assets and liabilities to make investment and credit decision is quite faulty as there are other yardsticks that are available for use by investors (e.g. earning power) to make investment decision. Similarly, since creditors are aware that the entity needs not to dispose its assets to pay them interest (where applicable) and the principal amount on maturity, then economic values may not be relevant to them. The probability of repayment can be effectively established using other yardsticks, like current and acid test ratios.

MacNeal's deductive model obviously gives rise to the existence of several types of cost or values in a single balance sheet at one time. The theory preferred economic values of assets, which according to him, reflects economic truth. But the market value of some assets, such as work in progress, can not be determined through the market forces of demand and supply and so MacNeal suggested replacement cost in place of the market prices. Still, replacement costs and market prices cannot be used in the case of some assets, like goodwill and other intangibles, and therefore to overcome this shortcoming MacNeal said historical cost can be used. The problem is being created here because the total figure for balance would be a mixture or concoction of at least three types of costs viz market prices, replacement costs and historical costs. Therefore, the final balance sheet figure or total wouldn't make meaningful sense.

MacNeal also suggested that depreciation should be charged on present economic value of assets rather than on historical cost. But since in most cases fixed assets appreciates rather than depreciates, then there would not be any depreciation charges for most assets as the market values of used assets tends to be higher than their historical costs. The cost of production will not comprise of the assets' cost used for production.

Finally, Himayun (2007) noted that the proposal will make valid comparison of financial statement data overtime difficult. If comparative information is not revised overtime or even if it is revised, the different methods that can be subjectively selected for value revision at balance sheet date will hamper valid comparism.

2.3 Inductive Theory

Inductive accounting theory involves drawing a generalized conclusion from specifics and therefore, generalized accounting principles are induced from the best current accounting practice. This means accountants observe practice and from the observed practice, accounting rules or principles are formulated. Hence, a theorist inductively derives goals from accounting practice and uses these goals to suggest improvement in current practice.

In inductive accounting theory, emphasis is paid on the status-quo (current accounting practice) to highlight where changes are most needed and where they are feasible. Ijiri (1975), a prominent inductivist, argued that changes suggested as a result of inductivism have a much better chance of being accepted and actually implemented than changes envisaged through a deductive method. He argued further that goals or policies developed through deductive methods, rather than an inductive study of an existing system, are seldom implemented because they do not rhyme with organizational requirements or conditions but are only consistent convictions or preferences of their proponent.

In diagrammatic form, inductive reasoning can be shown as follows:

• Observations • Hypothetical phenomenon • Non-empirical concept • (O)	• General statements • (x)	• O gives rise to X • X is induced from O • Many Xs may be induced • Implication of X goes beyond O. • (X)

The above shows that in induction, a general statement (X) is induced from some empirical observations, hypothetical phenomena or non-empirical concepts (O). Consequently, O (observations etc) gives rise to X (an improvement method or policy). This means the policy is induced from the observation though its implication may go beyond it. In this case, inductive theory contribute by coming up with X as an explanation of O.

Inductivists are basically conservatives because they examine extant accounting practice and try to rationalize or even justify their major elements. Prominent Inductivists include Hatfield (1927), Littleton (1953) and Ijiri (1975) and asserts their preference for inductive model because inductive reasoning derives goals implicit in the behaviour of an existing system, purposely not to maintain the status-qou or be pro-establishment, but to highlight where changes are most needed and therefore feasible. Changes are only acceptable to existing systems if they come as a result of such systems' inductive study.

The inductive school of thought comprise of several theorists, the most prominent being Littleton and Ijiri. This paper will discuss the work of Ijiri (1975).

IJIRI (1975)

Ijiri is a prominent inductivist who advocates and justifies the conventional historical cost accounting. His support for conventional accounting practice led him to develop three axioms which, he claims, conventional accounting rests upon. The three axioms are as follows:

Axiom of control: the set of all resources under the control of an entity at time **t** can be identified uniquely at that time or later.

Axiom of quantity: all resources under the control of an entity at time **t** can be uniquely partitioned into classes of resources at that time or later in such a way that for each class a nonnegative and additive quantity measure is defined. This measure has the property that two sets of resources in the same class are treated as being substitutes in the uses of resources if and only if their quantities are the same.

Axiom of exchange: every change in the set of resources under the control of the entity can be classified uniquely as it occurs either as terminator of an old simple exchange or an initiator of a new simple exchange with an estimated terminator.

Ijiri claims that the present accounting practice revolves around the axioms of control, quantities and exchange. Apart from the above, everything else in accounting is a mere computational procedure.

Ijiri expresses his theory in the following structure:

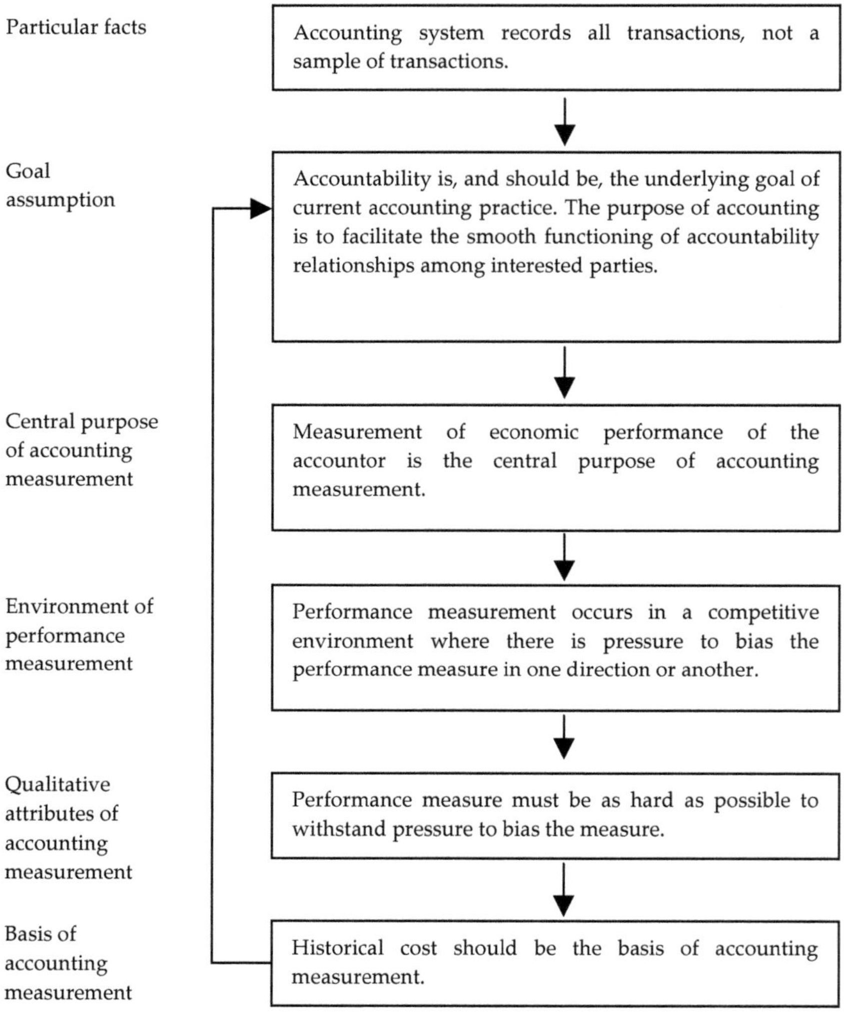

Ijiri's (1975) Inductive Theory

Particular facts

In the view of Ijiri's theory, accounting record covers all aspects of business transaction and therefore emphasized that accounting records every transaction. The rationale for this is that those in control of business must account for every thing to the owners and therefore asserts that accounting system must record every transaction, and not a sample of transactions.

Goal Assumption

Ijiri inductively derives the goal implicit in the current accounting practice, which according to him is accountability, though he uses this goal to suggest improvement in practice. He identified three parties that are involved in accountability relationship viz accountee, accountor and the accountant. The accountability relationship being a product of stewardship accounting; requires the accountor (manager) to report to the accountee (shareholders/owners) for his (accountor's) activities and its result. For this purpose, the accountor maintained a detailed record of his activities. An accountant joins this relationship as a third party, to help the accountor account for his activities and supplies information to the accountee. Consequently, Ijiri feels that accountability is, and should be the underlying goal of current accounting practice, and the purpose of accounting is to facilitate the smooth functioning of accountability relationship between the interested parties (accountee, accountor and the accountant).

Central Purpose of Accounting Measurement

In an accountability relationship, the accountor is responsible to the accountee for achieving the goals of the accountor. Consequently, the accountor relies on the accountant to supply information to the accountee on the accountor's progress towards achievement of the goals set by the accountee. The accountant uses accounting to evaluate the accountor in relation to the target set by the accountee. Therefore, the central purpose of accounting measurement shall be the measurement of economic performance of the accountor.

Environment Performance Measurement

Performance measure must be hard enough to withstand pressure to bias the measure in one direction or the other. To achieve this, Ijiri develops a concept called "hardness" of a measure. A "hard" measure is one constructed in such a way that people can not disagree with it easily, for example cash balance. A soft measure is one that can be easily pushed in one direction or another for instance, goodwill. To make measurement less flexible, Ijiri further added three more ingredients first, measurement should be based on verifiable facts. Second, the measurement process must be well specified and third, the number of justifiable rules should be restricted.

Bases of Accounting Measurement

Ijiri proposed that the bases of accounting measurement should be historical cost principle. His justifications are that firstly, proper functioning of accountability rests on proper records of past activities. This is satisfied by historical cost principle which requires the recording of all actual transactions. Secondly, historical cost principle is more objective than other bases of measurement such as net realizable value and replacement cost. Though such methods may be useful in some cases, they are highly subjective. In addition they (net realizable values and replacement costs) are based on actions (buying and selling at the balance sheet date) that the entity doesn't normally intend to undertake. He therefore reinforces the going concern convention. This stand also discards he conservatism convention that provided for the recording of inventory not at cost but at net realizable value if that is lower than the recorded cost.

Criticism of Ijiri's Inductive theory

Ijiri's inductive theory recognized the implicit objective of accounting and thus tries to maintain the status-quo though he proposed an improved version of the system. However, Ijiri's theory has some flaws and can be criticized on the following grounds.

The major problem of Ijiri's model is the inductive nature of the theory itself. Inductive reasoning entails a study of a particular system and formulating a generalized statement based on findings but since social, economic and accounting facts are not homogenous, then attempting to generate a general statement from an inductive study may result in a problem as the heterogeneous nature of business circumstances may make the generalized statement inapplicable.

The Ijiri's model has its first assumption stating that accounting system records all transactions and not a sample of transactions. It further argued that, managers maintain accounting records primarily for outside users. This is erroneous (as observed by Chandler, 1977) since in most cases, accounting records can be maintained even if outsiders may not be interested in them. For instance, the huge public expenditure incurred by government parastatals are fully recorded but the primary purpose of maintaining such records cannot be ascribed to usage by outsiders. Therefore, the assertion by Ijiri that accountants maintain accounting records primarily for outside users does not hold true.

Ijiri's theory is based on three axioms – control, quantity and exchange on which he claims conventional accounting is based. Of interest is the axiom of exchange, an action through which the entity forgoes control over some resources to gain control over some other resources. Exchanges include both market exchange (buying and selling) and production exchange (consumption of raw materials to produce finished goods). However this axiom fails to capture issues like donations received by an entity, since the entity gained control over the item received without foregoing control over any of its resources.

In addition, what sort of asset is gained when an entity expends on research and development? How does the axiom of quantity (the measure of quantity) apply to research and development? How do the axioms of Ijiri explain accounting treatments of intangibles such as goodwill, patents and copyrights?

As a supporter of historical cost concept and therefore an advocator of the conventional accounting system, the axioms of Ijiri allow the recording of actual transactions only, and assets values are net revised in consonance with changes in market prices of the assets. In addition to ruling out hypothetical transactions, Ijiri's theory also discards the conservatism convention, which requires the adjustment of inventories and marketable securities if their market prices are lower than their recorded costs.

This position in reality may hamper the effectiveness of financial reports. While recording the historical cost of assets may not have long-term negative results, since the hidden profit can be released terminally, there is no justification whatsoever for willingly overstating the prices of inventory and marketable securities. Apart from overstating profits, creditors (due to high current and acid test ratios) may be misled to take a decision, which if furnished with real prices of inventory and marketable securities may decide otherwise. Ijiri needs to prove that financial statements prepared on the bases of neglecting current costs as well as conservatism convention are not harmful to the users.

Summary, Conclusions and Recommendations

Accounting theory by reasoning can be either deductive or inductive. In the inductive method, goal assumptions are used to develop generalized statements meant for wide application. This is the approach being used to develop accounting policies which regulate accounting practice. More often than not, deductive reasoning doesn't lend support to current accounting practice but reforms them in a revolutionized way. In inductive reasoning, systems are studied internally and the result is used to suggest how to improve the current accounting practice. Unlike deductive reasoning, inductive reasoning is mostly pro-administration and maintains the status-quo.

From the preceding discussion, the paper concludes that reasoning plays an important role in the development of accounting theory. The various works of deductive and inductive theorists testified to this by using reasoning to develop policies or explain phenomenon which shapes the development of accounting and regulates its practice.

Since accounting theory is now dominant at shaping practice, the paper recommends that theorists need to place an equally high level importance on the issues of reliability and objectivity in developing accounting theory using either deductive or inductive reasoning. If financial statements are prepared without cognizance to changing price level, then the resulting report may be misleading and therefore not objective. But if on the other hand, current prices are used without restrictions, the reports may be biased and their reliability becomes questionable.

References

Anthony, R.N. and Reese, J.W. (1983): *Accounting: Text and Cases*. Irwin Publishers, USA.

Belkaoui, A. (1985), *Accounting Theory*.Harcout Brace, San Diego

Cunning, J.B. (1929): *The Economics of Accountancy.* The Ronald Press Company, New York.

Chambers, R.J. (1966): *Accounting, Evaluation and Economic Behaviour* Prentice Hall. Englewood Cliffs, New Jersey

Chandler Jr., A.D. (1977): *The Visible Hand-The Managerial Revolution in American Business.* Harvard University Press. Cambridge.

Dandago, K.I. (2001): Financial Accounting Simplified. Adamu Joji Publishers. Nigeria

Dandago, K.I. (2006): Advanced Accounting Theory, A lecture note for Ph.D. Accounting Class. Department of Accounting, Bayero University, Kano..

Hamid, K.T. (2006): Classification of Accounting Theory Levels. A Paper presented at Ph.D. Accounting Seminar series. Department of Accounting, Bayero University, Kano.

Hatfield, H.R. (1927): *Accounting.* D.A. Appleton and Company. New York.

Himayun, K. (2007): Normative Accounting Theories @ www.ssrn.com.

Hendrieksen, A.S. and Van Breda, M.(2001):*Accounting Theory* McGraw-Hill Book Company, Singapore,5th Edition

Ijiri, Y. (1975): *Theory of Accounting Measurement. Studies in Accounting Research.* American Accounting Association. Sarasota, Florida.

Kenneth, M.S. (1982): *Accounting Theory.* Grid Publishing Inc. Columbus

Littleton, A.C. (1953): Structure of Accounting Theory. Monograph No. 5. American Accounting Association. Sarasota, Florida

MacNeal, K. (1939): *Truth in Accounting.* Scholars Book Company, Texas.

Millichamp, A.H.(1990): *Foundation Accounting - An Instruction Manual for Accounting Students* DP Publications Ltd. Aldine Place, London.

Paton, W. A. (1922): *Accounting Theory.* The Ronald Press Company, New York.

Riahi-Belkaoui, A. (2000): *Accounting Theory,* Thomson Learning, London.

Roslender, R. (2004): Accounting for Intellectual Capital: rethinking its theoretical underpinnings. *Measuring Business Exellence*Vol.8, No 1, pp38-45

Sterling, R. (1990): Positive Accounting: An assessment. *Abacus.* Vol. 26 (No.2): 97-135.

Sweeney, H.W. (1936): *Stabilised Accounting.* Harper & Brothers. New York.

Upton, W.S. (2001), *Business Financial Reporting: Challenges from the New Economy,* Financial Accounting Standards Board, Norwalk, CT.

Vernon, K. (1986): *Accounting Theory*. John Wiley and Sons. New York

Watts, R. L. and Zimmerman, J. L. (1986): Positive Accounting Theory, Prentice Hall. Englewood Cliffs, New Jersey.

Wolk, I.H., Tearney, M.G. and Dodd, J.L.(2001):*Accounting Theory: A conceptual and Institutional Approach,* South Western College Publishing,

Thomson Learning Centre, Cincinnati, Ohio, USA, 5th Edition.

Wood F. and Sangster A. (1999) *Business Accounting* Pearson Education Ltd. London.

Chapter 13

Accounting and Social Change

Muhammad Liman Muhammad

Introduction

Accounting has been defined in several ways by several authors. For instance, the Accounting Terminology Bulletin No. 1 as cited in Hendriksen and Van Breda (2001) defines accounting as "the art of recording, classifying and summarizing in a significant manner and in terms of money, transactions and events which are, in part at least, of a financial character, and interpreting the results thereof". In a similar manner, the American Accounting Association (1966:1) gives the latest and widely accepted definition of accounting as "the process of identifying, measuring and communicating economic information to permit informed judgments and decisions by the users of the information". This definition implies that accounting is a process, the outcome of which is the information. Therefore, whichever way accounting is defined, the fundamental message emanating from the definitions is that it is a source of financial information for different categories of users.

According to Moore (1967), social change is a significant alteration over time in the behavioural pattern and culture. Schaefer (2001) posits that a change that has notable social consequences can be viewed as significant alterations in the people's way of life. Examples of such changes include, among others, the emergence of slavery, the industrial revolution and advent of money. In addition, Kornblum & Smith (2000) offer a more comprehensive definition of social change as "variations over time in the ecological ordering of populations and communities, in pattern of roles and social interactions, in structures and functioning of institutions and in the cultures of societies". This definition considers any variation in the issues identified as constituting a social change and not until the variations are of significant dimensions. Thus, a reconstitution of the council of the Nigerian Accounting Standards Board (NASB) to accommodate more members like the Chartered Institute of Taxation of Nigeria (CITN) and the Association of National Accountants of Nigeria (ANAN) is a social change.

Though according to Glautier & Underdown (1986), accounting history dates back to the era of civilization, it is obvious that the practice of accounting has undergone tremendous changes. Like in any other profession, the dynamism in the socio-economic environment within which accounting operates might not only necessitate but could also greatly influence changes in accounting principles, practices and procedures. The primary goal of accounting is the provision of relevant information for rational economic and business decisions by the users of the information. The information needs of different category of users vary from user to user and from time to time. As a result, accounting principles and practices have not remained rigid but appear to move with the tide of the changing needs and expectations of the people. Could it then be said that accounting is a product of its socio - cultural environment?

Several countries of the world, in accordance with their own peculiarities, enact laws to regulate the practice of accounting. For instance, the Companies and Allied Matters Act (CAMA) 1999 (as amended), the Banks and Other Financial Institutions Act (BOFIA) 1999 (as amended), and several other legislations were enacted in Nigeria, to make provisions to govern the practice of accounting in the light of changing circumstances. Similarly, the Accounting standards setting bodies set and review standards when situations demand. In recognition of the influence of social change on the practice of accounting, the NASB constitution and operating procedure (1982) specifically states that the Board is established to, among other things, review from time to time, the standard developed by the Board in the light of changes in the social, economic and political environment (Dandago, 2001).

This paper, therefore, examines the relationship between accounting and social change. To accomplish this, the paper largely adopts the documentary source of data obtained particularly from relevant textbooks and journals. Accordingly, the rest of the paper is divided into four parts. Part two covers the evolution of accounting thoughts and practices; part three is on the impact of social changes on accounting practices and methods; part four is on the impact of inflation on accounting information; and part five concludes the paper.

The Evolution of Accounting Thoughts and Practices

According to the American Accounting Association (AAA, 1970), accounting history involves the study of evolution in accounting thought, practices and institutions in response to changes in the environment and societal needs, as well as the effects the evolution in turn has on the environment. Many notable accounting historians have in their various studies failed to evaluate the accounting practices of the past in the context of the socio-economic environment of the time. Therefore, there are calls that a new accounting history should place emphasis on the interpretational understanding of the intertwining of accounting with its social, economic and political environment (Uche, 2002). All these suggest that there is an interrelationship between accounting and its larger environment. Kripke (1985) describes accounting as an art and technique by which economic events are abstracted into figures or numbers that can be classified by periods through arithmetical addition and subtraction, and compared with the number of the same economic entity for different periods and with the number of other entities for the same and different periods. He also posits that accounting is not a discovery but a creation, that is, an agreed set of technique, whose selection legislates its meaning and thus determines how people are permitted to see the world. Kripke (1985) believes that the usefulness and correctness of accounting information depends on what one intends to achieve. Thus, the diversity of users needs necessitates a timely review of accounting practices and methods in response to the socio-economic changes and legislative provisions.

While Hopwood (1990) states that, to some, accounting is too rigid a discipline protected and shielded from the pressures of the world by professional conservatism and an inadequate knowledge basis, Napier (2006) opines that accounting has changed, is changing, and is likely to keep changing in the future. Napier posits that accounting methods, techniques, ideas and practices as well as the role and significance of accounting within and between individuals and organizations have never remained static. In a similar manner, Hopwood (1976) argues that the purposes, processes and techniques of accounting, its organizational and social roles as well as the way in which the result, that is, accounting information is used have never been static. Hopwood opines that accounting has evolved and would continue to evolve in relation to changes in economic, social, technological and political environments of organizations. Thus, Hopwood describes accounting as having had, and hopefully still having the potential of being a responsive and adaptive calculative technology that can relate to and facilitate broader processes of enterprise and social development.

According to Napier (2006), accounting change is essentially a function of environmental change. Jones & Mellett (2007) describe accounting as an instrument of change that reflects the changing pattern of societal forces. From the traditional viewpoint, according to Napier (2006), accounting may have an effect on its environment, but the predominant direction of influence is from the environment to accounting. Consistent with this, a major recognition of recent researches in accounting is that accounting is not just reflective but constructive since it works to shape the environment and not a mere effect thereof (Napier, 2006). In Napier's view, accounting impacts on the environment by making possible particular modes of actions such as budgeting, identification of cost centres, and pursuit of other economic goals. Accounting also plays the role of making things visible in an organization through records that are kept containing events and transactions which create the possibility for an ever-present observability (Hopwood, 1990). The history of accounting, according to Glautier and Underdown (1986), reflects the evolutionary pattern of social developments that shows the extent to which accounting is a product of its environment and at the same time a force for changing it. This implies that though accounting practices are influenced by environmental changes; accounting also impacts on the behaviours of the various users of accounting information thereby contributing in reshaping the society. Littleton (1933: 361) describes the influence of environmental changes on accounting, thus:

> Accounting is relative and progressive. The phenomena which form its subject matter are constantly changing. Older methods become less effective under altered conditions; earlier ideas become irrelevant in the face of new problems. Thus surrounding conditions generate fresh ideas and stimulate the ingenious to devise new methods. And as such ideas and methods prove successful, they in turn begin to modify surrounding conditions. The results we call progress.

Littleton's emphasis was on the extent to which accounting methods and practices are responsive to the environment in which such methods and practices emerged. Littleton states that accounting is a design which time is constantly changing. To be progressive, according to Solomon (1995) in Napier (2001), is to have improvement over time, particularly the gradual perfection of humanity. Thus, accounting is making progress as it responds to social changes and improves in its method and practices. According to Broadbent & Guthrie (1992), changes in practice are seen as manifestation of functional or useful progress and system improvements. That accounting is progressive could imply that present practices are better than the past practices or present practices originate from past practices. For instance, Lee (1979) studied Distillers Company Limited (DCL) from 1981-1984 and concluded that before 1900, the information provided annually to the shareholders was not only extremely limited, but also presented in a rudimentary form with little additional explanation and analysis.

According to the Committee on Accounting History (1970), accounting history is worth teaching as part of the overall cultural formation of future accountants in order to be able to particularly stress that the presently acceptable practices of accounting have not been immutable over the decades and centuries of environmental change. This shows that the committee also believes that changes in the practice and methods of accounting are not spontaneous but a response to environmental changes. Similarly, Lister (1984) describes accounting history as a series of disconnected episodes rather than a coherent development. However, Napier (1989) argues that it is not the disconnections in the episodes or events that matters but a systematic investigations of such episodes, which is not impossible. The disconnection may be attributable to the fact that historical events do not take place consistently; and one event may not be determined by the other. For example, the advent of money, the industrial revolution and economic depression like that of 1930s in the US, are among the social changes that accounting had to respond to independently in the light of the challenges they posed. Since these events are not interdependent, developments in accounting history cannot follow a logical order. In line with this, Stamp (1980) also argues that the development of accounting standards should be evolutionary (i.e. based on environmental or social changes) and not based on a deterministic, authoritarian or normative approach. In their contribution, Miller, Hopper & Laughlin (1991) observe that rather than considering the history of accounting as a natural evolution of administrative technologies, it is increasingly being viewed as the formation of a particular complex of rationalities and modes of intervention among many. They see such a complex as originating out of diverse materials and in relation to heterogeneous range of issues and events. These events and issues are the socio-economic or environmental circumstances that influence accounting practice and methods, and form the basis of developments in accounting history.

Describing the scientific method of research, McCullers & Schroeder (1982) opine that there are clear limitations that would inhibit its application in accounting research. They identify the influence of people (social issues) and volatility in the economic environment as the factors that would make it impossible to hold the research variables in accounting constant. Walgenbach, Hanson & Dittrich (1988) also argue that since accounting is more of an art than a science, accounting principles are not unchangeable laws like those in the physical sciences. They describe accounting principles as guides to action which may be changed by altering a specific principle or formulating new ones to fit changed economic circumstances and business practices.

Accounting Research study (ARS) No.11, as cited in Hendriksen and Van Breda (2001), describes accounting postulates as basic assumptions or fundamental propositions concerning the economic, political and sociological environment in which accounting must operate. Similarly, the American Institute of Certified Public Accountants (AICPA) 1958 posits that postulates are the basic assumptions on which principles rest, and they are necessarily derived from the economic and political environment as well as the modes of thought and customs of all segments of the business community. All these relate accounting to its socio-economic and cultural environment.

Social Changes and Accounting Practices and Methods

This section identifies some of the significant social changes and examines how such changes have impacted on accounting practices and methods.

The Invention of money

Accounting is concerned about measurement, which is, assigning monetary values to accounting items. Monetary unit provides the best basis for measurements in accounting, particularly where aggregation is necessary (Hendriksen & Van Breda, 2001). Both trade and accounting, according to Glautier & Underdown (1986), predate the invention of money which they opine began to circulate in the sixth century B.C. Unlike trade by barter, money facilitated and encouraged the expansion of trade among different communities. The use of money as a common denominator for measurement necessitated the emergence of monetary unit as a fundamental concept or postulate in accounting. This concept limits the type of accounting information that would be needed about an enterprise as it provides that only that information that can be quantified or expressed in monetary terms should be identified and communicated. Glautier & Underdown (1986) posit that the communication of information about a business entity in monetary terms is the basis of modern financial accounting theory and practice.

The Arabic Influence

The emergence of the Arabic system of numerals also played a great role in shaping accounting practices. The Arabic numerals made possible the expression and recording of accounting items in figures or numbers. Hendriksen & Van Breda (2001) trace the origin of Arabic numerals to the Arabs, which they say was spread to Europe by Arab scholars and some Europeans who had stayed among the Arabs. The Arabic numerals are generally used by most countries of the world today for recording events, transactions and activities, whether in financial or cost and management accounting.

The Italian Renaissance

The rebirth of Italy is a turning point in the history of accounting. According to Glautier and Underdown (1986), though the practice of book-keeping existed as early as 4500 BC, it remained primitive until the introduction of the Italian method, which became known as double entry system. They opine that the origin of the accounting procedures and concepts being applied today in the orderly recording of business transactions is traceable to the practice during the early part of the Italian renaissance, whose economic expansion provided the conditions for the emergence of double entry (Carnegie & Napier, 1996). This led to the first publication on double entry system by Luca Pacioli in 1494, in whose book entitled "Summa de Arithmetica, Geometrica, Proportioni et Proportionalita" (Everything about Arithmetic, Geometry and Proportions) a section was dedicated to double entry system. Hendriksen and Van Breda (2001) opine that such developments in accounting in Italy were facilitated by the application of Arabic numerals and series of advances in mathematics brought to Europe by the Arabs. Hendriksen and Van Breda (2001) also trace the origin of some vocabularies in accounting like debits, credits, journal entries, ledgers, accounts, trial balances, balance sheet, and income statement to the renaissance.

Tracing developments in accounting, Littleton (1993) identifies four areas of differences between the practices of Italian cities and current methods and theory thus:

(i) **Objective:** Up to the 16th century, the primary objective of accounting was only to provide information for owners of businesses, who are essentially single proprietors. Therefore, accounts were treated as confidential documents unlike today where the presence of several users necessitate the publication of accounts of some organizations; provisions of relevant and reliable accounting information; as well as application of uniform standards of reporting.

(ii) **Entity Concept:** Most proprietors, during the Italian era, never made clear separation between personal and business affairs in their accounting records. This is against the entity concept, which requires that there should be a clear distinction between the affairs of owners of a business and that of the business. Though this concept is still being violated particularly by many small business enterprises today, most large companies, especially public ones apply the concept.

(iii) **Periodicity and Going Concern Concepts:** Unlike today, these concepts were lacking because most business ventures were of short duration or only survive up to the point their specific trading objectives are realized. The calculation of profit was not made on annual basis as practiced today but on completion of the venture. Therefore, there was no need for accruals and deferrals. Since fixed assets were rarely used, calculation of depreciation was unnecessary. In the case of businesses organized for longer periods of time, there was little need for demonstration of stewardship by way of calculation and reporting of the results of business operations periodically since the owners were in regular contact with the affairs of their businesses.

(iv) **Monetary Unit:** In the accounting practices of the Italian cities, there was lack of a single monetary unit in contrast to what is obtainable today where each country has its monetary unit serving as a common denominator. Besides, regional economic grouping like the European Union, adopts Euro dollar as a common currency by means of which accounts can also be prepared. Also, the Economic Communities of West African States (ECOWAS) has a proposal for common currency.

Despite the above developments, De Rover (1955) describes the period between 1494 and 1800 as the period of stagnation for accounting. However, this does not seem to be correct since the introduction of double entry bookkeeping and subsequent publication of a book by Luca Pacioli happened in 1494. Besides, the industrial revolution, which significantly impacted on accounting, started within this period. Peragallo (1983) describes the period between 1458 and 1558 as a period when writers focused on the mechanics of bookkeeping as developed by businesses but did not attempt to develop a theory of double entry or go beyond the bookkeeping needs of the mercantile firm. He refers to the period between 1559 to 1795 as an era when the critique of bookkeeping as a new element emerged, and as a result, research into the subject area of double entry bookkeeping began.

The Industrial Revolution

According to North (1981) significant changes in population growth, standard of living, replacement of agriculture with industry and service, specialization, division of labour, interdependence and technology took place between 1750 and 1830. Hendriksen and Van Breda (2001) opine that probably a period of good weather in Britain permitted a series of good harvest that made food prices to fall and therefore, enabled people to enjoy better nutrition and health. The longevity of the people increased as a result of good health and awareness of the need for personal hygiene. The increased population brought about increased demand for goods. Production increased significantly to meet rising demand. Old methods of production were replaced by new ones as a result of technological advancement. As manufacturing companies sprang up, more capital became necessary, and this led to increase in the number of banks in order to provide required financial assistance.

The industrial revolution necessitated mass production of goods, and as a result, management of companies needed a detailed accounting information to be able to determine the costs of production and also provide guide in valuation of inventory, pricing of finished goods, as well as cost control. Management needed cost information for decisions making more than ever before. Therefore, cost and management accounting is largely a product of the industrial revolution. This is consistent with the view of Glautier and Underdown (1986) who trace the origin of management accounting to the industrial revolution.

As a result of extensive use of fixed assets by companies, both for production and distribution, the application of the going concern concept as it relates to the accounting treatment of fixed asset became operational. The increased use of fixed assets was accompanied by a significant increase in the cost of production and distribution, thereby making depreciation of fixed assets highly necessary.

Large capital requirements by companies necessitated the separations of ownerships from management. This brought about the need for the periodic reporting of results of operations and financial positions of companies to their owners as opposed to the venture system. Financial information was not only then needed by management but also by different categories of users like shareholders, creditors and government, among other users for their decisions. This development also necessitated and brought about the statutory audits of companies by independent but competent auditors who attest to the truth and fairness of financial statements in order to lend more credence to them (financial statements). The industrial revolution stimulated the need for more detailed record of cost and the growth of corporation as a result created a demand for financial statements, external audit and professional accountants (Carnegie & Napier, 2006). It also brought about the establishment of the London Stock Exchange in 1773 and New York Stock Exchange in 1792.

The Rise of Investors

The increase in the number of investors between 1900 and 1930 in the US also played a role in reshaping the practice of accounting. According to the New York Stock Exchange Fact Book (1959) as cited in Hendriksen & Van Breda (2001), the average number of shares listed on the exchanges in 1900 was about 60 million and this rose to 180 million in 1917 and 1,212 million in 1930. Hendriksen and Van Breda observe that the rise of the investors necessitated the change in the objective of accounting from that of presenting information to management and creditors to that of providing financial information for investors and stockholders. They also opine that the rapid growth in the widespread ownership of corporations, particularly during the first years after the First World War, created new needs for accounting information. The change in the objective of financial statements, according to them, led to an increased emphasis on the income statements; a need for full disclosure of relevant financial information, by presenting a more comprehensive and complete financial statements and increasing the use of foot notes; as well as placing emphasis on consistency in reporting, especially with regards to income statement. All these changes were necessitated by the events of the time.

The 1929 Crash and Great Depression of the 1930s

The New York Stock Exchange continued to make tremendous progress up to 1929. The performances of many American companies were above average, and the economy was in a boom up to 1929. Many new industries were established thereby reducing the unemployment rate. Labour productivity was high and prices of products were stable. According to Hendriksen & Van Breda (2001), Car production rose from 485,000 in 1913, through 1,934,000 in 1919, to 5,622,000 in 1929. These greatly motivated individuals and institutions to invest in stocks.

However, by the last quarter of 1929, events in the stock market took a new but unfavourable turn as stockholders within the period lost not less than $15 billion (Malkiel, 1985). This development dragged the US economy from boom to the depression of 1930s thereby causing a decline in private investment of up to 90% as well as a fall in production by 56% (Hendriksen & Van Breda, 2001). According to

Gordon (1974), within this period, more than 9,000 banks shut their doors. And by 9th March 1933, all the banks were closed.

Though several factors could be and were responsible for the depression, the accountants and accounting practices of the period were not spared. Means & Berle (1932) as cited in Hendriksen & Van Breda (2001) believe that the lack of uniformity in the accounting practices was responsible for the downfall, and also claim that where the application of accounting standards are not strict, and there are no rules imposed by law, directors and their accountants may create figures in a manner they choose or prefer. They also argue that accountants have failed to put in place a series of standard rules. In a similar manner, the New York Stock Exchange also reacted to the crash by criticizing the lack of uniformity in accounting practice of the period, particularly in the areas of depreciation and consolidation where no rules existed then. Firms were accused of making excessive charges for depreciation and too conservative in undervaluing inventory, and were therefore requested to provide adequate and understandable information that would enable stockholders to determine the true value of their investments and not such information capable of misleading them (Hoxsey, 1929).

These developments brought about series of regulations designed to govern accounting practices. Some of such regulations include the Emergency Banking Act of 1933, the Glass Steagal Banking Act creating the Federal Deposit Insurance Corporation to provide insurance for bank deposits in 1933, and the establishment of the Securities and Exchange Commission of 1934, which provides for disclosure of specific financial and other information required to be made public and kept up to date by means of periodic financial statements. In addition, by 1936, the Committee on Accounting Procedure was created to issue pronouncements on matters of accounting principles and procedures.

The Development of the Computer

The development of computer has brought about a revolution in information technology. Like other social, environmental or technological changes, the development of computer has also impacted on accounting profession. The emergence of computers has refined the procedures for applications of earlier developed accounting principles and has significantly facilitated accounting practice. E – Accounting and e – auditing techniques are today practiced by organizations and professional firms in preparing accounts and conducting audit exercises. These facilitate timely and accurate processing of financial data for the production of required accounting information.

Reorganization of the Nigerian Accounting Standards Board

The NASB has been in existence since 1982 to issue accounting standards that would regulate accounting practices in Nigeria. To give backing to the Board, it was formally established by an Act of the National Assembly in July, 2003. The board is statutorily empowered to promote and enforce compliance with the standards developed or reviewed. The inspectorate unit of the Board has the power to obtain any information on any matters specified in a written notice served upon the Company and/or its auditors, and can enforce compliance by carrying out any examinations and enquiries to ascertain whether or not the provisions of the Act, or any regulation made, are being complied with. The unit is also empowered to impose such sanctions as may be prescribed by the Board.

Where the Board obtains a notice of non compliance with any applicable SAS in the preparation of financial statements by the Company Directors and Chief Accounting Officers, and the financial statement is not withdrawn and amended within 60 days, such officers shall be liable to appropriate penalties. Similarly, a Company's External Auditor shall be held liable for issuing an unqualified audit report even in the presence of apparent non compliance with any applicable SAS. These make the application and compliance with accounting standards not just persuasive but compelling on all practitioners. Certainly, this is capable of improving accounting practice in Nigeria.

Further, the composition of the membership of the Board, which cut across various bodies, agencies, and institutions as well as the introduction of more members like the Chartered Institute of Taxation and the Association of National Accountants of Nigeria has made it more representative. This is expected not only to ensure that relevant accounting standards are issued as and when necessary, but also assists the Board to monitor compliance with the standards.

The Impact of Inflation on Accounting Information

Financial statements are prepared with a view to providing a true and fair view of the results of operations and financial positions of organizations in order to serve as genuine and reliable guide for decision making. One way by which this can be achieved is by having a stable monetary unit; but this appears to be a mirage because of the problem of inflation prevalent in most economies, particularly those of developing countries like Nigeria. Though fluctuations in the value of money are regarded as the major cause of accounting distortions, Kokubu & Sawabe (1996) report that Takatera does not completely consent to this as he believes the problem can be addressed by applying the principles of accounting for price level changes. According to Wolk, Teaney & Dodd (2001), accountants in the US have since around 1920s realized the potential impact on accounting information of the effects of price changes, whether specific or general in nature. However, in spite of distortions in accounting information caused by changing prices, McCullers & Schroeder (1982), Glautier & Underdown (1986), Walgenbach, Hanson & Dittrich (1988), Anao (1989), Millichamp (1989), Wood & Sangster (1999) Hendriksen and Van Breda (2001), Dandago (2001) and Muhammad (2002) observe that the historical cost accounting is still widely accepted and applied by many business enterprises because of its acclaimed greater objectivity and verifiability.

In response to changing prices, the American Accounting Association (AAA) issued a supplementary statement No.2, Price Level Changes and Financial Statements in 1951, which recommends that financial statements be stated in units of general purchasing power to supplement historical cost statements. The American Institute of Certified Public Accountants (AICPA) in its Accounting Research Study No. 6 in 1961 also supported general price level adjusted statements. Similarly, the statement of standard accounting Practice (SSAP) 7 was issued in the United Kingdom in 1974, which also recommended a supplementary statement to be attached to the financial reports of companies in terms of their current purchasing power at the end of the accounting period. SSAP 7 was withdrawn in 1978, while SSAP 16, "Current Cost Accounting" was published in 1980 to also address the problem of accounting for inflation. In the same vein, though the Nigerian Accounting Standards Board has not issued any Statement of Accounting Standard specifically designed to address the problem of accounting for inflation, it is making frantic effort to do so. In the meantime, NASB adopts the International Accounting Standards (IAS) 29, which is on "Financial Reporting in Hyperinflationary Economies".

Conclusion

It is obvious that several changes have taken place in the accounting practices and methods in different parts of the world. This paper has attempted to establish the intertwining of developments in accounting and social change. In addition to the views of several scholars, who see a positive relationship between accounting and its environment, social or economic, the paper identifies major social changes such as the introduction of Arabic numerals, the Italian renaissance, the Industrial revolution and the great depression of 1930s in the US, among others, and assesses the impact such changes had on accounting.

It is apparent from the discussion that developments in accounting are in response to environmental and social changes of the time. Hence, accounting is a product of the changing societal needs; it is a highly dynamic discipline. As a social service, accounting practices and methods would remain inseparable from events in the environment. Therefore, in order to remain relevant, accounting has been responding, and must continue to respond to the social changes. However, since accounting is not and cannot be mechanical in nature or a natural science, whose laws have universal applications, developments of accounting principles or concepts should take cognizance of the peculiarities of different environments and changes therein.

References

Anao A.R. (1989), *An Introduction to Financial Accounting,* Ikeja: Longman Nigeria Ltd

American Accounting Association (AAA, 1966), *A Statement of Basic Accounting Theory,* in Glautier M.W.E & Underdown, B. (1986), *Accounting Theory and Practice,* London: Pitman Publishing 3rd Edn.

Barle, A.A. & Means, G.C. (1932), *The Modern Corporation and Private Property,* New York: Jovanovich, in Hendriksen, E.S. & Van Breda, M.F. (2001), *Accounting Theory: Text and Reading,* New York: McGraw Hill, 2nd edn.

Broadbent, J. & Guthrie, J. (1992), "Changes in the public sector: A review of recent 'Alternative' Accounting Research", *Accounting, Auditing & Accountability Journal,* Vol.5, No.2

Carnegie, G.D. & Napier, C.J. (1996), "Critical and Interpretive Histories: Insights into Accounting's Present and Future through its Past", *Accounting, Auditing & Accountability Journal,* Vol.9, No.3

Dandago, K.I. (2001), *Financial Accounting Simplified,* Kano: A.J. Publishers

________"Must Historical Cost Accounting Continue to Dictate Financial Reporting in Nigeria?", in Ezejelue, A.C. & Okoye, E.A. (eds), *Accounting: Issues and Readings,* Nigeria Accounting Association (NAA)

De Rover. R. (1955), "New Perspectives on the history of Accounting", *The Accounting Review,* July

Glautier, M.W & Underdown, B. (1986), *Accounting Theory and Practice,* London: Pitman Publishing 3rd edn.

Gordon, R.A. (1974), *Economic Instability and Growth: The American Record,* New York: Harper & Row

Hendriksen, E.S. & Van Breda, M.F. (2001), *Accounting Theory: Text and Reading,* New York: McGraw Hill, 5th edn

Hopwood, A.G. (1976), "Editorial: The Path Ahead. Accounting", *Organizations and Society,* Vol. 1

________(1990), "Accounting and Organization Change", *Accounting, Auditing & Accountability Journal,* Vol.3, No.1

Hoxsey, J.M.B. (1930),"Accounting for Investors" *Journal of Accountancy,* in Hendriksen, E.S. &Van Breda, M.F. (2001), *Accounting Theory: Text and Reading,* New York: McGraw Hill, 2nd Edn

Jones, M.J. & Mellett, H. J. (2007), "Determinants of Changes in Accounting Practices: Accounting and the UK Health Service", *Critical Perspectives on Accounting,* Vol. 18.

Kokubu, K & Sawabe, N. (1996), "The Past, Present and Future of Accounting: A Review Essay of Accounting, Organizations and Society: the Inside and Outside of Accounting by Sadao Takatera". *Accounting Organizations and Society,* Vol.21

Kornblum, W.& Smith, C.D. (2000), *Sociology in a Changing World,* New York: Harcourt College Publishers, 5th Edn.

Kripke, H.(1985), "Accounting: What Does it all means? The Commission's Biggest Failure" in Zeff, S.A. & Keller.. T.F. (eds) *Financial Accounting Theory,* New York; McGraw Hill Inc. 3rd Edn.

Lee, T.A. (1979), "Company Financial Statements: An Essay in Business History 1840-1950", in Lee, T.A. & Parker, R.H. (1979) (eds), *The Evolution of Corporate Financial Reporting,* Nairobi: Thomas Nelson.

Lister, R. (1984), "Accounting as History", *International Journal of Accounting,* Vol. 18, No. 2

Littleton, A.C. (1933), *Accounting Education to 1900.* New York: American Institute Publishing Co

Malkiel, B.G. (19850 *A Random Walk Down Wall Street.* New York: W.W. Norton & Co. 4th Edn.

McCullers, I.D. & Schroeder, R.G. (1982), *Accounting Theory,* New York: John Wiley Son

Miller, P., Horper, T. & Laughlin, R.G., (1991), "The New Accounting History: an Introduction", *Accounting Organizations and Society,* Vol. 16. No. 5/6

Millichamp, A.H. (1989), *Foundation Accounting: An Instructional Manual for Accounting Students,* London: DPP Publishers.

Moore, H.E. (1967), *Orders and Change: Essay in Comparative Sociology,* New York: Wiley

Muhammad, L. M. (2002), " Valuation of Fixed Assets by Business Enterprises in Nigeria" in Ezejelue, A.C. & Okoye, A.E. (eds), *The Nigerian Perspective,* Nigerian Accounting Association

Napier, C.J. (2001), "Accounting History and Accounting Progress", *Accounting History,* Vol.6, No.2

_______(2006), "Accounts of Change: 30 Years of Historical Accounting Research", *Accounting Organizations and Society,* Vol.31

New York Exchange Fact Book (1959), in Hendriksen E.S. & Van Breda, M.F. (2001), *Accounting Theory: Text and Reading,* New York: McGraw Hill 2nd Edn.

North, D.C. (1981), *Structure and Change in Economic History,* New York: WEW Norton & Co.

Peragollo, E. (1938), *Origin and evolution of Double Entry Bookkeeping,* New York: American Institute Publishing.

Schaefer, T.R. (2001), *Sociology,* New York: McGraw Hill Companies, 7th Edn

Solomon, R.C. (1995), "Progress", in Napier, C.J. (2001), "Accounting History and Accounting Progress", *Accounting History,* Vol.6, No.2

Stamp, E. (1980), *Corporate Reporting: Its Future Evolution,* Toronto: London Institutes of Chartered Accountants.

Uche, C.U (2002), "Accounting History Research: Some Theoretical Issues", in Anao, A.R. & Uche, C.U. (eds) *Research Design and Implementation in Accounting and Finance,* Benin: University of Benin Press.

Walgenbach, P.H., Hanson, E.I & Dittrich, N.E. (1988), *Financial Accounting: An Introduction,* London: Harcourt Brace Jovanovich. Inc. 5th Edn.

Wolk, H.I., Tearney, M.G. & Dodd, J.L. (2001), *Accounting Theory: A conceptual and Institutional Approach,* Cincinnati: South – Western Publishing, 5th Edn.

Wood, F. & Sangster, A (1999), *Business Accounting,* London: Pitman Publishing, 8th Edn.

Chapter 14

Issues in Behavioral Aspects of Accounting

Junaidu Muhammad Kurawa

1. Introduction

Behavioral aspect of accounting is that segment of accounting that seeks to foster an understanding of those elements of human behavior, both cognitive (perceived) and affective (emotional) that influence the decision making process in all accounting contexts and settings. In essence, the behavioral aspect of accounting focuses its attention at investigating the decision makers and their choices from individual, group, organizational and market perspectives in order to provide explanation(s) on the behavior of accountants, including auditors and non-auditors (other stakeholders) regarding how users of accounting information are influenced by various accounting functions and reports.

It is a special area of accounting addressing such aspects as human information processing behavior, judgement quality, accounting problem(s) created by users and providers of accounting information and the decision making skills of users and producers of accounting information. The Behavioral aspect of accounting encompasses a broad range of topics or sub-disciplines such as investments, judgement and decision making, risk taking behavior and analysis, financial management, managerial accounting and control, budgeting, auditing, accounting information processing and systems, strategic planning, tax accounting, financial reporting, financial statement analysis, accounting organization and society, government and non-profit accounting, issues in international accounting, disclosure laws and standards among others.

Research in Behavioral aspects of accounting and auditing has evolved through three phases. The initial phase covers the period between the mid-1960s to mid-1970s; the second phase covers the mid-1970s to mid-1980s and the third phase covers the mid-1980s to date. In the initial period covering mid- 1960s to early 1970s, research in this field was inspired mostly by practice and policy issues. In managerial accounting, it focused on the impact of control systems and budgetary standards on the performance of employees. In financial accounting, it focused on the type of information to supply to external decision makers and how best to measure and disclose that information. In auditing, it focused on how to perform audits more effectively and efficiently and how best to report audit reports to external users.

In the second stage, covering mid- 1970s to the mid- 1980s, research in this field paid more attention to constructing models of individual decision makers, evaluating the extent to which individual decision judgement and decisions departed from the constructed normative models.

Since the mid 1980s, the research focus has shifted from documenting the shortcomings of human judgement in accounting and auditing settings to understanding (and reducing or eliminating) those shortcomings. A major shift of this period has been from viewing the decision maker as a passive converter of inputs to outputs, to viewing the decision maker as a diagnostician (problem identifier) especially in the auditing domain.

Having regard to the discussion above, this paper examines the contributions of scholars in the most notable area of behavioral aspect of accounting, namely, financial reporting and management fraud. The aim of the paper is to provide an insight into the dimensions and relative importance of behavioral accounting traits on financial reporting and management fraud, and how accounting practice could be enhanced through a better understanding of the behavior of individuals and organizations. The paper adopts documentary review of secondary data as its methodology. The paper is divided into five sections including the introduction. The next section discusses the major concepts of behavioral aspect of accounting. Section three reviews the content and contributions of behavioral accounting issues within the area of financial reporting and management fraud. Section four discusses the expectation of users and preparers of financial information. And the last section concludes the paper and offers some recommendations.

2 Literature Overview

2.1 Definition of Concepts of Behavioral Aspect of Accounting

As indicated within the introduction, the behavioral aspect of accounting is a special area of accounting addressing such issues as human information processing behavior, judgment quality, accounting problem(s) created by users and providers of accounting information and the decision making skills of users and producers of accounting information. In discussing these issues, it is necessary to define certain behavioral traits that are most often used in the behavioral accounting literature. These traits are relevant in understanding the behavior of users and preparers of accounting information. They include analytical ability, amiable disposition, driverability and expressionism. Also defined is management fraud, which is an abnormal accounting behavior, analyzed in the subsequent section.

Analytical ability: this behavioral trait is noted for the ability to gather and review data. It is typical of people in technical positions such as engineering, accounting and information technology. Details and accuracy are important to these people, and they take great pride in providing information that is correct. Therefore users and providers of accounting information that possess a high level analytical ability form the back bone of the accounting family that are recognized today as diagnosticians. They are wanted on both side of the coin.

Amiable disposition: This behavioral trait is noted within highly supportive individuals interested in establishing and maintaining relationships, who are agreeable and congenial with great skills in achieving consensus within the accounting family. They can effectively facilitate groups and bring sides together to develop a win/win solution. Producers of accounting information would want the users of this information to possess a high level of this trait. Though it is not always the case.

Driverability trait: individuals that possess the ability to control, direct, lead, manage, regulate, supervise or oversee the affairs entrusted upon them are regarded as having this behavioral trait. It implies, having the driving force behind getting things done in the accounting family. These types of individuals are result-oriented and are motivated by goals. They typically gravitate to positions of recognition and status. Drivers are effective at time management, and seem to possess an innate ability to devote just the right amount of time and effort to things that need to be done. They rarely struggle with making decisions. Both producers and users of accounting information share this trait.

Expressionism—Is the ability of the individual to express emotional experience rather than impressions of the external world. Individuals having this trait are visionary and good at grasping the big picture. They are truly the "politicians" in the accounting family, establishing and using contacts extensively. They possess such qualities like indicative tendencies, suggestive capabilities, eloquent and revealing proficiencies and denotative styles.

Management fraud: This is a behavioral problem which entails deliberate action committed by management that injures investors and creditors through misleading financial statements. It can also represent a scheme designed to deceive the users of accounting information which is accomplished using fictitious documents and representations that support fraudulent financial statements. It is an accounting problem created by producers of accounting information.

2.2 Financial Reporting and Management Fraud

Financial accounting information is the product of corporate accounting and external reporting systems that measure and routinely disclose audited, quantitative data concerning the financial position and performance of publicly held firms. Sabari, (2004) argues that, audited balance sheets, income statements, and cash flow statements, along with supporting disclosures, form the foundation of the firm-specific information set available to investors and regulators. In recent times however, references to false financial statement are increasingly frequent over the last few years, resulting in the high incidence of corporate failure locally and internationally. Falsifying financial statements primarily consists of manipulating elements by overstating assets, sales and profit, or understating liabilities, expenses, or losses. When a financial statement contains falsifications so that its elements no longer represent the true picture, we speak of fraud. Management fraud can be defined as "deliberate fraud committed by management that injures investors and creditors through misleading financial statements" (Eliott and Willingham, 1980). Wallace (1995), contested that fraud is "a scheme designed to deceive; it can be accomplished with fictitious documents and representations that support fraudulent financial statements".

The exact number of business failures that are actually caused by fraud in Nigeria can not be accurately predicted, but undeniably lots of businesses, especially small firms, go bankrupt each year due to fraud losses. Losses can occur in almost any area of accounting. It includes losses in cash, accounts receivable, expenditures for services, and inventory among others. Fraud is not just a problem in large firms. It occurs more frequently in small businesses because of their weak internal control. Fraud in a small firm has a greater impact, as the firm does not have the resources to absorb the loss (Wells, 1997). In a global economy and multinational trade, the trend of international fraud through fraudulent financial reporting affects all countries (Vanasco, 1998).

Most techniques for manipulating profits can be grouped into three broad categories – changing accounting methods, fiddling with managerial estimates of costs, and shifting the period when expenses and revenues are included in results (Worthy, 1984). Other false financial statements include cases where documents are manipulated as in, recording revenue on shipments after year-end by backdating shipment documents, altering test documents, and producing false work reports. Other common fraudulent schemes are asset misappropriation schemes like the theft of company assets (e.g. cash and inventory) and fraudulent management of receivables (Comer, 1998).

The study of Vanasco (1998) examines the role of professional associations, governmental agencies, and international accounting and auditing bodies in promulgating standards to prevent fraud in financial statements and other white-collar crimes. It also examines several fraud cases. The cases examined show that the cash, inventory, and related party transactions are prone to fraud. Auditors assign a high-risk index to the potential misappropriation of inventory, cash defalcation, and conflict of interest. Typical financial statement fraud techniques involved the overstatement of revenues and assets (Beasley, Carcello, and Harmanson 1999). Over half the frauds involved overstating revenues by recording revenues prematurely or fictitiously. Many of those revenue frauds only affected transactions recorded right at the end of significant financial reporting periods (i.e. quarter-end or year-end). About half the frauds also involved overstating assets by understating allowances for receivables, overstating the value of inventory, property, plant and equipment and other tangible assets, and recording assets that did not exist.

Corporate falsification can also be classified as that committed by insiders for the company (violation of government regulations, i.e. tax, securities, safety and environmental laws). Senior managers might perpetrate financial statement falsifications to deceive investors and lenders or to inflate profits and thereby gain higher salaries and bonuses. Higson (1999) analysed the results of 13 interviews with senior auditors/ accountants on whether their clients report suspected fraud to an external authority. Although some companies do report it, quite a number seem reluctant about reporting.

Similarly, the study of Bonner *et al.* (1998) examines whether certain types of financial reporting fraud result in a higher likelihood of litigation against independent auditors and develops a new taxonomy to document types of fraud that includes 12 general categories. They study found that auditors are more likely to be sued when the financial statement frauds are of types that most commonly occurs or when the frauds arise from fictitious transactions. Auditors' sensitivity with respect to clients' ethical status and their assessment of the likelihood of fraud is examined by Abdolmohammadi and Owhoso (2000). The results indicate that senior auditors were sensitive to ethical information, e.g. regarding clients' service to the community, in making their assessment of the likelihood of fraud, deeming such clients less likely to have committed fraud.

Recent work has attempted to build models to predict the presence of management fraud. Results from logit regression analysis of 75 fraud and 75 no-fraud firms indicate that no-fraud firms have boards with significantly higher percentages of outside members than fraud firms (Beasley, 1996). Similarly, Hansen, McDonald, Messier, and Bell (1996) use a powerful generalized qualitative-response model to predict management fraud based on a set of data developed by an international public accounting firm. The model includes the probit and logit techniques. An experiment was conducted to examine the use of an expert system developed to enhance the performance of auditors (Eining, Jones, and Loebbebke 1997). Auditors using the expert system exhibited the ability to discriminate better among situations with varying levels of management fraud risk and made more consistent decisions regarding appropriate audit actions. Green and Choi (1997) presented the development of a neural network fraud classification model employing endogenous financial data. A classification model created from the learned behaviour pattern is then applied to a test sample. During the preliminary stage of an audit, a financial statement classified as fraudulent signals the auditor to increase substantive testing during fieldwork. Fanning and Cogger (1998) use an artificial neural network to develop a model for detecting management fraud. Using publicly available predictors of fraudulent financial statements, they find a model of eight variables with a high probability of detection.

In the same vein, Summers and Sweeney (1998) investigate the relationship between insider trading and fraud. They find, with the use of a logit model, that in the presence of fraud, insiders reduce their holdings of company stock through high levels of selling activity as measured by either the number of transactions, the number of shares sold, or the Naira amount of shares sold. In another study Beneish (1999) investigates the incentives and the penalties related to earnings overstatements primarily in firms that are subject to accounting enforcement actions by the Securities and Exchange Commission (SEC) in the United States. He finds that the managers are likely to sell their holdings and exercise stock appreciation rights in the period when earnings are overstated, and that the sales occur at inflated prices. The evidence suggests that the monitoring of managers' trading behaviour can be informative about the likelihood of earnings overstatement.

Abbot, Park and Parker (2000) on the other hand, examine and measure the audit committee independence and activity in mitigating the likelihood of fraud. Using the logistic regression analysis they find that firms with audit committees which are composed of independent directors and which meet at least twice per year are less likely to be sanctioned for fraudulent or misleading reporting.

3. Expected Behavior of Users and Producers of Financial Information

In this section an attempt is made to relate the expectations of users and producers of financial information having regard to the behavioral trait identified above and the reviewed behavioral issue. We shall attempt to answer such questions as - do producers of financial information mislead its users? The behavioral accounting traits discussed earlier will be used to explore the relationship between the expectation of the users and that of the producers of accounting information.

3.1 Do Producers of Accounting Information Mislead Its Users?

Several studies have been conducted in the area of income asymmetry or income smoothing with varying position on whether producers of accounting information deliberately mislead the users of these information. It has been established by scholars that the earnings reported on firms' financial statements are generated by adjusting cash flows, in principle to reflect the firm's future cash flow prospects. Scholars like Chan, Jegadeesh, and Lakonishok (2000), and Xie (2001) have provided evidence that firms choose income-increasing accounting methods or report high accounting adjustments (accruals) to improve investor perceptions artificially.

Pincus and Wasley (1994) find that voluntary accounting changes tend to be made by firms that have been experiencing poor prior accounting performance, and that these changes tend to increase earnings. In another study, Hand, Hughes, and Sefcik (1990) find that firms undertake fictitious transaction partly to 'window dress' their earnings. Similarly, Amir and Ziv (1997) discovered that, firms that choose to adopt newly-mandated changes earlier in the adoption period are those for which the changes are more income increasing. They argued that, upward manipulation of earnings is stronger at the time of new issues of equity and prior to heavy insider trading.

The studies of Burgstahler and Dichev (1997) and DeGeorge, Patel, and Zeckhauser (1999), established and confirm that, managers adjust earnings to meet anticipated income levels such as, past levels, and analysts forecast levels. The motive is essentially to influence the external user of the information positively.

From these discussions, it is possible to agree that producers of accounting information sometimes mislead the users of such information. This position will be clearer if the motive for the misrepresentation is known. But because several reasons could be responsible for the misinformation the user need only to have a better understanding of the behavioral traits and the expectations of the producers of such accounting information to be able to use the information wisely.

The fundamental objective of corporate firms is to maximize the market value of their firm. This underscores the main objective of external accounting information dissemination. Basically, the producers of accounting information aim at creating financial information that has four major important factors (qualities) embedded in it. They target relevance, i.e., the accounting information should be relevant to decision making. The second major factor is faithful representation, which replaces the term reliability in the previous framework, meaning that information should be complete, verifiable, and neutral. The third major factor is comparability (including consistency), which would enable users to identify similarities in and differences between two sets of economic phenomena. In other words, users are provided with opportunity to compare likes with likes. The last major factor is understandability, meaning that users who have a reasonable knowledge of business and economic activities or financial accounting should be able to comprehend the meaning of the information. Additionally producers of accounting information do not exclude relevant financial information because of complexity or difficulty for some users to understand. Where any of these qualities has been compromised, it is assumed not to be deliberate. With this background, users of accounting information must understand and possess the following skills to be able to analyze and use these accounting information with high degree of caution and utility.

Users of accounting information must possess a high degree of analytical ability to enable them to collect and review relevant accounting information. They must be highly conscious of all details and the accuracy of the accounting information they wish to use. Reliance must not be placed on the trust and judgment of the producer of such accounting information.

Users of accounting information are expected to possess some degree of amiable disposition. They should be agreeable and congenial to the producers of accounting information's main motive of faithful representations of facts unless otherwise proven to the contrary in applying analytical ability skills.

Users of accounting information must possess a high degree of driverability trait. In essence they should have a focus (goal) with which to direct and force the producers of accounting information to produce and make available complete, verifiable and neutral information for accurate decision making.

Users of accounting information must possess high degree of vision and suggestive capabilities. In other words, they should be able read between the lines in terms of intention of the producer of accounting information and the quality of the information provided. This is about reading the mind of the producer through understanding his emotional experience rather than the impression given by the information itself. All that glisters is not gold.

4. Conclusions and Recommendations

In examining and discussing the behavioral aspects of accounting issues, certain conclusions can be drawn from the previous sections:

- That research in behavioral aspects of accounting has evolved over time, with differing objectives and focus, related to the phases of its development. The current focus is on diagnostic ability (problem identification) especially in the auditing domain.
- That, producers of accounting information sometimes mislead the users of such information. Several motives could be responsible for the misrepresentation, which includes upward manipulation of income and improved investor perception
- Falsification of financial statements has led to a high incidence of corporate failure. This has been attributed to management fraud resulting from insider activities committed with the intent to deceive the users of financial information.
- Above all, the behavior of producers of accounting information is tied to the four major aspects of quality of financial information. It could best be understood through a better comprehension of the major behavioral traits inherent in the user/ producer of accounting information relationship.

Based on these conclusions, the following recommendations are hereby proffered.

- Users of accounting information should strive to gain a good understanding of the fundamental behavioral traits in accounting in order to be able to use this accounting information with a high degree of caution and utility.
- Users of accounting information must possess a high degree of analytical ability to enable them to collect and review relevant

accounting information. They must be highly conscious of all details and the accuracy of the accounting information they wish to use.

- Users of accounting information are expected to possess some degree of amiable disposition. They should be agreeable and congenial to the producers of accounting information main motive of faithful representations of facts.
- Users of accounting information must possess high degree of driverability trait. In essence they should have a focus (goal) with which to direct and force the producers of accounting information to produce and make available complete, verifiable and neutral information.
- Users of accounting information must possess high degree of vision and suggestive capabilities. In other words, they should be able read between the lines in terms of intention of the producer of accounting information and the quality of the information provided.
- Above all, accountants and managers must place ALLAH first in the discharge of their duties. They must allow their conscience and the teaching of their religion to guide their conduct. This will impact positively in eliminating sharp practices committed by these key individuals, and reduce the high incidence of corporate failures.

References

Abbot, J.L., Park, Y., Parker, S. (2000), "The effects of audit committee activity and independence on corporate fraud", *Managerial Finance,* Vol. 26 No.11, pp.55-67.

Abdolmohammadi, J.M., Owhoso, D.V. (2000), "Auditors' ethical sensitivity and the assessment of the likelihood of fraud", *Managerial Finance,* Vol. 26 No.11, pp.21-32.

Amir, E. and Ziv, A. (1997), Recognition, disclosure, or delay: Timing the adoption of SFAS no 106, Journal of Accounting Research 35, 61–81.

Beasley, M. (1996), "An empirical analysis of the relation between board of director composition and financial statement fraud", *The Accounting Review,* Vol. 71 No.4, pp.443-66.

Beasley, S.M., Carcello, J.V., Hermanson, D.R. (1999), *Fraudulent Financial Reporting: 1987-1997: An Analysis of US Public Companies,* Research Report, .

Beneish, M.D. (1999), "Incentives and penalties related to earnings overstatements that violate GAAP", *The Accounting Review*, Vol. 74 No.4, pp.425-57.

Bonner S.E. (1998). Fraud type and auditor litigation. An analysis of SEC accounting and auditing enforcement releases (Eds),*The Accounting Review*, Vol. 73 No.4, pp.503-32.

Burgstahler, D. and Dichev, I. (1997), Earnings management to avoid earnings decreases and losses, Journal of Accounting and Economics 24, 99–126.

Chan, K., Jegadeesh, N.and Lakonishok, J. (2000), Earnings quality and stock returns: The evidence from accruals, University of Illinois. USA

Comer, J.M. (1998), *Corporate Fraud*, 3rd ed., Gower Publishing, Aldershot, .

DeGeorge, F., Patel, J. and Zeckhauser, R. (1999), Earnings manipulations to exceed thresholds, Journal of Business 71, 1–34.

Eining, M.M., Jones, D.R., Loebbecke, J.K. (1997), "Reliance on decision aids: an examination of auditors' assessment of management fraud", *Auditing: A Journal of Practice and Theory*, Vol. 16 No.2, pp.1-19.

Elliot, R., and Willingham, J. (1980), *Management Fraud: Detection and Deterrence*, Petrocelli, New York, NY, .

Fanning, M.K., Cogger, K.O. (1998), "Neural detection of management fraud using published financial data", *International Journal of Intelligent Systems in Accounting, Finance and Management*, Vol. 7 No.1, pp.21-41.

Green, B.P., Choi, J.H. (1997), "Assessing the risk of management fraud through neural-network technology", *Auditing: A Journal of Practice and Theory*, Vol. 16 No.1, pp.14-28.

Hand, J., Hughes, P. and Sefcik, S. (1990), Insubstance defeasances - Security price reaction and motivations, Journal of Accounting and Economics 13, 47–89.

Hansen, J.V., McDonald, J.B., Messier, W.F., Bell, T.B. (1996), "A generalized qualitative-response model and the analysis of management fraud", *Management Science*, Vol. 42 No.7, pp.1022-32.

Higson, A. (1999), "Why is management reticent to report fraud? An exploratory study", *22nd Annual Congress of European Accounting Association*, Bordeaux, .

Pincus, M. and Wasley, C.(1994), The incidience of accounting changes and characteristics of firms making accounting changes, Accounting Horizons 8, 1–24.

Sabari, M. H., (2004), A Comparative Analysis of Corporate Reporting in Nigeria and the United States., Proceedings of the Second National Conference on Ethical Issues in Accounting: Prudence , Transparency and Accountability Vol. 2.,pp187-199

Summers, S.L., Sweeney, J.T. (1998), "Fraudulently misstated financial statements and insider trading: an empirical analysis", *The Accounting Review*, Vol. 73 No.1, pp.131-46.

Vanasco, R. R. (1998), "Fraud auditing", *Managerial Auditing Journal*, Vol. 13 No.1, pp.4-71.

Wallace, W.A. (1995), *Auditing*, South-Western College Publishing, Cincinnati, OH., .

Wells, J.T. (1997), *Occupational Fraud and Abuse*, Obsidian Publishing, Austin, TX., .

Worthy, F.S. (1984), "Manipulating profits: how it's done?", *Fortune*, Vol. 25 pp.50-4.

Xie, H. (2001), The mispricing of abnormal accruals, Accounting Review 76.

Chapter 15

Equity Theories and Objectives of Financial Reporting

Aliyu Sulaiman Kantudu

Introduction

In modern economic societies, economic activities are conducted by companies instead of proprietorship, partnership or small enterprises. The change in size is coupled with change in the objective of business enterprises and public perception of the role of these institutions. Social responsibility of the corporation has gained increase attention and there is therefore a need to orient the conceptual and structure of framework of accounting to accord wider responsibility of modern corporations. This is so, because the enterprise interfaces with the owners in the owners' equity accounts.

Consequently, several deductive theories have developed over time, which attempted to depict the relationship between enterprises and owners and are found useful in interpreting nonlegal rights and interests in the owners' equity accounts as well as in determining certain component of income (Wolk, Francis and Tearney, 1991). The theories which, explain the focus that financial reporting of an enterprise should take are referred to the equity theories (proprietary, entity, residual equity, fund, commander and enterprise). While the proprietary theory views the owners and the firm as identical, entity conceives the business enterprise as an entity or institution in its own right, with the firm and its owners as separate beings. The residual equity on the other hand, recognizes only the equity shareholders as the recipient of the accounting information for decision making. However, under the fund theory, interest is on social control agencies (government agencies) and the overall process of credit extension and investment. The commander theory focuses on management. Lastly, the enterprise theory focuses on all the stakeholders or interested participants in an organization.

However, accounting standards setting bodies whether national or international, in setting accounting standards focus their attention and dwell their standards to some overall objectives of financial reporting so that the standards satisfy the characteristics of being coherent, meaningful and relevant. Thus, the issues usually raised are whether the objectives of financial reporting can adequately be defined without relating these objectives to specific user groups? Do users have different needs with respect to the nature of the reported information and/or with respect to the extent of that information or not? (Wolk, Tearney and Dodd, 2001) Financial Reporting therefore restricts itself to information in a normal set of financial statements, that is, a balance sheet, a statement of income, and a statement of retained earnings, together with various footnotes and supporting schedules. Notes and supplementary schedules may contain additional information that is relevant to the needs of users about the items in the balance sheet and income statement, such as disclosures about the risks and uncertainties affecting the enterprise and any resources and obligations not recognized in the balance sheet (IASC, 1989). Although financial statements may include information about plans, new products, projected capital expenditures, and the like, this is generally presented in such a way that it is definitely separated from the ordinary financial statements (Mautz and Sharaf, 1961). Fundamental questions are how much information and what form of presentation are necessary to enable users to form opinions and take decisions which are competent to them (Flint, 1982).

One of the tasks of accounting therefore is to reduce information overload contained in the company's financial statement to manageable and understandable proportions. On the other hand, the summarization and condensation may be carried to such an extreme that useful comparisons and distinctions are lost or concealed. Obviously too much or too little detail may be harmful (Mautz and Sharaf, 1961and Kantudu 2005). Flint (1982); and Hendriksen and Van Breda, 1998) state that the fundamental questions in financial reporting are from which users' standpoint have the accounts to be considered and what level of understanding is to be assumed on the part of those who have to form opinions and take decisions. Thus, one could not be strong this, is because, there seems to be no state of opposition existing between the real economic interests of different user groups (Troberg and Ekholm, 1995).

Therefore, information that is provided to owners of capital as a basis for their capital-allocation decisions is also relevant to other users. The interests of all users in information about an enterprise have economic dimensions and should therefore be satisfied by such information which is necessary for establishing the enterprise's intrinsic value.

Although, Wolk. Tearney and Dodd (2001) note that the equity theories, previously, received considerable attention, today they play secondary role to newer, empirical research approach. The problem with the equity theories according to Wolk's thesis is that, the relationship between the firm and its owners, while important, does not really provide a complete enough base from which to define and interpret all enterprise events. However, other writers in their attempt to find relevance to the equity theories in financial reporting advocated for the selection and consistent application of one equity theory by the firm (Merino, 1993). It is against this background that, this study is conducted with a view to determine whether or not the equity theories find relevance in today's business setting.

For the purpose of this paper the method of analysis adopted is descriptive analysis. The study, thus, relies heavily on the use of secondary data, whereby text books, journal articles, internet, etc provides material for the study.

The main objective of this paper therefore is to examine the equity theories in the light of objective of financial reporting as set by accounting standards setting bodies, in order find out the relevance or otherwise of the equity theories in today's business arrangements. In order to achieve this novel objective the paper is divided into three sections. Section one is an introduction. Section two presents a conceptual framework and literature review. Section three contains the summary and conclusions drawn from the results.

Literature Review and Conceptual Framework

The Concept of Equity Theories

The equity theories of accounting are normative-deductive theories based on the relationship between the firm and its owners. These theories were developed in the early eighteen and nineteen century to provide consistent deductive basis for all accounting transactions and events, by taking a view of the enterprise i.e. the relationship between the firm and its owners. The theories were expected to be of use to accounting standard setters. The equity theories proposed so far include: (a) the proprietary theory; (b) the entity theory; (c) the residual equity theory; (e) the fund theory; (f) the commander theory; and (g) the enterprise theory. The theories are briefly explained in the next subsections.

The Proprietary Theory

In the proprietary theory the owner is at the center of interest. That is, the proprietary theory assumes that the owners and the firm are virtually identical. The proprietary theory, attempted to bring the absentee owner to center stage when viewing the enterprise (Merino, 1993). Under this theory, the absentee ownership claims were legitimized by measuring profits available for distribution to owners rather than the notion that earnings and capital belonged to the firm itself. Thus net income accrues directly to the owners, that is, it represents an increase in the wealth of the proprietors. The proprietorship is considered to be the net value of the business to the owners, it is thus, a wealth concept (Hendriksen, 1982).

In the expanded form, the shareholder owns all the firm's liabilities, and the difference between their assets and liabilities represents the shareholder's interest or equity and as such the balance sheet equation would be: Assets – (Liabilities = Owners equities. This means that, income represents the owners increase in both net assets (assets minus liabilities) and owners' equities arising from operations during the period.

As promising as this theory seems to be, it was criticized of having vary narrow scope of applicability, in accounting theory (Hendriksen, 1982). It is thus adaptable best to the single proprietorship form of organization, because in this form there is generally a personal relationship. The proprietary theory is not so readily applicable to the corporate form of organization as it is to the single proprietorship and the partnership. Under such uni-stranded model of firm-owner relationship, the relevant information system is simple informal, all focus is on what belong to, contributed by or distributed to the proprietor.

The Entity Theory

Under the entity theory, business enterprises are generally conceived as an entity or institution in its own right. It is a separate legal being with power to own assets and to create liability.

Consequently, the entire assets including the net income belong to the firm while creditors and equity holders are treated as investors in the firms' assets, with different rights and claims. The balance sheet equation is given by: (Assets = (Equities (Including liabilities). However, Paton and Littleton (1940) observe that "it has become almost axiomatic that the business accounts and statement are those of the entity rather than those of the proprietor, partners, investor or other parties or group concerned. One implication of entity theory is that accounting information is of very little relevance to those who contract with the firm.

Residual Equity Theory

The residual equity theory is based on the premise that, since the equity holders are ultimate risk takers within an enterprise, their interest in the firm in the firm should be paramount. This is because they serve as a buffer or protector for all groups with prior claims on the firm, such bondholder and preferred stock. The underlying assumption of this theory is that information appropriate for decision-making purposes such as that helpful in predicting cash flows must be supplied to the residual equity holders. In the residual equity theory, changes in asset valuation, changes in income and in retained earnings, and changes in interest of other equity holders are all reflected in the residual equity of the common stockholders. The specific equities include the claims of creditors and the equities of preferred stockholders. The balances sheet equation would be:

Assets = E specific Equities (liabilities and preferred stock) = Residual Equity

The equity of the common stockholders in the balance sheet should be presented separately from the equities of preferred stockholders and other specific equity holders. According to Hendriksen (1982, 457), the residual equity point of view is a concept somewhere between the proprietary theory and the entity theory.

The objective of the residual equity approach is to provide better information to common stockholders for making investment decisions. In a going-concern situation, the current value of common stock is dependent primarily upon the expectation of future dividends. Future dividends are dependent upon expectations of total receipts less specific contractual obligations, payments to specific equity holders, and requirements for reinvestment. Since financial statements are not generally prepared on the basis of possible liquidation, the information provided regarding the residual equity should be useful in predicting possible future dividends to common stockholders including liquidation dividends (Hendriksen, 1982).

The Fund Theory

The fund theory came about as a result of the inherent weaknesses and inconsistencies of both the entity and proprietary theories (Vatter, 1947). Under this theory, a fund is simply a group of assets and related obligations devoted a particular purpose, which may or may not be that of generating income (Goldberg, 1965). Thus, fund theory, is most applicable to the governmental and not-for-profit making organizations where endowment funds, encumbrances, and special asset groups often devoted to specific and separate purposes prevail (Wolk, Tearney and Dodd, 2001). The balance sheet equation, in the fund theory is given by summation of assets equals summation of restriction of assets (Assets = Restrictions of Assets).

The equation is so, because, the restriction on the assets arise from both liabilities and invested capital. Thus, the invested capital has to maintain intact unless specific authority for partial or total liquidation is sought.

The Commander Theory

The commander theory's focus is on management, that is, the commander of the firm's resources. This theory was very much concerned with the fact that management needs information to carry out its control and planning functions on behalf of owners. Hence, the commander theory might really be viewed as being applicable to management accounting rather than financial accounting, though, the manager in his fiduciary role can transpose the commander view to the investor (Clark, 1993).

The Enterprise Theory

The enterprise theory, which is of recent origin, is based on a broader concept than either proprietary or entity theory. According to the enterprise theory, accounting may be thought of as a social theory of accounting, that is, the firm is considered to be a social institution operated for the benefit of many interested groups. From an accounting point of view, this would mean that the responsibility of proper reporting would not only extend to stockholders and creditors, but also many other groups and the general public. This concept of the firm is, according to Hendriksen (1982), most applicable to the large modern corporation that has been obliged to consider the effect of its actions on various groups and on society as a whole.

Enterprise Theory vs Proprietary and Entity Theories

Since the fund and commander theories are found to be adoptable to government/not-for-profit organizations and sole proprietorship/partnership respectively, and the residual equity which focus only on the firm. This section would be devoted to appraising the enterprise theory (the newer concept) against the proprietary and entity theories.

The deficiencies of both proprietary theory and entity theory as a framework for analyzing business behaviour were summarized by Vatter (1947) thus:

> Neither the proprietary theory nor the entity theory is a wholly satisfying frame of reference for accounting. Each is vulnerable in that is it adopts a personality as is its focus of attention. The difference between them is mostly whether the person (for whom the book are kept and to whom the reports are made) is the proprietor or proprietor in their human selves, or whether real people must be viewed abstract or in the guise of a fictional entity, corporate or otherwise. The weakness in these personalized bases for accounting is that the content of accounting reports will tend to be affected by personal analysis, and issue will be decided not by considering the nature of the problem but upon some extension of personality. To reach or support conclusion that are for the most part mere expediencies.

In other wards the proprietary theory and entity theory trivialize issue about business enterprises-decision processes in business organization are overlooked, and the importance of information system to modern organization structure is misplaced as there is a failure to recognize the diversity of uses of such information. They also fail to notice emergence of large public owned corporations where management no longer considers the shareholders as the only beneficiaries from corporate existence and survival. Consequently, Suojanen (1954) suggested that in the case of larger corporation an enterprises theory would be more appropriate. He explained the Enterprises theory as follows:-

The enterprises is conceives as a decision-making centre for those who are participants, however fleeting or intimate may be their contact with it is as an organization. The decision made in the enterprises affects, in one way or another, the stockholders, the employee the creditors, the customers, various governmental and social control agencies such as the security and Exchange commission and the new York stock Exchange and the most ephemeral of the group Known as the 'public'

The Enterprises theory is based on a broader concept than either proprietary or entity theory. Under Enterprises theory, a business enterprise is seen as an organization which is an embodiment of decision making process. Also since the decision organizations affect every participant are themselves decision- makes thus a large corporation is viewed as clearing house through which transfer payment are arrange among participants and conditions for organizational survival are specified in terms of the methods of motivating organization participants (Cyert and March 1963). The participants are human being vision and perception and therefore are frequently in the processes of taking decision one of which is the decision to belong' to the enterprise. Thus, the enterprise theory is not oriented toward a particular interest in an organization but interest of all participants. Moreover, enterprise theory provides a useful base for a study of the role of the information system in an organization. Thomas (1980) describes this important link thus:

> Taking the a foregoing perspective, in which shareholders are only one of a number of groups who provide resources or contribute towards continued accounts as being to provide information that enable existing and potential participants to decide whether or not they wish too participate with organization.

Furthermore, the link between enterprise theory and accounting information is greatly enriched when one look at the objectives for published accounting reports. Rappaport (1964) has enunciated four basic objectives for external corporate reporting as:

- the management of large business corporations have a reporting obligation segments of society affected by their decision i.e. investors, employees, customers, supplies, local communities and the public at large.
- Those groups with a legitimate interest in the corporation should be providing with information essential to arriving at rational judgments concerning the equitable sharing corporate benefits.
- In the interest of economy progress, these groups which are responsible allocating resources in our economy should be provide with information which will promote efficient allocation.
- In the interest of sustaining our basic values, information which is likely to influence socially desirable behavior and discourage undesirable behaviour should be reported e.g. calling attention to monopoly profits to preserve pluralism in the industry sector of our economy or calling attention to environment destruction by and economic operator

The enterprise theory, therefore, broadness the information obligation of firms, that is, from satisfying the shareholders to that of satisfying all member in the organization who participate in the creation of it wealth as well members and institutions who are affected by the externalities of organization's activities e.g. the public.

The equity theories of accounting as mentioned earlier are normatively –deductive theories, which seek to explain the relationship between enterprises and their owners, and could provide interesting insights into some accounting problem. However, they were criticized for being limited in scope and not sufficiently global to permit their intensive use in solving fundamental accounting problems (Wolk, Tearney and Dodd, 2001). The next subsection of the paper focuses on the objectives of financial reporting.

Objectives of Financial Reporting

The starting point for any field of study is to set forth its boundaries and determine its objectives (Hendriksen and Van Breda, 1998).Thus, objectives of financial reporting is one of important areas to consider in the general framework of the concept of financial reporting. Buzby (1978) also notes that any rational development of accounting requires a well conceived, clearly delineated and generally accepted set of objectives. He further argued that it is the objectives that established the purpose of accounting and defined the limits of its boundaries.

Similarly, Glautier and Underdown (1986), notes that the failure to establish a conceptual framework for financial reporting purposes rests precisely in the failure to direct financial reporting practices toward the needs of external users. Ellis (1972) and Buzby (1978) stated that, currently, no single set of objectives commands consensus among accountants and users. However, there is reasonable wide consensus that, one of the prime, albeit broad objectives of accounting is to provide relevant information to users for the purpose of making economic decisions relative to the reporting enterprise. He further said that, there seems to be a growing awareness that many financial statement users seek information that can aid then in the prediction of key enterprise variables, such as earning power.

Hendriksen (1977) argue that, in addition to emphasis on the specific needs of users of financial statements, discussion of accounting objectives should focus on one of the three levels of accounting theory thus: (a) syntactic, (b) semantic and (c) behavioural. Consequently, Arthur Young and Company in Hendriksen (1977) noted that the primary objective of financial statements should be to communicate reliable financial information concerning an enterprise business transaction, including: the resulting assets, liabilities, and ownership equities; and indication of profit or loss there from (derived by deducting costs and expenses from related revenues). He further notes that ... the overall purpose of financial statements is to communicate information concerning the nature and value of the economic resources of a business enterprise, the interests of creditors and the equity of owners in the economic resources, and the changes in the nature and value of those resources from period to period.

Having viewed the objectives of financial reporting from the point of view of authors, efforts would now be geared towards the standards setters and review their perception of the objectives vis-à-vis the equity theories.

Appraisal of the Objectives of Financial Reporting of some Countries

In the United States, the objectives of financial reporting are defined in the Statement of Financial Accounting Concepts (SFAC) No. 1 as to provide information useful for making economic decisions (FASB 2005, art. 34). Financial reporting is expected to provide information about an enterprise's financial performance during a period and about how management of an enterprise has discharged its stewardship responsibility to owners FASB (2005, para. 50). This is because it is the owners who reappoint or replace management the (stewardship objective).

Looking at these two objectives, the first is defined more closely as information useful to investors and creditors and other users in making rational investment, credit, and similar decisions and for predicting, comparing, and evaluating potential cash flows to them in terms of amount, timing, and related uncertainty. Thus, by bringing investors and creditors side by side may rather be interpreted as a support for the entity theory, or potentially the residual equity theory. The objective of the residual equity approach therefore is to provide better information to common stockholders for making investment decisions. The information provided regarding the residual equity according to Hendriksen and Van Breda, (1998) is useful in predicting possible future dividends to common stockholders including liquidation dividends. The second objectives in line with FASB, lends supports to the proprietary theory. What is very clear as in the USA's standards is that the owners are at the center of interest.

However, in Britain, which is said to be characterized, by something called 'managerial capitalism' (Bryer, 1993). That is, management was separated from the owners because company ownership was characterized by passive investments, that is, lack of dominant or controlling owner(s). As a consequence, financial reporting was carried out more on management terms than owner or any other user group terms. Consequently, the case for statutory regulation and disclosure of financial information during the nineteenth century was defeated on the ground of 'confidentiality' (Bryer, 1993).

In Britain, the objective of financial statements, according to Accounting Standards Board (1991, art. 12-13), is to provide information about the financial position, performance and financial adaptability of an enterprise that is useful to a wide range of users in making economic decisions. ASB states further that financial statements prepared for this purpose meet the common needs of most users and went a head to itemized the users as present and potential investors, employees, lenders, suppliers, and other trade creditors, customers, governments and their agencies and the public. These users use financial statements to satisfy some of their different needs for information (ASB, 1991, art. 9). In listing a wide range of users, ASB's position seems to support the enterprise theory, according to which the firm is considered to be a social institution operated for the benefit of many interested groups. This means that the responsibility of proper reporting does not only extend to stockholders and creditors but also to other groups and the general public.

While, the second objective of financial statements as stated by ASB is that financial statements should show the results of the stewardship of management, that is, the accountability of management for the resources entrusted to it. This objective seems to contradict the enterprise theory and rather lends support for the proprietary theory. This position is also in line with the requirements of the UK's Companies Act of 1976 that, the accounts are to be laid before the company in a general meeting. The management has a general obligation to report on their stewardship to the stockholders and guard the interest of the stockholders. A similar view was expressed in the Report of the Inflation Accounting Committee (1975) in which it was stated that it was a "traditional tenet of accounting that the main objective of published financial statements is to enable the directors to give an account of their stewardship of the shareholders' funds to the shareholders". On a whole, one can say that the focus of British as it relates to objectives of financial report is on the proprietary.

Similarly, in the European Union countries, the objectives of financial reporting, according to the Fourth European Community Council Directive (art.2), is that the annual accounts shall give a true and fair view of the company's assets, liabilities, financial position and profit or loss. The composition of the annual accounts is defined as the balance sheet, the profit and loss account and the notes on the accounts, and it is stated that these documents shall constitute a composite whole. A cursory look at this objective reveals that no specific user group is singled out in the Directive. The conclusion to be drawn is that the meaning of the 'true and fair view' convention should primarily be determined on the basis of the information needs of the owners. Furthermore, 'a true and fair view' to the owners is not necessarily different from 'a true and fair view' to other users.

In contrast, the Finnish accounting thinking has been largely influenced by Professor Martti Saario with respect to determining the result (profit/loss) in the income statement (Gray, 2000). That is to say, the business enterprise is viewed as a mean for the owner to achieve profits. The primary objective of financial reporting in Finland is thus defined as determining the net income (result) of the accounting period and owners′ equity, specifically the amount of owners′ equity which can be distributed (Committee on the Renewal of the Accounting Act 1990, 91).As a consequence, the objective of the income statement calculation is to determine the amount of profit which can be distributed, that is, the result of the accounting period is not calculated for the sake of determining the profit of the enterprise but to determine how much profit the owner has made on his business. This view constitutes a strong support for the proprietary theory.

However, Nigeria, like many other countries in the world, has its local standards setting body, the Nigeria Accounting Standard Board, which is shouldered with the responsibility of issuing out standards. The objectives of financial reporting, is contained in SAS 2 i.e. information to be disclosed in financial statements. SAS 2(Part 4(10): 1985) states the objective of financial reporting as the provision of all accounting information that will assist users to assess the financial liquidity, profitability and viability of a reporting entity should be disclosed and presented in a logical, clear and understandable manner. Similarly, Part 2 (1) went on to list the following as users of accounting information: firms, organizations or enterprises, individuals, financial institutions or group of investors, managers, employees and customers, governments and regulatory bodies and quasi-government establishments. Thus, the information expected to be provided in financial statements are those that are quantitative and qualitative in nature to aid their users in making informed economic decisions (SSAS 2: Part 1). Impliedly; this means that there are no major differences in the information needs between different user groups. Furthermore, listing a wide range of users seems to support the broad form of the enterprise theory, that is, accounting is thought of as a social theory of accounting, that is, the firm is considered to be a social institution operated for the benefit of many interested groups.

The International Accounting Standards Board (IASB) being the apex accounting body, issue out standards which member nations are expected to comply with. In its framework for the preparation and presentation of financial statements, IASB (2005: article 12) states that the objective of financial statements is to provide information about the financial position, performance and changes in financial position of an enterprise that is useful to a wide range of users in making economic decisions. The standard went further to state that financial statements prepared for this purpose meet the common needs of most users, and the economic decisions that are taken by users require an evaluation of the ability of an enterprise to generate cash and cash equivalents and of the timing and certainty of their generation (IASB, 2005: art. 13, 15). Users in this context are specified by the standards as present and potential investors, employees, lenders, suppliers and other trade creditors, customers, governments and their agencies and the public.

The above can be interpreted to imply that there are no major differences in the information needs between different user groups. Furthermore, listing a wide range of users seems to support the broad form of the enterprise theory, that is, accounting is thought of as a social theory of accounting, that is, the firm is considered to be a social institution operated for the benefit of many interested groups.

In specifying the information needs of different users, IASB (2005: art. 9), however, states that users use financial statements in order to satisfy some of their different needs for information. This makes the impression that the needs for information differ among users, at least to some extent. This leaves the observer somewhat puzzled.

The extent of information to be reported could logically be determined by the needs of the dominant user group and/or the (indirect) payer of that information, that is, typically the owners. This position is indirectly supported by the IASC statement that financial statements also show the results of the stewardship of management, or the accountability of management for the resources entrusted to it. According to IASC (1989, art. 14), those users who wish to assess the stewardship or accountability of management do so in order that they may make economic decisions; these decisions may include, for example, whether to hold or sell their investment in the enterprise or whether to reappoint or replace management. Assuming a non-distress situation, the company acts of most Western industrialized countries provide only the owners with the right to reappoint or replace the management. Therefore, the IASC position can be interpreted as a support for the proprietary theory, that is, the proprietor or owner is at the center of interest. That is, the assets are assumed to be owned by the proprietor, and the liabilities are the proprietor's obligations. Revenues are increases in proprietorship and expenses are decreases.

On the other hand, IASB (2005: art. 103) states that if users are mainly concerned with the operating capability of the enterprise, a physical concept of capital should be used. The operating capability may be of interest to many different users but only the owners have a direct executory power to reappoint or replace management. This supports the proprietary point of view. On the basis of the discussions above, one can conclude that it would be desirable that IASB would be more clear and specific on the issues of reporting objectives and user needs than what is currently is on the ground.

Users of Financial Reports and their Information Needs

Financial reporting is not an end in itself. It is a means of communicating to the users of financial reports information that is useful in making choices among alternative uses of scarce resources. Thus, the objective stems largely from the needs and interests of those users. Potential users of financial reports and their information needs include (IASB, 2005; and FASB, 2006):

Equity investors. Equity investors in an entity are interested in the entity's ability to generate net cash inflows because their decisions relate to the amounts, timing, and uncertainties of those cash flows. To an equity investor, an entity is a source of cash in the form of dividends (or other cash distributions) and increases in the prices of shares or other ownership interests. Equity investors are directly concerned with the ability of the entity to generate net cash inflows and also with how the perception of that ability affects the prices of its equity interests.

Creditors. Creditors, including purchasers of traded debt instruments, provide financial capital to an entity by lending cash (or other assets) to it. Like investors, creditors are interested in the amounts, timing, and uncertainty of an entity's future cash flows. To a creditor, an entity is a source of cash in the form of interest, repayments of borrowings, and increases in the prices of debt securities.

Suppliers. Suppliers provide goods or services rather than financial capital. They are interested in assessing the likelihood that amounts an entity owes them will be paid when due.

Employees. Employees provide services to an entity; employees and their representatives are interested in evaluating the stability, profitability, and growth of their employer. They are interested in information that helps them to assess the entity's continuing ability to pay salaries and wages and to provide incentive payments and retirement and other benefits.

Customers. To its customers, an entity is a source of goods or services. Customers are interested in assessing the entity's ability to continue to provide those goods or services, especially if they have a long-term involvement with, or are dependent on, the entity.

Governments and their agencies and regulatory bodies. Governments and their agencies and regulatory bodies are interested in the activities of an entity because they are in various ways responsible for seeing that economic resources are allocated efficiently. They also need information to help in regulating the activities of entities, determining and applying taxation policies, and preparing national income and similar statistics.

Members of the public. An entity may affect members of the public in a variety of ways. For example, an entity may make a substantial contribution to the local economy by providing employment opportunities, patronizing local suppliers, paying taxes, and making charitable contributions. Financial reporting may assist members of the public and their representatives by providing information about the trends and recent developments in the entity's prosperity and the range of its activities, as well as the entity's ability to continue to undertake those activities.

Given the number of the users as well as their information needs one should expect the financial statements to be of a general purpose consisting of quantitative and qualitative information to aid users in making informed economic decisions.

Summary and Conclusion

This paper, reviews the equity theories and the objectives of financial reporting. Similar, the objectives of financial reporting as set by some countries, including IASB, was also analyzed. The users and the information needs were also highlighted. The paper finds that accounting authorities in most countries and IASB seem to present definitions of the objectives of financial reporting which are very similar to one another. That is, providing information useful for making economic decisions, as one of the principal objectives of financial reporting. With respect to users of financial information, these accounting authorities present a wide range of users which seems to render support for the enterprise theory. The U.S. differs from the others in that investors and creditors are specifically mentioned among the users thus, indicating some support for the entity theory or the residual equity theory. A second principal objective of financial reporting presented by local accounting authorities and IASB is to provide information about the results of the stewardship of management, that is, the accountability of management for the resources entrusted to it. This reporting objective seems to support the proprietary theory view. The guidelines regarding financial reporting and users provided by the local accounting authorities as well as FASB and IASB seem to revolve on the issues of the objectives of financial reporting, user groups, and user needs. Some of the propositions presented seem to support the entity theory or perhaps the residual equity theory, while others support the enterprise theory, or the proprietary theory.

The author is of the opinion that there exists no state of opposition between the real economic interests of different user groups. On the basis that owners of capital in an enterprise are concerned with managing their capital in the best possible way, information with which they are provided as a basis for their capital-allocation decisions is also relevant to other users. The interests of all users in information about an enterprise have economic dimensions and should therefore be satisfied by such information which is necessary for establishing the enterprise's intrinsic value. Last, the equity theories which were developed some decades back, though, very relevant in today's business arrangements, the enterprise theory is found to be more relevant to the current information needs of users of financial reports of entities. Thus, accounting standards setting bodies should pay more attention to the enterprise theory, which is broader in concept, when coming up with the objectives of financial reporting in the future.

References:

FASB (2006): Conceptual Framework for Financial Reporting: Objective of Financial Reporting and Qualitative Characteristics of Decision-Useful Financial Reporting Information Financial Accounting. *Standards Board of the Financial Accounting Foundation* July 6, 401 Merritt 7, Po Box 5116, Norwalk, Connecticut.

Accounting Principles Board (1970) '*Statement No.4: Basic Concepts and Accounting Principles Underlying Financial Statements of Business Enterprises'*. New York: American Institute of Certified Public Accountants.

Accounting Standards Board (1991) '*Exposure Draft: Statement of Principles*'. London: The Institute of Chartered Accountants in England and Wales.

Accounting Standards Steering Committee (1975) 'The Corporate Report' - a discussion paper published for comment. London.

Bryer, R.A. (1993) 'The Late Nineteenth-Century Revolution in Financial Reporting: Accounting for the Rise of Investor or Managerial Capitalism', *Accounting, Organizations and Society,* Vol. 18, No. 7/8: 649-690.

European Economic Community (1978) Fourth Council Directive. Brussels: EEC.

International Accounting Standards Committee (1989) *Framework for the Preparation and Presentation of Financial Statements*. London: IASC.

Financial Accounting Standards Board (1978) '*Statements of Financial Accounting Concepts for Business Enterprises No. 1: Objectives of Financial Reporting by Business Enterprises'*. Stamford, Connecticut: FASB.

Flint, D. (1982) True and Fair View in Company Accounts. London: The Institute of Chartered Accountants of Scotland: Gee & Co (Publishers) Limited.

Hendriksen, E.S. (1982) Accounting Theory. Homewood, Illinois: Irwin.

The Sandilands Report (1975) *Inflation Accounting,* Cmnd 6225, London: HMSO.

Buzby S.L. (1982). The Nature of Adequate Disclosure *In* McCullers and Schroeder, *Accounting theory,* John Wiley and Sons Inc. PP550-656.

Ellis R.G. (1972). On a View from a Financial Analyst *Corporate Financial Reporting, The Issues, the Objectives and some New Proposals* Edited by Rappaport and Revise. Commerce cleaning House Inc. N.Y. PP.57.

Epstein, B. J. and A.A. Mirza (2002). *Interpretation and Application of International Accounting Standards,* Wiley IAS, John Wiley and Sons, INC. New Jersey.

Glautier M.W.E. and Underdown (1986). *Accounting Theory and Practice* ELBS/Pitman publishing London PP.426-447.

Hendriksen, E. A. and F. M. Van Breda (1992). *Accounting Theory,* McGraw-Hill International Edition.

Moonitz, (1961). "On the Basis postulates of Accounting. *Accounting." Research Study* No.1 New York AICPA PP.27

NASB (1984). *Disclosure of Accounting Policies (SAS 1),* Published by the Nigerian Accounting Standard Board.

NASB (1985). *Information to be disclosed in Financial Statement (SAS 2),* Published by the Nigerian Accounting Standard Board.

OftenHeimer J.L. (1999). "Cutting financial Reports down to size". *Journal of Accountancy* March. PP.45-47.

Wood, F. and Sangster A. (2002). *Business Accounting 2,* Ninth Edition Pearson Education Limited London, England.

Robert, P. (1999). "Prospective financial statements a glimpse of future". *Journal of Accountancy* July, PP.35-40.

Revsine, L., D. W. Collins, and Johnson. W. B. (2002). *Financial Reporting and Analysis.* Pearson Education Inc. Upper Saddle River, New Jersey.

Wolk, H., M. Tearney, and Y. J. Dodd (2002). *Accounting Theory: A Conceptual and Institutional Approach,* South–western Thomson earning U.S.A.

Troberg, P and Ekholm, B (1995): Objectives of Financial Reporting: Are User Needs Different? *Working paper* Swedish School of Economics and Business Administration

NSE (2004). The NSE Daily Official Listing.

Nobes, C. (1999). Towards a General Model of the Reasons for International Differences in Financial Reporting, *In*: *International Accounting and Comparative Financial Reporting*, edited by Nobes, C. (1999), Edward Elgar Publishing Limited, Cheltenham.

Nobes, C.W., and Parker, RH. (1998). *Comparative International Accounting*, 5th, London, Prentice Hall.

O'Brien, P.C. (1998). "Discussion of International Variation in Accounting Measurement Rules and Analysts' Earning Forecast Errors." Journal of Business Finance and Accounting Vol. 25 No, (9 and 8), pp 1249-1254.

Rappaport, A. (1964)."Establishing objective for published corporate Accounting Report." *Accounting Review,* April. PP. 99 and 951.

Rappaport A. and Learner E. (1969).A Framework for financial reporting by diversified companies In McCullers and Schroeder (1982) *Accounting theory*. John Wiley and Sons Ltd. PP.656.

Soper F.J., and Dolphin, R. (1964). "Readability and Corporate Annual Reports." *The Accounting Review* April. PP.358-362.

Smith, J.E. and Smith, N.P. (1971). "On Readability: A measure of the performance of the communication function of financial Reporting". *The Accounting Review*. July. PP.552-561.

Selected Bibliography

Abbot, J.L., Park, Y. and Parker, S. (2000), "The effects of audit committee activity and independence on corporate fraud", *Managerial Finance,* Vol. 26, No.11, pp.55-67

Abdel Khalik, A. R. and Ajyinka, B. B. (974), *Empirical Research in Accounting: A Methodological View Point,* Sarasota: AAA.

Abdel-Magid, M. F. (1981),"The theory of Islamic banking: Accounting Implications", *The International Journal of Accounting Education and Research* 17 (1): 79-102.

Abdolmohammadi, J.M. and Owhoso, D.V. (2000), "Auditors' ethical sensitivity and the assessment of the likelihood of fraud", *Managerial Finance,* Vol. 26 No.11, pp.21-32.

Accounting Principles Board (1970), '*Statement No.4: Basic Concepts and Accounting Principles Underlying Financial Statements of Business Enterprises'*. New York: American Institute of Certified Public Accountants.

Accounting Standards Board (1991), *'Exposure Draft: Statement of Principles'*,London: The Institute of Chartered Accountants in England and Wales.

Achleitner, A. (2000), International-Accounting-Standards: in Campbell, J. E., Hermanson, H. M. and

McAllister, J. P. (eds), "The High Road: Obstacles to International Accounting Standards Convergence", *The CPA Journal* ,May.

Adams, R.A. (2001).*Public Sector Accounting and Finance made Simple,* Lagos: Corporate Publishers Ventures.

Adams, H. L. (1981), "Should the Big 8 Teach Communication Skills?" *Management* Accounting, PP37-40.

Adelberg, A. H. (1982), "An Empirical Evaluation of the Communication of Authoritative Pronouncements in Accounting", *Accounting and Finance,*pp73-94.

Adelberg, A. H. and Farrelly, G. E. (1989), "Measuring the Meaning of Financial Statement Terminology: A Psycholinguistic Approach", *Accounting and Finance.*

Adelberg, A. H. (1979a), "Narrative Disclosures Contained in Financial Reports: Means of Communication or Manipulation?", *Accounting and Business Research*, pp 179-190.

Adelberg, A. H. (1979b), "A Methodology for Measuring the Understandability of Financial Report Messages", *Journal of Accounting Research*, pp565-592

Ahmad, H.A (2003), "A review of Ethical Concepts in relation to the work of State Accountant General: A Case Study of Kano State, in Dandago, K.I. and Tanko, A.I.(eds): *Proceedings of the 1st National Conference on Ethical Issues in Accounting,* organized by the Department of Accounting, Bayero University, Kano-Nigeria.

Ali, A. and Hwang, L. S. (2000), "Country-specific factors related to financial reporting and the value relevance of accounting data", Journal *of Accounting Research,* 38 (1), 1 – 21, Spring. June.

American Accounting Association (1971), "Report of the Committee on the Behavioural Science Content of the Accounting Curriculum", Accounting Review Supplement, 46.

American Accounting Association (1977), Committee on Concepts and Standards for External Financial Reports, Statement on Accounting Theory and Theory Acceptance, American Accounting Association

Amir, E. and Ziv, A. (1997), "Recognition, disclosure, or delay: Timing the adoption of SFAS No 106", Journal of Accounting Research 35, 61–81.

Anao A.R. (1989), An *Introduction to Financial Accounting,* Ikeja: Longman Nigeria Ltd

Andrews, J. D. and Koester, R. J. (1979), "Communication Difficulties as Perceived by the Accounting Profession and Professors of Accounting", *Journal of Business Communication*, Pp 33-42

Anthony, R. N., and Reece, J. S. (1975), Management Accounting*: Text and Cases*, Homewood, IL: Irwin. United Kingdom.

Anthony, R.N. and Reese, J.S. (1983): *Accounting: Text and Cases,* Irwin Publishers, USA.

Anyafo, A.M. (2004),"Transparency and Accountability in Intergovernmental Financial Relations: A Literary Essay on State-Local Governments Joint Account Operation in Nigeria", *Bayero International Journal of Accounting Research.*1 (1), 24-35.

Asaolu T.O., Oladele, P.O. and Oladoyin, A.M. (2005), *"An assessment of the ethical values of honesty and integrity in accounting establishments, The case of Obafemi Awolowo University (O.A.U)"*; in Dandago K.I and K.T. Hamid (eds), *Honesty and Integrity,* Department of Accounting, Bayero University, Kano, Nigeria, Gidan Dabino Publishers.

Avard, S. L. and White, J. H. (1986), "Readability Study of Principles of Financial Management Text Books", *Journal of Financial Education,* Pp53-63

Baffa, A.U. (2004), "Issues on Principles of Transparency and Accountability in Nigeria", *Bayero International Journal of Accounting and Research. Vol. 1 Number 1,* pp81 – 86

Bailey, W.T. (1973), "The Realm of Meaning", *Communication, Language and Meaning: Psychological Perspective, in* Miller, G.A.(ed) ,New York: Basic Books.

Bailey, W.T. (1982), "An Appraisal of Research Designs Used to Investigate the Information Content of Audit Reports", *Accounting Review* V.57:141-146.

Baker, H. E. III, and Kare, D. D. (1992), "Relationship Between Annual Report Readability and Corporate Financial Performance", *Management Research News 4,* pp1-4.

Barker, R. G. (2003), "Global accounting is coming", Harvard *Business Review,* April 24 – 25.

Barle, A.A. and Means, G.C. (1932), *"The Modern Corporation and Private Property",* in Hendriksen, E.S. and Van Breda, M.F. (eds), *Accounting Theory: Text and Reading,* New York: McGraw Hill, 2nd edition.

Barnett, A., and Leoffler, K. (1979), "Readability of Accounting and Auditing Messages", *Journal of Business Communication, Pp49-59.*

Bean, V. L., and Watanabe, J. E. (1990), "Techniques for Improvement of Communication Skills: accounting Students and Graduates Rate Effectiveness", Accounting *Educators' Journal.* pp 36-45.

Bearer, W. H., Kennelly, J. W and Voss , W. M (1968), "The Predictive Ability as a Criterion for Evaluation of Accounting Data" *Accounting Review,* Sarasota: AAA

Beasley, M. (1996), "An empirical analysis of the relation between board of director composition and financial statement fraud", *The Accounting Review*, Vol. 71 No.4, pp.443-66.

Beasley, S.M., Carcello, J.V. and Hermanson, D.R. (1999), *Fraudulent Financial Reporting: 1987-1997: An Analysis of US Public Companies*, Research Report.

Beaver, W.H. (1989), Financial Reporting: An Accounting Revolution, second edition (EagleWood Cliff, N.J: Prentice-Hall Inc.)

Bedford, N., and Baladouni, V. (1962), "A Communication Theory Approach to Accounting", Accounting *Review*, pp650-659

Belkaou, A. (1993), *Accounting Theory*, Dryden Press, Britain, 3nd Edition

Belkaoui, A. (1978), "Linguistic Relativity in Accounting", Accounting, *Organizations and Society*, pp 97-104.

Belkaoui, A. (1985), "The Professional Linguistic Communication of Accounting Concepts: An Experiment in Sociolinguistics", *Journal of Accounting Research*, volume 18, no. 2. PP362-374

Belkaoui, A. (1995), *"The Linguistic Shaping of Accounting"*, Connecticut: Westport Quorum Books

Belkauoi, A. (1981), *Accounting Theory*, New York: Harcourt Brace Javonvich.

Bello, M.S. (2004), "Usury as an Ethical Problem: The Islamic Banking Perspective", in Dandago, K.I. and Tanko, A.I.(eds), *Proceedings of the 2nd National Conference on Ethical Issues in Accounting*, Organized by the Department of Accounting, Bayero University, Kano-Nigeria

Bello, M.S. (2003), "How Ethical is Accounting Income Smoothing? An Empirical Investigation", *in Dandago, K.I. and Tanko, A.I.(eds), Proceedings of the First National Conference on Ethical Issues in Accounting*, organized by the Department of Accounting Bayero University, Kano-Nigeria, 6-10 January 2003, pp.113-129

Beneish, M.D. (1999), "Incentives and penalties related to earnings overstatements that violate GAAP", *The Accounting Review*, Vol. 74, No.4, pp.425-57

Beynon, M.J., Clatworthy, M.A. and Jones, M.J. (2004), "The prediction of profitability using accounting narratives: a variable precision rough sets approach", *International Journal of Intelligent Systems in Accounting, Finance and Management,* Vol. 12, pp. 227-42.

Bloom, R. (2000), "An analysis of Two vision statements on international accounting standard setting", *The Ohio CPA Journal,* January – March 24-26.

Blumer, H. (1969), *Symbolic Interactionism: Perspective and Method.* Englewood Cliffs, N. J.: Prentice-Hall, Inc.

Bonner, S.E. (1998), "Fraud type and auditor litigation: An analysis of SEC accounting and auditing enforcement releases", *The Accounting Review,* Vol. 73 No.4, pp.503-32.

Bringerg, J. G and Nath, B. (1975), "Implications of Behavioral Science for Managerial Accounting", *Accounting Review* (Jan), Sarasolu :AAA.

Broadbent, J. and Guthrie, J. (1992), "Changes in the public sector: A review of recent 'Alternative' Accounting Research", *Accounting, Auditing & Accountability Journal,* Vol.5, No.2

Brower, B. W. (1993), *"Dispositional Ethical Realism"* Ethics, Vol. 103, No. 2; Chicago, University of Chicago Press

Bryan, S.H. (1997), "Incremental information content of required disclosures contained in management discussion and analysis", *The Accounting Review,* Vol. 72 No. 2, pp. 285-301

Bryer, R.A. (1993),"The Late Nineteenth-Century Revolution in Financial Reporting: Accounting for the Rise of Investor or Managerial Capitalism", *Accounting, Organizations and Society,* Vol. 18, No. 7/8: 649-690.

Bryne, G. (1937), "To what Extent can the practice of Accounting Be Reduced to Rules and Standards?" Journal of Accountancy

Burgstahler, D. and Dichev, I. (1997),"*Earnings management to avoid earnings decreases and losses",* Journal of Accounting and Economics 24, 99–126

Burton, J. C., Palmer, R. E. and Kay, R. S. (1981), *A Hand book of Accounting and Auditing,* London: Warren, Gorham and Lamont

Buzby S.L. (1982), "The Nature of Adequate Disclosure *In* McCullers and Schroeder", *Accounting theory,* John Wiley and Sons Inc. PP550-656.

Campbell, J. E., Hermanson, H. M. and McAllister, J. P. (2002), "The high road: Obstacles to international accounting standards convergence", *The CPA Journal,* May 20 – 24.

Canning, J. B. (1923), *Tax Economics of Accounting,* New York: The Ronald Press.

Caplan, E.H. (1972), "Accounting Research as an Information Source for Theory Construction", in Sterling, R.R.(ed), *Research Methodology in Accounting,* Scholars Books Co.

Carnegie, G.D. and Napier, C.J. (1996), "Critical and Interpretive Histories: Insights into Accounting's Present and Future through its Past", *Accounting, Auditing & Accountability Journal,* Vol.9, No.3

Chambers, R. J., (1993), "Positive Accounting Theory and the PA Cult", *Abacus,* Vol. 29, No. 1, pp. 1-29.

Chambers, R.J. (1955), "Blueprint for a Theory of Accounting", *Journal of Accounting Research,* Vol. 6, No.5

Chambers, R.J. (1966), *Accounting, Evaluation and Economic Behaviour,* Prentice Hall, Englewood Cliffs, New Jersey

Chan, K., Jegadeesh, N. and Lakonishok, J. (2000), Earnings quality and stock returns: The evidence from accruals, University of Illinois. USA

Chandler Jr., A.D. (1977), *The Visible Hand-The Managerial Revolution in American Business,* Cambridge: Harvard University Press.

Charon, J. M. (1979), *Symbolic Interactionism: An Introduction, an Interpretation, Integration*. Englewood Cliffs, New Jersey: Prentice-Hall, Inc.

Cherry, C. (1961), *On Human Communication: A Review, A Survey and A Criticism*. New York: Science Editions Inc.

Choi, F., Frost, C. and Gary, K. (2002), *International Accounting,* Prentice Hall, New Jersey, 4th edition

Christenson, C. (1983), *"The Methodology of Positive Accounting",* The Accounting Review (January), pp1-22

Chua, W.F. (1986), "Radical Developments in Accounting Theory", The Accounting Review, Vol.LXI, No. 4 October

Clatworthy, M. A. and Jones, M. J. (2006), "Differential patterns of textual characteristics and company performance in the chairman's statement" *Accounting, Auditing & Accountability Journal,* Vol. 19, No. 4, pp. 493-511

Comer, J.M. (1998), *Corporate Fraud,* Aldershot: Gower Publishing Ltd, Third Edition.

Cooper, D. J. and Hopper, T. M. (1990), *Critical Account,* London: The Macmillan Press

Cooper, D.J. and Sherer, M.J. (1984), "The Value of Corporate Accounting Reports: Arguments for a Political Economy of Accounting," *Accounting, Organizations and Society,* Vol. 9, No. ¾, pp 207-232.

Cottell, P.G. and Perlin ,T.M. (1990), *Accounting Ethics,* London: Qourum Books.

Cunning, J.B. (1929), *The Economics of Accountancy, New York:* The Ronald Press Company.

Dalhat, B.S. and Barnabas, A.O. (2003), "The Effects of Low Adherence to Ethical Standards of Accountants in Nigeria", in Danadago, K.I. and Tanko, A.I.(eds) *Proceedings of the First National Conference on Ethical Issues in Accounting,* organized by the Department of Accounting BUK From 6-10 January 2003, pp.102-112

Dandago, K.I. (2001), Financial *Accounting Simplified,* Kano-Nigeria: A.J. Publishers Ltd

Dandago, K.I. and Suleiman, D.M. (2005), *The role of internal auditors in establishing honesty and integrity. Are the watchdogs asleep?,* in Dandago K.I and K.T Hamid (eds), Honesty and Integrity, Department of Accounting, BUK, Kano; Gidan Dabino Publishers,

David, G. (1986), *Morals by Agreement,* Oxford: Oxford University Press

Davis, S. W., Krishnagopal, M. and Gareth, M.(1982), "The images that have shaped accounting theory", *Accounting, Organizations and Society* 7 (4): 307-18.

De Rover, R. (1955), "New Perspectives on the history of Accounting", *The Accounting Review,* July

Devine, C. T. (1960), "Research Methodology and Accounting Theory Formation". *The Accounting Review* (July) Sarosota: AAA.

Devitt, M. (1984), *Realism and Truth*, New Jersey: Princeton University Press.

Dillard, J. F. (1991), "Accounting as a Critical Social Science", *Accounting, Auditing and Accountability Journal* 4 (1): 8-27.

Duska, R. F. (1992), "Why be a Loyal Agent? A systematic Ethical Analysis" in Bowie N. E. and R. E. Freeman (eds) , *Ethics and Agency Theory*, New York: Oxford University Press

Dzinkowski, R. (2001)," Bridging the GAAP", *Financial Management*, March 28-29.

Eining, M.M., Jones, D.R. and Loebbecke, J.K. (1997), "Reliance on decision aids: an examination of auditors' assessment of management fraud", *Auditing: A Journal of Practice and Theory*, Vol. 16 No.2, pp.1-19.

Elliot, R., and Willingham, J. (1980), *Management Fraud: Detection and Deterrence*, Petrocelli, New York, NY.

Enthoven, A. J. H. (1973), *Accountancy and Economic Development Policy*, New York: American Elseir.

Epstein, B. J. and Mirza, A.A. (2002), *Interpretation and Application of International Accounting Standards*, John Wiley and Sons, INC, New Jersey.

Esthel, .S. and Van Breda, M.F. (2001), *Accounting Theory: Text and Reading*, New York: McGraw Hill, 2nd edition

Fanning, M.K., Cogger, K.O. (1998), "Neural detection of management fraud using published financial data", *International Journal of Intelligent Systems in Accounting, Finance and Management*, Vol. 7 No.1, pp.21-41.

Financial Accounting Standards Board (1978) '*Statements of Financial Accounting Concepts for Business Enterprises No. 1: Objectives of Financial Reporting by Business Enterprises*'. Stamford, Connecticut: FASB.

Fishman, J. A. (1972), *The Sociology of Language*, USA, Rowley, MA: Newbury House.

Fleischman, R.K. and Tyson, T.N. (1993), "Cost Accounting the Industrial Revolution: The present State of Historical knowledge" *Economic History Review,* Vol. 46, No.3.

Flint, D. (1982), True and Fair View in Company Accounts. London: The Institute of Chartered Accountants of Scotland: Gee & Co (Publishers) Limited.

Flory, S. M., Phillips, T. J., Reidenbach, E. R. and Robin, D. P. (1992), *"A multidimensional Analysis of Selected Ethical Issues in Accounting* ",The Accounting Review; Vol. 67 No. 2 http://www.jstor org/journals/aaasoc.html

Flower, J. (1997), "The future shape of harmonization: the EU versus the IASC versus the SEC", *The European Accounting Review* (6)2, 281 – 303.

Gambling, T. (1974), *Societal Accounting,* London: George Allen and Unwin.

Gambling, T. and Karim, R.A. A.(1991), *Business and Accounting Ethics in Islam,* London: Mansell Publishing Limited.

Garrido, P., Leon, A. and Zoio, A. (2002), "Measurement of formal harmonization progress: The IASC experience", The *International Journal of Accounting,* Pp 37, 1 – 26.

Gazdar, G. (1979), *Pragmatics: Implicature, Presupposition and Logical Form,* New York: Academic Press.

Gernon, H. and Meek, G. K. (2001), *Accounting: An International Perspective (5th ed.).* New York: Irwin/McGraw-Hill.

Gilman, S. (1939), *Accounting Concepts of Profit,* New York: Ronal Press

Glautier, M. W and Underdown B. (1970), *Accounting Theory and Practice,* Great Britain: Pitman Publishing Ltd.

Glautier, M.W and Underdown, B. (1986), *Accounting Theory and Practice,* London: Pitman Publishing, 3rd edition.

Gonedes, N. J. (1972), "Efficient Capital Markets and External Accounting", *The Accounting Review (Jan),* Sarasota: AAA

Gordon, R.A. (1974), *Economic Instability and Growth: The American Record,* New York: Harper & Row

Gornik-Tamaszewski, S. and McCarthy, I. (2003), "Cooperation between FASB and IASB to achieve convergence of accounting standards", *Review of Business,* Spring 52 –59.

Gray, R., Kouhy, R. and Lavers, S., (1995), "Corporate Social and Environmental Reporting: A Review of the Literature and a Longitudinal Study of UK Disclosure", *Accounting, Auditing and Accountability,* Vol. 8, No 2, pp.47-77.

Green, B.P. and Choi, J.H. (1997), "Assessing the risk of management fraud through neural-network technology", *Auditing: A Journal of Practice and Theory,* Vol. 16 No.1, pp.14-28.

Hamid, K.T. (2004),"Prudence Transparency and Accountability in The Nigerian Banking Industry: A Means for Building Customer Confidence",in Dandago K. I. and Tanko, A. I.(eds), *Proceedings of the 2nd National Conference on Ethical Issues in Accounting,* Organized by the Department of Accounting, Bayero University, Kano-Nigeria

Hansen, J.V., McDonald, J.B., Messier, W.F. and Bell, T.B. (1996), "A generalized qualitative-response model and the analysis of management fraud", *Management Science,* Vol. 42, No.7, pp.1022-1032

Haried, A. A. (1972), "The Semantic Dimension of Financial Statements", *Journal of* Accounting *Research,* pp 376-391.

Haskins, C.W. (1904), *Business Education and Accountancy,* New York: Harper and Brothers

Hatfield, H.R. (1924), "A historical defense of bookkeeping", *The Journal of Accountancy,* Vol. 37, No.4, pp.241-53

Hatfield, H.R. (1927): *Accounting.* D.A. Appleton and Company. New York.

Hendrieksen, A.S. and Van Breda, M.(2001), *Accounting Theory* McGraw-Hill Book Company, Singapore,5th Edition

Hendriksen, E. S. (1977); *Accounting Theory,* Homewood: R. D. Inwin 3rd Edition.

Hendriksen, E.S. & Van Breda, M.F. (2001), *Accounting Theory: Text and Reading,* New York: McGraw Hill, 2nd edition

Hendriksen, E.S. (1982), *Accounting Theory,* 1st edition, Homewood, III,: Richard D Irwin

Herbert, W.E. (1978),*Pragmatism Versus Ethical Conduct,* Qourum Books, USA.

Higson, A. (1999), "Why is management reticent to report fraud?: An exploratory study", *22nd Annual Congress of European Accounting Association,* Bordeaux.

Hill, C. (1999), *Competing in the Global Marketplace,* Irwin McGraw Hill, Boston, 3rd edition.

Hines, R (1988), "Financial Accounting: In Communicating Reality, We Construct Reality", *Accounting, Organizations and Society,* No. 3

Hofstede, G. (1991), *Cultures and Organizations: Software of the Mind,* McGraw-Hill Book Company, New York.

Holmes, J. (1992), *An Introduction to Sociolinguistics,* Harlow Essex, United Kingdom: Longman Group UK Limited.

Hopper, T. and Powell, A. (1985), "Making sense of research into the organizational and social aspects of management accounting: A review of its underlying assumptions", Journal of Management Studies, Vol. 22, No. 5, September 1985.

Hopwood, A.G. (1976), "Editorial: The Path Ahead Accounting", *Organizations and Society,* Vol. 1

Hoxsey, J.M.B. (1930),"Accounting for Investors", *Journal of Accountancy,* in Hendriksen, E.S. and Van Breda, M.F. (eds), *Accounting Theory: Text and Reading,* New York: McGraw Hill, 2nd Edition

Idoko, O.G. (1998), *Corporate Social Responsibility Accounting Practice.* Unpublished M.Sc. Accounting Thesis, ABU Zaria.

Idris, J. S. (1987), "The Islamization of the sciences: its philosophy and methodology", *The American Journal of Islamic Social Sciences* 4 (2): 201-208, International Institute of Islamic Thought (IIIT)

Ijiri, Y. (1975), *Theory of Accounting Measurement: Studies in Accounting Research,* American Accounting Association. Sarasota, Florida.

Ijiri, Y. and Robert, J. (1966), "Reliability and Objectivity of Accounting Methods", *in* Wolk, I. H., Tearney, M. G. and Dodd, J. L. (2001), *Accounting Theory: A Conceptual and Institutional Approach,* South Western College Publishing, Thomson Learning Centre, Cincinnati, Ohio, USA, 5th Edition.

International Accounting Standards Committee (1989), *Framework for the Preparation and Presentation of Financial Statements,* London: IASC.

Investor Relations Business (2002), FASB, IASB to Converge Standards, *Investor Relations Business*, 2002, Pp11-18.

Iwan, T. and M. Gaffikin (2000), The Shariate Accounting: An Ethical construction of Accounting Knowledge, *IBFNET*

James, W.P. (1965), *The Foundation of Financial Accounting,* Baton Rouge: Louisiana State University Press, USA.

Jensen, M., and Meckling, W (1986), "Theory of the Firm: Managerial Behavior, Agency Costs and Ownership Structure," Journal of Financial Economics, 3(4), pp305-360.

Johnson, I.E (1996),Public Sector Accounting and Financial Control, Surulere: Financial Training

Jones, M.J. and Mellett, H. J. (2007), "Determinants of Changes in Accounting Practices: Accounting and the UK Health Service", *Critical Perspectives on Accounting,* Vol. 18.

Kadmon, N. (2001), *Formal Pragmatics*, Oxford: Blackwell.

Kam, V. (1986), *Accounting Theory,* New York: John Wiley and Sons Ltd

Kantudu, A.S. (2004), *"The Relevance Of Auditors' Report In Enhancing Management Accountability In Nigeria",* in Dandago K.I. and Tanko A.I.(eds), *Prudence, Transparency and Accountability,* Department of Accounting, BUK, Kano: Gidan Dabino Publishers.

Kantudu, A.S. (2006), Application of Employee retirement Benefits by Quoted Firms in Nigeria, An Unpublished Ph.D. Theses submitted to Department of Accounting, Ahmadu Bello University, Zaria-Nigeria.

Kaplan, S.E., Pourciau, S. and Reckers, P.M.J. (1990), "An examination of the effect of the president's letter and stock advisory service information on financial decisions", *Behavioural Research in Accounting*, Vol. 2, pp. 63-92

Katz, J.J. (1966), *The Philosophy of Language*, London: Harper & Row.

Kelinger, F. N, (1964), *Foundations of Behavioural Research*, New York: Holt, Rinhart & Winston.

Kempson, R. (1988), Grammar and conversational principles. in Newmeyer, F. (ed.): Linguistics: *The Cambridge Survey, Vol. II. Cambridge*, Eng.: Cambridge University Press, pp. 139-163.

Kieso, D. E; and Weygandt, J. J. (1983), *Intermediate Accounting*, New York: Wiley & Son Inc. 4th Ed.

King, J. B. (1989), "Confronting Chaos", *Journal of Business Ethics* - January

Kleekämper, H.; Kuhlewind, M. and Alvarez, M. (2002), "The Convergence of Generally Accepted Accounting Principles and International Financial Reporting Standards", Anderson: Anderson University.

Kohler, E. L. (1936) "Theories and Practice" *The Accounting Review* (Sept), Sarota: AAA.

Kokubu, K and Sawabe, N. (1996), "The Past, Present and Future of Accounting: A Review Essay of Accounting, Organizations and Society: the Inside and Outside of Accounting by Sadao Taketera". *Accounting Organizations and Society*, Vol.21

Kornblum, W. and Smith, C.D. (2000), *Sociology in a Changing World*, New York: Harcourt College Publishers, 5th Edition.

Kripke, H.(1985), "Accounting: What Does it all means? The Commission's Biggest Failure" in Zeff, S.A. &

Keller.. T.F. (eds) *Financial Accounting Theory*, New York; McGraw Hill Inc. 3rd Edition.

Kuhn, T. S. (1970), "The Structure of Scientific Revolution" *International Encyclopedia of Unified Science*, Chicago: University of Chicago Press. 2nd Enlarged Ed.

Laboury, W. (1964), Phonological Correlates of Social Stratification. In: Belkaoui, A. (1995), *The Linguistic Shaping of Accounting,* Connecticut, USA. Westport Quorum Books.

Ladd, D. R. (1963), *Contemporary Corporate Accounting and Public,* Honewood: Richard D. Irwin.

Larson, K. (1996), Implications of Measurement Theory on Accounting Concept Formulation. *In*: Wolk, I. H., Tearney, M. G. & Dodd, J. L. (2001), *Accounting Theory: A Conceptual and Institutional Approach,* South Western College Publishing, Thomson Learning Centre, Cincinnati, Ohio, USA, 5th Edition.

Larson, R. K. and Kenny, S. Y. (1999): The harmonization of international accounting standards: Progress in the 1990s? *Multinational Business Review*, Spring Pp1-12

Larson, R. K. and Larson, L. L. (2001): Coming to terms with international accounting standards. *Internal Auditor*, February Pp 43 – 47.

LaShaw, M. N. (2004): *The Convergence of Generally Accepted Accounting Principles and International Financial Reporting Standards*, Anderson University.

Lee, T.A. (1979), "Company Financial Statements: An Essay in Business History 1840-1950", in Lee, T.A. & Parker, R.H. (1979) (eds), *The Evolution of Corporate Financial Reporting,* Nairobi: Thomas Nelson.

Lehman, C.R. (1992), Accounting's Changing Roles in Social Conflict, New York: Markus Weiner Publishing, Inc. 1992.

Lemon, A.J., and Cahan, S.F., (1997), "Environmental Legislation and Environmental Disclosures: Some Evidence From New Zealand", *Asian Review of Accounting*, Vol. 5, No. 1, pp. 78-105.

Lister, R. (1984), "Accounting as History", *International Journal of Accounting,* Vol. 18, No. 2

Littleton, A. C., (1953), Structure of Accounting Theory, Monograph No. 5. Sarasota, Florida: American Accounting Association

Littleton, A.C. (1933), *Accounting Revolution to 1900,* New York: American Institute Publishing Co. 2nd edition.

Machlup, F. (1955), "The Problem of Verification in Economics", *The Southern Economic Journal.*

MaClenahen, J. S. (2002), GAAP goodbye? PWC's CEO wants to scrap rules-based accounting for global guidelines. *Industry Week* http://www.findarticles.com

MacNeal, K. (1939), *Truth in Accounting,* Philadelphia: University Pennyslvania Press.

MacNeal, K. (1970, [1939]), Truth in Accounting, Lawrence, Kansas: Scholars Book Co.

Madsen, P. (1995), "A Theoretical Ground for the Practice of Business Ethics; A Commentary", Business Ethics Quality, Vol. 5, No. 3 http://www.jstor.org/journals/pdc.html

Mainoma, M.A. (2002), "Adequacy of Accounting Information to Users" in Ezejelue, A.C. AND Okoye A.E. (eds), *Accounting: The Nigerian Perspective,* Nigerian Accounting Association

Malkiel, B.G. (19850 *A Random Walk Down Wall Street.* New York: W.W. Norton & Co. 4th Edition.

Mamman, S. (2004), Disclosure of Corporate Social Responsibility Performance in Accounting Reports,*The Nigerian Journal of Accounting Research,* Dept. of Accounting, ABU, Zaria, Vol.1 No. 1, pp 14-21

Martinson, O. B. and Ziegenfus, D. E. (2000), Looking at what influences ethical perception and judgment,*Management Accounting Quarterly,* Fall, pp 41-47.

Mattessich, R. (1964), *Accounting and Analytical Methods: Measurement and Projection of Income and Wealth in the Micro and Macro-Economy,* Homewood, Illinois: Richard D. Irwin Inc.

Matthews, M. R. and Parera, M. H. B. (1996), *Accounting Theory and Development,* London: Chapman and Hall.

Mautz, R. K. (1965), *"Challenges to Accounting profession", The Accounting Review,* Vol. 40 ,No. 2 http://www.jstor.org/journals-/aaasoc.html

May, O.G. (1927), "Principles of Accounting", *Journal of Accountancy,* November

McCullers, I.D. and Schroeder, R.G. (1982), *Accounting Theory,* New York: John Wiley Son.

McDonald, D. (1967), Feasibility Criteria for Accounting Measures, *In:* Wolk, I. H., Tearney, M. G. & Dodd, J. L. (2001), *Accounting Theory: A Conceptual and Institutional Approach,* South Western College Publishing, Thomson Learning Centre, Cincinnati, Ohio, USA, 5th Edition.

McDonald, D. L. (1972), *Comparative Accounting Theory,* Reading: Addison-Wesley.

Miller, P., Horper, T. and Laughlin, R.G., (1991), "The New Accounting History: an Introduction", *Accounting Organizations and Society,* Vol. 16. No. 5/6

Millichamp, A.H. (1989), *Foundation Accounting: An Instructional Manual for Accounting Students,* London: DPP Publishers.

Millichamp, A.H.(1990), *Foundation Accounting - An Instruction Manual for Accounting Students* DP Publications Ltd. Aldine Place, London.

Mobley, S. C, (1970) "The challenges of socioeconomic Accounting" *Accounting Review,* Sarosota: AAA.

Moonitz, (1961),"On the Basis postulates of Accounting. *Accounting," Research Study* No.1 New York AICPA PP.27

Moore, H.E. (1967), *Orders and Change: Essay in Comparative Sociology,* New York: Wiley

Moran, R. T., Harris, P. R., Stripp, W. G. (1993), *Developing the global organization,* Houston: Gulf Publishing.

Morgan, G. and Linda S.(1980), The case for qualitative research. *Academy of Management,* 5 (4): 491-500.

Morris, C. W. (1938), 'Foundation of the theory of signs', in *International Encyclopaedia of Unified Science* 1, No. 2, O. Neurath, R. Carnap, C. Morris, eds. Chicago: University of Chicago Press, pp. 1-59.

Most, K. S. (1982), Accounting Theory, second edition (Columbus: Grid Publishing)

Most, K.S. (1982), *Accounting Theory,* Grid Publishing Inc., Columbus USA, 2nd Edition

Mueller, G. (1997), Harmonization Efforts in the European Union, *In: International Accounting and Finance Handbook,* edited by Choi, F. (1997), Wiley and Sons, New York, 7th edition.

Mueller, G. G. (1967) "Accounting within a Macroeconomic Framework", *International Accounting,* New York: Macmillan.

Mueller, G.; Gernon, H. and Meek, G. (1991), Accounting – an International Perspective; Richard D. Irwin, Inc; Homewood, 2nd edition

Muhammad, L. M. (2002), " Valuation of Fixed Assets by Business Enterprises in Nigeria", in Ezejelue, A.C. & Okoye, A.E. (eds), *The Nigerian Perspective,* Nigerian Accounting Association

Muhammad, L.M. (2004). The Impact of Internal Audit on Accountability in Nigerian Organisations.In Dandago, K.I. and Tanko, A.I.(eds), *Proceedings of the 2nd National Conference on Ethical Issues in Accounting,* Organised by the Department of Accounting, Bayero University, Kano-Nigeria

Muhammad, L.M.(2005).The Status of Prudence, Accountability and Transparency in Nigerian Companies. *Bayero International Journal of Accounting Research.*1 (2), 176-189.

Napier, C.J. (2001), "Accounting History and Accounting Progress", *Accounting History,* Vol.6, No.2

NASB (1984), *Disclosure of Accounting Policies (SAS 1),* Published by the Nigerian Accounting Standard Board

NASB (1985), *Information to be disclosed in Financial Statement (SAS 2),* Published by the Nigerian Accounting Standard Board.

Ness, K.E., and Mirza, A.M., (1991), "Corporate Social Disclosure: A Note on a Test of Agency Theory", *British Accounting Review,* Vol. 23, No. 3, pp. 211-217.

Neuman, W.L. (2003), *Social Research Methods: Qualitative and Quantitative Approaches, International Student Edition,* USA: Pearson Education Inc.

Nobes, C. (1999), Towards a General Model of the Reasons for International Differences in Financial Reporting, *In Nobes, C.(ed), International Accounting and Comparative Financial Reporting,* Cheltenham: Edward Elgar Publishing Limited

Nobes, C. and Parker, R. (2000): Comparative International Accounting, *Financial Times-* Prentice Hall, Hartlow.

Nobes, C.W., and Parker, RH. (1998). *Comparative International Accounting*, 5th, London: Prentice Hall.

Nobes, C; Mueller, G; Gernon, H; and Meek, G. (1997): Accounting an International Perspective, Richard D. Irwin, Inc; Chicago, 4th edition.

Nolan, J. (1972), "Wheat Study Members Assess Product". *The Journal of Accountancy,* June, in Hendriksen,

Esthel,.S. & Van Breda, M.F. (2001), *Accounting Theory: Text and Reading,* New York: McGraw Hill, 2nd edn

North, D.C. (1981), *Structure and Change in Economic History,* New York: WEW Norton & Co.

O'Brien, P.C. (1998),"Discussion of International Variation in Accounting Measurement Rules and Analysts' Earnings Forecast Errors", *Journal of Business Finance and Accounting,* Vol. 25 No, (9 and 8), pp 1249-1254.

Odoh, C.M. & Nwadialo, E.O. (2004), "Auditor's Liability to the Third Party: A Landmine for Nigerian Auditors", in Dandago, K.I. & Tanko, A.I. (eds), Prudence, Transparency and Accountability, proceedings of the Second national Conference of Ethical Issues organized by the Department of Accounting, Bayero University, Kano, Nigeria.

OftenHeimer, J.L. (1999), "Cutting financial Reports down to size", *Journal of Accountancy,* March, PP.45-47

Oliverio, M. E. (2000), The new structure of international accounting standards, *The CPA Journal,* May, Pp20-26, 91.

Orijioke, B.A.M (2002),"Corporate Governance in Nigeria", a paper presented at Mandatory Continuing Professional Development (MCPD) of the Association of the National Accountants of Nigeria (ANAN)

Palepu, K.G., Healy, P.M. and Bernard V.L. (2000), *Business Analysis and Valuation,* South-Western College Publishing, Ohio, USA

Panchapakesan, S., & McKinnon, J., (1992), "Proxies for Political Visibility: A Preliminary Examination of the Relation Among Some Potential Proxies", *Accounting Research Journal,* Spring, pp. 71-80.

Partee, B. H. (1999), "Semantics" in R.A. Wilson and F.C. Keil, eds., *The MIT Encyclopedia of the Cognitive Sciences.* Cambridge, MA: The MIT Press.

Patilo, J. W. (1965), *The Foundation of Financial Accounting,* Balton Ruge: Louiscana State University Press.

Paton, W.A. (1922), *Accounting Theory,* New York: Accounting Studies Press

Paton, W.A. and Littleton, A.C. (1940), "An Introduction to Corporate Accounting Standards," Sarasota, Fla: American Accounting Association.

Peragollo, E. (1938), *Origin and evolution of Double Entry Bookkeeping,* New York: American Institute Publishing.

Pincus, M. and Wasley, C.(1994), The incidience of accounting changes and characteristics of firms making accounting changes, Accounting Horizons 8, 1–24.

Practer, P. (1998), International accounting standards, *The CPA Journal* 68(7), 14-20.

Radebaugh, L. and Gray, S. (1997), I*nternational Accounting and multinational enterprises,* John Wiley and Sons, New York, 4th edition

Radebaugh, L., and Daniels, J. (2001), *International Business, Environment and Operations,* Prentice Hall, London, 9th edition

Ragab, I. A. (1993), Islamic perspectives on theory building in the social sciences, *The American Journal of Islamic Social Sciences* ,10 (1): 1-22.

Rappaport, A. and Learner, E. (1969), "A Framework for financial reporting by diversified companies ",in McCullers and Schroeder (ed) ,*Accounting theory,* John Wiley and Sons Ltd, PP.656.

Rappaport, A. (1964),"Establishing objective for published corporate Accounting Report", *Accounting Review,* Reaction and motivations, Journal of Accounting and Economics 13, April, pp 47–89

Revsine, L., Collins, L. D. and Johnson, W. B. (2002), *Financial Reporting and Analysis,* New Jersey: Pearson Education Inc., Upper Saddle River.

Riahi-Belkaoui, A. (2000), *Accounting Theory,* Thomson Learning – Business Press, Padstow, Cornwall, 4th edition.

Riahi-Belkaoui, A. (2000), *Accounting Theory,* London: Thomson Learning.

Riahi-Belkaoui, A. (2002), *International Financial and Managerial Accounting,* Westport, CT: Quorum Books.

Ritzer, G. (1975), "Sociology: A Multiparadigm Science", *The American Sociologist.*

Roberts, C.; Weetman, P. and Gordon P. (1998), International Financial Accounting – a comparative approach, *Financial Times, London:* Pitman Publishing

Romal, J. B. and Hibschweiler, M. A. (2002), *"Improving Professional ethics: Steps for Implementing Change,* the CPA Journals, New York: New York State Society of CPAs

Roslender, R. (2004)," Accounting for Intellectual Capital: rethinking its theoretical underpinnings", *Measuring Business Exellence*Vol.8, No 1, pp38-45

Ruder, D. (2001), "Worldwide Convergence in Accounting", *Auditing, and Independence Standards,* S. 1-22,

Sabari, M. H., (2004), "A Comparative Analysis of Corporate Reporting in Nigeria and the United States", in Dandago, K.I. and Tanko, A. I.(eds), *Proceedings of the Second National Conference on Ethical Issues in Accounting: Prudence , Transparency and Accountability* Vol. 2.,pp187-199

Samuels, J.; Piper, A. (1985), *International Accounting: A survey,* London: Croom Helm.

Schaefer, T.R. (2001), *Sociology,* New York: McGraw Hill Companies, 7th Edn

Schultz, J. and Lopez, T. (2001), "The impact of national influence on accounting estimates: Implications for international Accounting Standard-setters", *The International Journal of Accounting,* 36, pp. 271-290.

Scott, D. R. (1941), "The Basis for Accounting Principles", *Accounting Review, December*

Sempier, R. N., Chandler, R. and Dalessio, A. (1991),"Harmonization of Auditing Standards". In F. D. S. Choi(ed), *Handbook of International Accounting,* New York: John Wiley & Sons Inc., Pp14-24

Shahul, J. (1998), "Critical Financial Analysis and Accounting for Stakeholders", *Critical Perspective on Accounting,* Vol. 9, No. 2, pp 235-249

Smith, J.E. and Smith, N.P. (1971), "On Readability: A measure of the performance of the communication function of financial Reporting", *The Accounting Review,* July, PP 552-561.

Smith, M. and Taffler, R.J. (1995), "The incremental effect of narrative accounting information in corporate annual reports", *Journal of Business Finance and Accounting,* Vol. 22, No. 8, Pp1195-216

Smith, M. and Taffler, R.J. (2000), "The chairman's statement – a content analysis of discretionary narrative disclosures", *Accounting, Auditing & Accountability Journal,* Vol. 13, No. 5, pp. 624-46

Solomon, R.C. (1995), "Accounting History and Accounting Progress", *Accounting History,* Vol.6, No.2

Soper F.J., and Dolphin, R. (1964),"Readability and Corporate Annual Reports", *The Accounting Review,* April, PP358-362.

Sorter, G. H. (1941), "An Event Approach to Basic Accounting Theory", *Accounting Review,* Sarosota: AAA

Stalnaker, R. (1972), "Pragmatics", in G. Harman and D. Davidson (eds.), *Semantics of Natural Language,* Dordrecht: Reidel, pp. 380-397.

Stamp, E. (1980), *Corporate Reporting: Its Future Evolution,* Toronto: London Institutes of Chartered Accountants.

Stanko, B. B. (2000), "The case for international accounting rules", *Business & Economic Review* July – September,. 21- 25.

Staubus, G. I. (1961), *A Theory of Accounting to Investors,* Berkeley, California: University of California Press.

Sterling, R. (1990)," Positive Accounting: An assessment", *Abacus,* Vol. 26 (No.2): 97-135.

Sterling, R. R. and Raymond, R. (1969), "A Valuation Experiment", in Wolk, I. H., Tearney, M. G. and Dodd, J. L. (eds), *Accounting Theory: A Conceptual and Institutional Approach,* South Western College Publishing, Thomson Learning Centre, Cincinnati, Ohio, USA, 5th Edition.

Sterling, R.R. (1970), "Theory Construction and Verification", The *Accounting Review,* Vol. 45

Stolowy, H. (1997), The definition of international accounting through textbook contents, a paper presented at the 8th world congress of the international association for accounting education and research (IAAER) Paris, France, October.

Street, D. L. and Gray, S. J. (1999),"How wide is the gap between IASC and U.S. GAAP? Impact of the IASC comparability project and recent international developments", *Journal of International Accounting, Auditing & Taxation* 8(1), 133-1

Street, D. L., Nichols, N. B. and Gray, S. J. (2000), "Assessing the acceptability of international accounting standards in the U. S.: An empirical study of the materiality of U. S. GAAP reconciliations by non-U.S. companies complying with IASC standard", *The International Journal of Accounting* 35 (1), 27 – 63.

Summers, S.L. and Sweeney, J.T. (1998), "Fraudulently misstated financial statements and insider trading: an empirical analysis", *The Accounting Review,* Vol. 73 No.1, pp.131-46.

Sutton, M. H. (1997), "Financial reporting in U.S. capital markets: International dimensions", *Accounting Horizons* 11(2), 96-102.

Swanda, J. R. (1990*),"Goodwill, Going Concern, Stocks and Flows: A Prescription for Moral Analysis"* Journal of Business Ethics Vol. 9 No. 9

Sweeney, H. W. (1936), *Stabilized Accounting,* New York: Harper & Brothers.

Sweeney, H. W. (1936), *Truth in Accounting,* Philadelphia: University of Pennsylvania Press.

Tearney, M. G. & Dodd, J. L. (2001), *Accounting Theory: A Conceptual and Institutional Approach,* South Western College Publishing, Thomson Learning Centre, Cincinnati, Ohio, USA, 5th Edition.

Tennyson, B.M., Ingram, R.W. and Dugan, M.T. (1990), "Assessing the information content of narrative disclosures in explaining bankruptcy", *Journal of Business Finance and Accounting,* Vol. 17 No. 3, pp 391-410.

The Sandilands Report (1975), *Inflation Accounting,* London: HMSO CMND 6225.

Tinker, A.M., Merino, B.D., and Neimark, M.D., (1982), "The Normative Origins of Positive Theories: Ideology and Accounting Thought", *Accounting, Organisations and Society*, Vol. 7, pp. 167-200.

Troberg, P and Ekholm, B (1995), "Objectives of Financial Reporting: Are User Needs Different?" *Working paper* Swedish School of Economics and Business Administration.

Uche, C.U (2002), "Accounting History Research: Some Theoretical Issues", in Anao, A.R. & Uche, C.U. (eds) *Research Design and Implementation in Accounting and Finance,* Benin: University of Benin Press.

Ullmann, S. (1957), *The Principles of Semantics.* Oxford: Basil Blackwell

Upton, W.S. (2001), *Business Financial Reporting: Challenges from the New Economy,* Financial Accounting Standards Board, Norwalk, CT.

Vanasco, R. R. (1998), "Fraud auditing", *Managerial Auditing Journal,* Vol. 13 No.1, pp.4-71

Vernon, K. (1986), *Accounting Theory,* New York: John Wiley and Sons

Walgenbach, P.H., Hanson, E.I and Dittrich, N.E. (1988), *Financial Accounting: An Introduction,* London: Harcourt Brace Jovanovich Inc., 5th Edition.

Wallace, W.A. (1995), *Auditing,* Cincinnati: South-Western College Publishing.

Watts, R. L. and Zimmerman, J. L. (1986), *Positive Accounting Theory,* New Jersey: Prentice Hall, Englewood Cliffs.

Watts, R.L. and Zimmerman, J.L., (1979), "The Demand for and Supply of Accounting Theories: The Market for Excuses", *The Accounting Review,* Vol. 54, No 2, pp. 273-305.

Watts, R.L. and Zimmerman, J.L., (1990), "Positive Accounting Theory: A Ten Year Perspective", *The Accounting Review,* Vol. 65, No 1, pp. 131-156.

Whittington, G., (1987), "Positive Accounting: A Review Article", *Accounting and Business Research,* Vol. 18, Autumn, pp. 327-336.

Wikipedia (2007a), *Semantics-pragmatics-syntax trinity,* Wikimedia Foundation, Inc

Wikipedia (2007b), *Pragmatics,* Wikimedia Foundation, Inc.,

Wikipedia, (2006), "http://en.wikipedia.org/wiki/positive-accounting"

William, O. E. and Murphy, P. E. (1990), *"The Ethics of Virtue: A Moral Theory of Marketing",* Journal of Macro Marketing; http://www.jstor org/journals/aaasoc.html

Wolk, I. H., Tearney, M. G. and Dodd, J. L. (2001), *Accounting Theory: A Conceptual and Institutional Approach,* South Western College Publishing, Thomson Learning Centre, Cincinnati, Ohio, USA, 5th Edition.

Wood, F. & Sangster, A (1999), *Business Accounting,* London: Pitman Publishing, 8th Edition.

Wood, F. and Sangster, A. (2002), Business *Accounting 2,* London: Pearson Education Limited, Ninth Edition.

Worthy, F.S. (1984), "Manipulating profits: how it's done?" *Fortune,* Vol. 25 pp.50-4

Xie, H. (2001), "The Mispricing of abnormal Accruals", *Accounting Review* 76

Yamey, B.S (1980), "Early Views on the Origins and Development of Book-keeping and Accounting," *Accounting and Business Research,* Special accounting History, Vol. 10, No. 37A

Yamey, B.S. and Littleton, A.C. (1956), *Studies into the History of Accounting,* London: Sweet & Maxwell

Zarzeski, M. T., (1996), "Spontaneous harmonization effects of culture and market forces on accounting disclosure practices", *Accounting Horizon Vol. 10,* March, PP16-20

Zeff, A.S. (1978), "the Rise of Economic Consequences," in McCullers, I.D. and Schroeder, R.G. (eds), *Accounting Theory,* New York: John Wiley Son.

Zeff, S. (2002), "Political Lobbying on Proposed Standards: A Challenge on the IASB", *Accounting Horizons,* Vol. 16 Issue 1, March Pp 43 and 49.

Zetf, A. S. (1978), "The Rise of Economic Consequences", *Journal of Accountancy,* New York: AICPA

About the Contributors

Associate Professor Aliyu Sulaiman Kantudu (alisukan@yahoo.co.uk) B.Sc., M.Sc., PhD. (Acct.), MBA, CNA, FICMA, MTMFA, is the immediate Past Head, Department of Accounting, Bayero University, Kano, Nigeria. He has been a Lecturer in Accounting and Finance in the Department of Accounting of the University, since 1992. He is currently a Visiting Associate Professor to a number of Universities and Institutions, including Ahmadu Bello University, Zaria; Kaduna State University; Usman Dan Fodiyo University, Sokoto; University of Maiduguri; Federal University of Technology, Yola; and the Nigerian Defense Academy, Kaduna. He is also an External Examiner to a number of Universities and Polytechnics in Nigeria. His areas of research interest include Advanced Accounting Theory and Practice: Financial and Corporate Accounting, Financial Reporting and Disclosure; and Corporate Finance, Investment and Portfolio Analysis. He is married with children.

Ahmed Bawa Bello (ahmedbawabello@yahoo.com), B.Sc., M.Sc. (Acct.), MBA (Finance), ACA, ACTI, is currently the Head, Department of Accounting, Federal University of Technology, Yola, Adamawa State, Nigeria. He is currently a PhD Accounting Research Student, in the Department of Accounting, Bayero University, Kano, Nigeria. He also serves as an External Auditor, Consultant and Financial Analyst to a number of Institutions and business organizations in Nigeria. His areas of research interest include Accounting Theory and Practice: Business Finance; Financial Accounting; Auditing and Investigation; Management Accounting and Business Valuation. He is married with children.

Ibrahim Magaji Barde (imbarde@yahoo.com), B.Sc., M.Sc. (Acct.), MBA, ATMFA, is a Lecturer in the Department of Accounting, Bayero University, Kano,Nigeria. Currently, he is a PhD Accounting Research Student, in the same Department. He is a Consultant with K.I. Dandago & Co. (Chartered Tax Practitioners, Fundraisers and Financial Analysts). His areas of research interest include Corporate Reporting and Disclosure; Financial Accounting; Quantitative Techniques in Accounting; and Management Information System. He is married with children.

Junaidu Muhammad Kurawa (jndmuhammad@yahoo.com), B.Sc., M.Sc. (Acct.), MBA, ATMFA, CPA, is a Senior Lecturer in the Department of Accounting, Bayero University, Kano, Nigeria. Currently, he is a PhD Accounting Research Student, in the same Department. He is a Consultant with K.I. Dandago & Co. (Chartered Tax Practitioners, Fundraisers and Financial Analysts). His areas of interest include Public Reporting and Accountability; Corporate Finance; Public Sector Accounting and Control; Cost and Management Accounting; and Management Information System. He is married with children.

Kabir Tahir Hamid (khtahir2004@yahoo.com), B.Sc., M.Sc. (Acct.), MBA, CPA, ATMFA, is a Lecturer in the Department of Accounting, Bayero University, Kano, Nigeria. Currently, he is a PhD Accounting Research Student, in the same Department. He is a Consultant with K.I. Dandago & Co. (Chartered Tax Practitioners, Fundraisers and Financial Analysts). His areas of research interest include Financial and Corporate Accounting; Quantitative Techniques in Accounting; Corporate Governance; Auditing, Investigation and Forensic Accounting; Taxation and Fiscal Policy; Green Accounting and Social Reporting; and Research Methodology in Accounting. He is married with children.

Associate Professor Kabiru Isa Dandago, B.Sc., M.Sc (Acct), MBA, PhD (Econs), ACA, MNIM, MNES, MIMC, is the Immediate Past Dean, Faculty of Social and Management Sciences, Bayero University, Kano-Nigeria (2004-2008). He is currently (since June 2008), the Chairman, Bayero Consultancy Services Unit of the same University. He has been a lecturer in Accounting in the Department of Accounting of the University since 1990. Dr Dandago has taught Cost Accounting, Management Accounting, Financial Accounting, Taxation, Auditing and Investigation, Public Finance, Business Mathematics, Mathematics for Social Sciences and Research Methodology in Accounting to various Undergraduate, Post Graduate Diploma and Masters Students. He has attended many national and international conferences on Accounting and related disciplines, including the 17th World Congress of Accountants (WCOA) and the 12th World Congress of Accounting Historians (WCAH). He has published many books and journal articles in Accounting, Taxation, Auditing, Industrialization and general

Management, which are enjoying wide readership in Nigeria and beyond. He is married with children.

Muhammad Aminu Isa (ameenueesa@yahoo.co.uk), B.Sc., M.Sc. (Acct.), CNA, ATMFA, is a Lecturer in the Department of Accounting, Bayero University, Kano, Nigeria. Currently, he is a PhD Accounting Research Student, in the same Department. His areas of research interest include Cost and Management Accounting; Capital Market Studies; Consolidation and Business Performance; and Corporate Reporting and Information Disclosure.

Muhammad Liman Muhammad (mohdliman2@yahoo.com), B.Sc., M.Sc. (Acct.), MBA, ATMFA, is a Senior Lecturer in the Department of Accounting, Bayero University, Kano,Nigeria. Currently, he is a PhD Accounting Research Student, in the same Department. He is a Consultant with K.I. Dandago & Co. (Chartered Tax Practitioners, Fundraisers and Financial Analysts). His areas of research interest include Taxation and Fiscal Policy; Cost and Management Accounting; Capital Structure and Corporate Taxation; and Public Sector Accounting. He is married with children.

Mashood Yinka Salaudeen (yin_salaudeen@yahoo.com), B.Sc., M.Sc. (Acct.), FCA, ACTI, is a Lecturer in the Department of Accounting, University of Abuja, Abuja-the Federal Capital of Nigeria. Currently, he is a PhD Accounting Research Student, in the Department of Accounting, Bayero University, Kano-Nigeria. His areas of interest include Advanced Accounting Theory and Practice; Capital Market Studies; Financial Accounting; Public Sector Accounting and Control; and Auditing and Investigation. He is married with children.

Index

A

Accounting Principles Board, 98, 102, 252, 255
Accounting Standards Board, 245, 252, 255
Accounting Terminology Bulletin, 203
Adam, 9
American Accounting Association, 97, 99, 105, 107, 156, 158, 162, 165, 172, 173, 180, 181, 182, 201, 203, 205, 216, 217, 256, 273
American Institute of Accountants, 101, 147
American Institute of Certified Public Accountants, 54, 102, 173, 208, 216, 252
Anglo-American Model, 56
Arab Society of Certified Accountants, 53
Association of National Accountants of Nigeria, 134, 204, 215
Auditing Standards Executive Committee, 102
Australia, 52, 53, 58
Australian Securities, 55

B

Balance Sheet, 28, 33, 191
Banks and Other Financial Institutions Act, 103, 142, 204
Barde, Ibrahim Magaji, 12, 15
Bayero University, Kano, v, 107, 122, 123, 124, 137, 201, 258, 264, 271, 272, 279, 280, 281
Belgium, 53
Bello, Ahmed Bawa, 13, 64, 109, 122, 125, 143, 144, 148, 258, 266, 279
Brazil, 53
Bureau De Change, 30

C

Cash Flows Statement, 53
Central Bank of Nigeria, 142, 178
Channel Islands, 53
Charge and Discharge System, 183
Chartered Institute of Taxation of Nigeria, 134, 203
Committee on Accounting History, 94, 207
Companies and Allied Matters Act, 14, 20, 34, 35, 37, 76, 103, 142, 177, 204
Companies and Allied Matters Decree, 31
Construction Contract, 23, 24
Consultative Group, 52
Contractor Financed Projects, 24
Current Operating Performance Concept, 24

D

Dandago, Kabiru Isa, i, ii, iii, iv, v, 9, 10, 19, 107, 122, 123, 124, 127, 131, 137, 138, 178, 180, 201, 204, 216, 218, 256, 257, 258, 261, 264, 266, 271, 272, 274, 279, 280, 281
Denmark, 53
Disclosure of Accounting Policies, 19, 20, 253, 271
Discount Houses, 30
Dispositional Ethical Realism, 128, 137, 259

E

Earnings per Share, 34
Economic Communities of West African States, 211
Efficient Market Hypothesis, 73
enterprise theory, 17, 145, 235, 238, 240, 241, 242, 243, 246, 247, 248, 251
Eve, 9

F

Federal Deposit Insurance Corporation, 214
Federal Ministry of Commerce, 19
Financial Accounting Standard Board, 139
Financial Accounting Standards Board, 54, 101, 102, 202, 252, 262
First World War, 213
Five -Year Financial Summary, 33
France, 47, 48, 50, 51, 52, 53, 66, 276
fund theory, 17, 235, 238, 240

G

General Accepted Accounting Principles, 142
Generally Accepted Accounting Principles, 20, 45, 58, 64, 76, 98, 142, 268
Germany, 47, 48, 49, 50, 51, 52, 53
globalization, iv, 44, 45
Great Britain, ii, 50, 51, 165, 263

H

Hamid, Kabir Tahir, 11, 14, 71, 116, 123, 137, 139, 201, 257, 261, 264, 280
Hausa, 76

I

Income Statement, 33
Industrial Relation Business, 57
Institute of Chartered Accountants of Nigeria, 19, 134
International Accounting Standard, 11, 45, 58
International Accounting Standards, 10, 19, 52, 60, 63, 68, 178, 247, 252, 253, 255, 262, 266
International Accounting Standards Board, 10, 63, 247
International Federation of Accountants, 52

International Financial Reporting Standards, 54, 55, 64, 178, 267
International Monetary Fund, 176
International Organization of Securities Commissions, 52
Ireland, 52, 53
Isa, Mustapha Ahmad, v, 11

J

Jega, Prof Attahiru M., v

K

Kaduna State University, v, 279
Kantudu, S. Aliyu, 10, 17, 43, 44, 64, 127, 138, 235, 236, 266, 279
Kurawa, 14
Kurawa, Junaidu Muhammad, 16

L

Life Insurance Enterprises, 29
Liquefied Natural Gas., 32

M

MacNeal, Kenneth, 166, 181, 187, 189, 201, 269
Malaysia, 53
Mexico, 50, 52, 53
Middle East, 48
Muhammad, Muhammad Liman, 12, 16, 106, 124, 219, 271

N

Naira, 25, 35, 227
National Insurance Commission, 31
New York Stock Exchange, 212, 213, 214
New Zealand, 53, 181, 268
Nigeria Accounting Standard Board, 247
Nigerian Accounting Standards Board, 10, 20, 41, 203, 215
Nigerian Deposit Insurance Corporation, 178
Nigerian Stock Exchange, 74, 77, 142, 144, 145
Non-Bank Financial Institutions, 31
Normative Accounting Theory, 153
Notes on the Accounts, 33

O

Oxford dictionary, 98

P

Profit and Loss Account, 33

R

Radda, Sadiqq Isa, v
residual equity theory, 17, 238, 239, 245, 251

S

Salaudeen, Yusuf M, 14, 151, 281

Securities Exchange Commission, 49
South Africa, 48, 53
Spain, 53
Statement of Accounting Standard, 20, 21, 22, 23, 25, 26, 27, 28, 29, 30, 31, 32, 33, 34, 35, 36, 37, 45, 103
Statement of Accounting Standard (SAS) 14, 32
Statement of Accounting Standards, 30, 76, 178
Statement of Cash Flows, 32, 33
Statement of Financial Accounting Concepts, 74, 103, 139, 244
Statement of Source and Application of Funds, 32
Statement of Standard of Accounting Practice, 45
Suleiman, Hajiya Dije Muhammad, v, 261

U

United States, 47, 48, 49, 50, 51, 52, 53, 54, 57, 95, 164, 171, 227, 233, 244, 274
Upstream activities, 30
Usmanu Danfodiyo University, Sokoto, v
Utilitarianism, 110, 121

V

Value Added Statements, 33
Value Added Tax, 33, 141

W

Wikipedia, 81, 84, 85, 91, 175, 182, 277, 278
World Bank, 176, 177, 178, 182
World Trade Organization, 53

www.ingramcontent.com/pod-product-compliance
Ingram Content Group UK Ltd.
Pitfield, Milton Keynes, MK11 3LW, UK
UKHW020220041026
15470UKWH00012B/785

9 781906 704223